In the Shadow of the Mexican Revolution: Contemporary Mexican History, 1910–1989

Translations from Latin America Series

Institute of Latin American Studies
University of Texas at Austin

In the Shadow of the Mexican Revolution: Contemporary Mexican History, 1910–1989

By
**Héctor Aguilar Camín
and Lorenzo Meyer**

Translated by Luis Alberto Fierro

 University of Texas Press, Austin

First Edition, 1993

Requests for permission to reproduce material from this work should be sent to Permissions, University of Texas Press, P.O. Box 7819, Austin, Texas 78713-7819

 The paper used in this publication meets the minimum requirements of American National Standard for Information Sciences—Permanence of Paper for Printed Library Materials, ANSI Z39.48–1984.

Library of Congress Cataloging-in-Publication Data

Aguilar Camín, Héctor, 1946–
    [A la sombra de la Revolución Mexicana. English]
    In the shadow of the Mexican revolution : contemporary Mexican history, 1910–1989 / by Héctor Aguilar Camín and Lorenzo Meyer ; translated by Luis Alberto Fierro.
        p.   cm. — (Translations from Latin America Series)
    Includes bibliographical references and index.
    ISBN 0-292-70446-1. — ISBN 0-292-70451-8 (pbk.)
    1. Mexico—History—20th century. I. Meyer, Lorenzo. II. Title. III. Series.
F1234.A22513 1993   93-5168
972.08—dc20   CIP

Contents

Preface

We began to write this book, separately, about 1983: Lorenzo Meyer in order to solve the practical problem of providing his students with a textbook on which to base his classes on contemporary Mexican history; Héctor Aguilar Camín in order to fulfill various academic and journalistic commitments that demanded a historical perspective on the present—all this in the midst of great doubts about the future, when the 1980s heralded the end of a period of Mexican postrevolutionary history.

The parallel efforts merged into a single task thanks to the initiative of Enrique Florescano in promoting in 1984 the production of an illustrated history of Mexico, from pre-Hispanic times until the Miguel de la Madrid administration, which was sponsored by the National Institute of Anthropology and History (INAH). We were assigned the volume on the twentieth century, which in Mexico really begins, as is well known, ten years after 1900, with the fall of Porfirio Díaz and the modest insurrection that led Francisco I. Madero to power and sacrifice.

We put together the texts we had each written separately, redistributed the task by periods and topics, and then wrote and rewrote the whole package from beginning to end. Another team, consisting of Ema Yanes, Antonio Saborit, Sergio Mastretta, and José Armando Sarignana, with the constant support of Jaime Bali from the Publications Department of INAH, simultaneously undertook the photographic research. They collected for our period nearly 1,500 photographs, of which only a small fraction were used and whose remaining wealth awaits a complementary editor in the INAH archives .

The first edition of the INAH illustrated history started precisely with the chapter on the twentieth century and was published in the format of weekly booklets in 1987. It was a spectacular failure, in part because the publication schedule was affected by the demons of inflation, pushing the printing costs for each booklet far beyond the budget. The entire history was meant to include, according to the initial plan, more than one hundred volumes; only forty were published, corresponding to the twentieth century. The second edition of the illustrated history was printed in 1988 by Editorial Patria in ten slender, inexpensive, and easy-to-handle volumes that were sold each week in large stores and super-markets, with great success.

From the beginning of our project, we had thought, however, that the history text itself had to fulfill its own destiny as a nonillustrated book: accessible to students, scholars, and the general public, in a single volume, in which an easy-flowing but rigorous history of the last eighty years of Mexico would be condensed. There was no such book in the intellectual and academic circles of Mexico when we began to write it, and there still isn't one. Thus grew our interest in publishing a new version, revised and expanded, without illustrations, so that it might circulate where the previous editions were unable to, among the traditional book readers, in bookstores and libraries, and in the classrooms and centers for research and teaching where such a book might have been in demand.

In the Shadow of the Mexican Revolution begins, as we have said, with the downfall of Porfirio Díaz in 1910, and it ends with the July 1989 elections: seventy-nine years of change and continuity, of innovation and reiteration. As we finish writing it, we have—as many Mexicans do—the impression that Mexico is moving forward to a new historical period, which dispels some of the most cherished traditions and the most intolerable vices of the historical legacy that we know as the Mexican Revolution. It is difficult to foresee where it will take us, but it is possible to recognize the roots of this Mexican society of the end of the millennium, with its rare and unique combination of old and new, memory and future, oppression and hope, authoritarianism and democracy.

This work was written as part of the academic tasks of the authors in their respective institutions: Lorenzo Meyer as Coordinator of the Program of Mexican-U.S. Studies at the Colegio de México, and Héctor Aguilar Camín as Director of Historical Studies at the National Institute of Anthropology and History (INAH). Without the understanding and support of Mario Ojeda, President of the Colegio de México, and of Enrique Florescano, Director of INAH (1983–1988), this book would not exist. And it exists, especially, so that it might someday fall into the hands of a particular group of future readers, to whom it is dedicated: Rosario, Lorenzo, Román, Mateo, and Catalina.

1.
In the Path of Madero:
1910–1913

They were not expecting it. The custom of peace was stronger than the evidence of change. *El Imparcial,* the first industrial journal of Mexico and a symbol itself of the enormous transformation that the country had experienced, guaranteed its readers in 1909: "A revolution in Mexico is impossible." Karl Bunz, the German envoy, wrote to his government on September 17 of that same year: "I believe, as does the press and public opinion, that a general revolution is not possible at all." Following his 1910 visit, Andrew Carnegie, the U.S. steel magnate, was left with only the following impression about the country's future: "In all of the corners of the Republic an enviable peace reigns." The Spanish poet Julio Sesto added his own meteorological certainty: "There is no black cloud on the horizon."

But the country had changed. During the previous decades, it had adopted more innovations than could be assimilated by a society such as Mexico's at the turn of the century. The deformed daughter of the liberal project, that society had been dreamed of fifty years before as republican, democratic, egalitarian, rational, industrious, open to innovation and progress. Fifty years later, it was oligarchic, dominated by *caciques* (political bosses), and authoritarian, slow, increasingly disjointed, introverted, jolted by innovation and productive changes, though still tied down by its colonial traditions. It still was, as it had been at the time of its independence a hundred years before, a Catholic society, based on *haciendas* and Indians, crisscrossed by corporative privileges, with a national industry encapsulated in the productive efficiency of the textile industry and the royal mines, and a trade that was just beginning to overcome the regional inertia of the markets.

Federalism had taken the operational form of *cacique* domination; democracy, the face of dictatorship; equality, the route of social immobility; progress, the shape of railroads and foreign investment; industriousness, the form of speculation, the appropriation of goods that increased private fortunes without contributing to the nation's accumulation. But the country had changed, and the innovations proved to be permanent.

Mexico experienced a productive restructuring in the thirty years before the 1910 revolution, which consolidated its northern frontier—a critical area in view of the U.S. expansion—and defined its incorporation into the world market. As a consequence of that change, foreign investment increased from 110 million pesos in 1884 to 3,400 million in 1910. A third of that injection of funds fueled the largest technological revolution of Porfirian Mexico: the construction of almost thirteen thousand miles of railroad tracks. A quarter of foreign investment accrued to mining, which saw its production multiplied from 40 million pesos in 1893 to four times as much in 1906. The rest, to a certain extent, was a by-product. Ramón Eduardo Ruiz writes:

> The mineral bonanza built cities, established the basis for the railroads, and helped commercial agriculture develop. Silver, gold, and copper mines dotted the landscape, and were later joined by lead, zinc and other industrial metal mines. Commercial agriculture for export modified the landscape of Yucatán (hemp), Morelos (sugar), Coahuila and Sonora (cotton, vegetables, chickpeas), and cattle empires oriented toward the U.S. market were established. In the Gulf, British and U.S. companies were in competition to exploit the rich oil fields. The textile plants aligned themselves in the Córdoba-Puebla-Mexico City corridor, and in Guadalajara, Durango, Nuevo León and Chihuahua, for a production that reached 45.5 million pesos in 1904. The black smoke of the smelters darkened the skies of Chihuahua and Monterrey, where 60 thousand tons of iron and steel were produced. There were also factories to produce the following: paper; beer; alcohol; tobacco for domestic consumption; a sugar industry financed by foreigners that bought the land, planted cane and mechanized the production; meat-packers; jute fabric; glycerine; dynamite; fine crystal; glass; hemp rope; cement; and soap.

Furthermore: between 1877 and 1911, the population of Mexico grew at an annual rate of 1.4 percent, while it had grown at an annual rate of .6 percent since the beginning of the nineteenth century. The economy grew at an annual rate of 2.7 percent, whereas in the previous seventy years the average growth rate, with upward and downward swings, had been negative or stagnant. The national income of 50 million in 1896 had doubled within ten years, and the per capita income, which in 1880 was growing at an annual rate of 1 percent, achieved a growth rate of 5.1 percent between 1893 and 1907. In the same period, exports increased sixfold, while imports grew by three and a half times. The chronic bankruptcy of public finances reached an end in 1895, when, for the first time, there was a surplus. Mexico could finally place its bonds in the international markets, and the national budget of 7 million pesos in 1896 increased to almost 24 million in 1906.

These are some of the figures of Porfirian progress. It is necessary to underscore them in order to remember that the revolution that Madero set loose was not the child of misery and stagnation, but rather of the disorder brought forth by boom and change: (1) Foreign investment developed cities and established productive empires, but it also generated inflation that affected the real wage of workers and the middle class; (2) the link with the North American market opened job opportunities and increased exports (sixfold between 1880 and 1910), but made the country vulnerable to the fluctuations of the U.S. economy, whose recession in 1907, for example, led to the repatriation of thousands of Mexican workers who had been fired from the factories and mines across the border; (3) the mining boom created cities and paid high wages, but altered entire regions, created floating, unstable, and restless populations, and sowed the seeds of an explosive nationalism, due to the anti-Mexican job discrimination; (4) the railroad shortened distances, reduced transportation costs, and unified markets, but it also multiplied the price of fallow land, enabling its dispossession, and segregated, by not reaching them, traditional centers of production and commerce, as well as the oligarchies that benefited from them; and (5) the agricultural modernization consolidated an extraordinarily dynamic sector, but it contributed to the destruction of the peasant economy, usurped the rights of the rural towns and communities, and thrust its inhabitants into the inclemency of the market, hunger, peonage, and migration.

While celebrating in 1910 the centennial of its independence, the country was experiencing a mixture of splits, or upheavals, and innovations that would cast it in the coming years into the maelstrom of civil war.

The Agrarian Split

The oldest of these splits affected the traditional peasant communities of the Center and South of the country. It was a struggle coming from afar, from the historical conflict of liberalism against the colonial order of corporative landholding that governed the system of land property held both by the clergy and by the indigenous communities.

The resistance by the clergy had marked the civilian discords of the nineteenth century. The resistance of the communities had flooded the period with agrarian rebellions (historian Jean Meyer has confirmed seventy rebellions in a preliminary review). The judicial climax in the matter was reached with the laws of disentailment (freeing from mortmain) of 1856, politically sanctioned by the Juarista victory over the French intervention and the restoration of the republic in 1867.

In 1895, stimulated by the impact of the railroad on the price of land, the Porfirian regime opened a new wave of disentailment with the law of vacant and idle lands, which facilitated the claims and appropriation of fallow land. The effect of that new liberalization of land on the social organization and the economy of the peasant communities was felt with particular virulence: the annual per capita consumption of corn in Mexico fell by 20 pounds between 1895 and 1910 (from 330 to 310 pounds); the average life span in those fifteen years fell from 31 to 30.5 years; in the final five years of the nineteenth century, infant mortality increased from 304 to 335 per thousand.

The alliance of the Porfirian establishment with the landowners and agricultural modernization meant the dispossession, retreat, and precarious subsistence of the peasant towns. But the resistance equaled the magnitude of the offensive, and it incubated in the first years of the 1910s the largest of the Mexican peasant rebellions. The conflict, begun a century before, received a name and a leader on the afternoon of September 12, 1909, when the men of Anenecuilco, a small town in the state of Morelos in the Center-South of the Republic, elected a new leader. He had just reached thirty years of age and had established ties with politicians from all over the state due to a recent and disastrous electoral campaign as a semi-independent candidate for governor of Morelos. He was a sharecropper of a *hacienda*, and he had some cattle and land; he bought and sold horses, and when there was no planting he roamed the towns of the Cuautla River with a pack of mules carrying merchandise. His name was Emiliano Zapata and he would become in due time first a leader, and then a legendary symbol of Mexican agrarianism.

The law of idle lands and the speculative trail of the railroad also subjected the most recent agrarian tract to dispossession and affronts, a region that proved no less resistant to modernization than the Morelos peasants: the members of the northern communities, inheritors of the old military colonies that dotted the frontier territories during the nineteenth century, as a sequel to the colonial garrisons that had consolidated the military expansion of the viceroyalty. These were towns that for generations had fought alone against the attacks of outlaws and Indians, until the definite pacification of the Apaches in 1880; they were communities built in isolation, self-defense, and regional pride. In the last years of the Porfiriato, those towns were subject to land speculation and the hegemony of regional oligarchic interests.

The speculation created by the boom in mining and agricultural invest-ments—generally by foreigners—took away land from the peasants. The consolidation of the new regional oligarchies took away their political independence and municipal autonomy. They thus lost their isolation and their territory, their independence and security in the rules of their own world, the capacity to decide who their authorities would be and to manage their immediate interests. They were the muleteers, farm workers, cowboys, northern people of horse and rifle, *gambusinos*, who complained in the following terms:

Namiquipa, Chihuahua: "We see with deep sorrow that those plots that we believe justly belong to us, because we have received them from father to son and have cultivated them with the constant work of more than a century, have been turned over to strange hands simply by presenting a claim and paying a few pesos."

Janos, Chihuahua: "Two leagues from Janos we find the prosperous Colony *Fernández Leal*, whose owners live with all comfort in the United States, while we, who have suffered the invasions of the barbar-ians whom our forefathers drove away, have not been able to secure these plots."

Santa Cruz, Sonora: "We cannot endure the injustice and abuse that the president and the treasurer heap upon us. There are men here who could assume authority, and in case that you (the governor) are inatten-tive to this, we shall see how we get rid of them. We are family men that would suffer upheavals if there were any unrest, but if it is unavoidable we will do it."

Additionally, the struggle against the Indians in the North during the Porfiriato included the "pacification" of the Mayo and Yaqui Indians of Sonora, a bloody war that disrupted the organizational forms of both tribes, rejected their ancient rights, and transferred their lands to white domination—the richest lands of the Northwest, fertilized by the only two rivers with a quasi-permanent waterflow in the arid Sonorense plains. These lands were colonized following an initial war against the Indians (1877–1880), but the Yaqui resistance to the occupation re-mained alive, irreducible, and uninterrupted during the whole period of the Porfiriato and the Revolution, part of which was fought with Yaqui troops and part in Sonora against Yaqui insurgents.

Closed Roads

The years prior to the Maderista explosion added other destabilizing factors to the deep split that was widening in the ancient agrarian and rural veins of Mexico. Between 1900 and 1910, several factors converged to darken the horizon of the middle classes and the budding working class that Porfirian development had created. Foreign investment reduced the income of these sectors by two mechanisms: the high inflation that was produced, and the new taxes that the government had to create in order to compensate for the tax exemptions created for foreign firms and financial drafts from abroad. The consolidation of regional oligarchies, which at the turn of the century began to add the monopoly of political power to their control of economic power, also reduced the space available for the middle classes. The intermediate positions in business, services, and, above all, public office, began to be taken by friends and family of those oligarchies. The pyramid of the monopoly reproduced itself, and both large cities and small towns saw their avenues of upward mobility being closed, as well as the deterioration of the most basic forms of local life.

Benjamin Hill, a Sonorense prototype of the sectors that had been passed over and were anxious to find a crack in the system, expressed the following view in 1908:

> A wave of fresh blood is indispensable to renew the stagnant blood that exists in the veins of the Republic, languishing with doddering old fools, in great part honorable remains of the past, but, if you will, mummies that materially obstruct our march toward progress.

And a small merchant, Salvador Alvarado, left this simple sketch of the coagulated local disintegration and the desire for change:

> I began to feel the need for change of our social organization since I was 19 years old, when, back in my town of Pótam, Yaqui River, I saw the police commissioner get drunk almost every day in the town pool, in the company of his secretary; of the local judge that was also the civil judge and fiscal agent; of the post office agent; and of some merchant or army officer, persons all of whom constituted the influential class of that small world.

Mined Territory

The mining vertigo and the industrial reactivation also led to the development under the Porfiriato of the first working-class battalions in Mexico, in the modern sense of the term. The northern mines attracted, with their high-paying jobs, migrants from all over the country; within months, they erected dozens of provisional cities, disorganized and noisy, marked by irregularity, discrimination, and the absolute will of the owners, generally North American or British. The foreign companies exploited the mines and controlled municipal life, they selected mayors, paid the police force, maintained the schools, dominated trade, and sometimes also purchased the cattle-raising and agricultural lands surrounding the mines that provided food for the miners. The most notable case of that vertigo was the Sonorense city of Cananea, almost on the Arizona border. The millions invested there by the adventurous Col. William C. Green, founder of the Cananea Consolidated Copper Company, transformed that semiabandoned town of only 100 inhabitants in 1891 into the center of copper production in Mexico. In only six years (1900–1906), the beckoning of copper lured into the dry hills of Cananea 14,000 inhabitants (the population was 891 at the turn of the century and 14,841 at the end of the Porfiriato). Starting with practically zero production, in those six years the mining vein provided for the introduction of sixteen active mines and the production of 14 million pesos in copper (the total production of Porfirian mining was 140 million pesos in 1906). In May 1906, Cananea had 5,360 Mexican workers and 2,200 foreign workers, the minimum wage was 2 pesos and the highest wage was 6 pesos, at a time when the minimum wage in the northern Pacific region of Mexico was 1.21 pesos and in the central region .59 pesos.

The workers of Cananea had begun their organization under the influence of Magonismo and of the radical smoldering that plagued the factories and mines on the other side of the border in California and Arizona, under the influence of anarcho-syndicalism, and the expansion of socialist currents in the United States. Toward the end of May 1906, their nationalism disturbed by the permanent job discrimination in favor of North Americans and threatened by a sudden increase in their workload, the budding labor organization of Cananea marshaled the accumulated turmoil and called for a strike. Their demands: five pesos of wages for eight hours of work, the firing of a *mayordomo* (foreman), the right to promotion for Mexicans according to their skills, and the hiring of at least 75 percent of Mexican workers by the company. This was June 1, 1906. The following three days were filled with strike, struggle, and repression; there were riots, looting, and fires, resulting in ten dead and a hundred arrested. Cananea saw the arrival of Arizona rangers and volunteers, five hundred Mexican soldiers, and the governor of Sonora, Rafael Izábal, who personally coordinated the pacification.

Peace was eventually reestablished, but not the legendary prestige of the mines in U.S. financial circles. The contraction of the U.S. markets the following year also contributed to the industry's collapse. Without credit or market, Cananea, the fabulous black pearl of Porfirian mining, ceased its operations in October 1907 and began to fire workers by the hundreds in order to restructure its plant and its installations. It reopened in April 1908, but it did not achieve profits again until the beginning of 1911, when the Maderista rebellion was irreversibly on its way.

Shipwreck in Río Blanco

The scandal of the Cananea strike in the dynamic mining sector was still fresh when a new one arose, this time in a traditional industrial sector, the textile factories of Río Blanco, Veracruz. There, after a protracted conflict with the owners over working conditions, the workers rejected a finding by President Díaz that established favorable regulations in their relationship with the firms, but that restricted their rights, particularly their political rights. On January 7, 1907, they refused to go back to their working places, and the front door of the firm was blocked by women, who stopped anyone wanting to enter. Agitation began with cheers for Juárez and jeers against the Spaniards and the French who controlled the factories, the businesses, and the privileges of the region. The rally continued in a store next to the factory, where an employee inflamed passions by shooting a worker. The worker died, and the store was looted and burned. The police came and were resisted. The rural police led a charge, machetes in hand, but they were also repelled with stones. The turmoil spread. The following morning, excited and provisioned by the looting, the strikers let the prisoners escape from the jail, and they marched toward the nearby town of Nogales with the purpose of "seeking arms." There, they also looted the municipal building, freed the prisoners, and continued their trek, still marching under the banner of Juárez. "We marched along, to the compass of slogans and songs," remembers a participant. "We felt free and the masters of our own destiny after suffering so much misery and oppression. It seemed like a festival."

The festival ended abruptly at dawn. At 1:30 in the morning on January 9, two companies of the 24th Army Battalion arrived at Santa Cruz, under the command of the undersecretary of war, Rosalino Martínez. During the course of that night, the soldiers combed the streets, controlled riots and rioters, and imposed a pax Porfiriana. Bernardo García Díaz writes:

> When morning broke on January 9, while the whistles of the
> factories of the district called workers to work again, continuous
> volleys sounded. Over the sinister scene of the burnt stores, the
> executions that the Porfirian plutocracy had ordered to serve as

examples were taking place. Of the 7,083 workers that toiled in the textile factories before the strike, on January 9 only 5,512 came back to work. The other 1,571 workers escaped from the region, were arrested, were injured, or were definitely dead.

Under the debris and the dead, the Cananea and Río Blanco strikes defined the Porfirian inability to digest the modern attempts at union organization and struggle. Confronted by the offspring of its own development—the new groups of workers that appeared with the productive advances of the old society—the Porfirian establishment did not seem to have any answer other than intolerance and repression.

The Presence of the North

In the thirty years of Pax Porfiriana, the North of Mexico underwent more permanent changes than in all of its previous history. The capitalist surge on the other side of the border and the investments on this side, the railroad that cut distances, the banks that facilitated credit, the oil boom in the Gulf, the mining boom in Sonora, Chihuahua, and Nuevo León, the industrial boom in Monterrey, the merchant and marine boom in Tampico and Guaymas, brought to the North in those years the material stimulus for a double and effective incorporation: on one hand, to the expanding U.S. market, and on the other, to the incomplete and growing network of what was beginning to be called the Mexican Republic. In those years, the North was a focus of investments and new productive centers that diversified its economic and human scene. That region saw the convergence in a rapid mix of traditional *haciendas* and export plantations, new mining and agricultural cities, high wages, a prosperous level of ranchers, cowboys, and free wage agricultural workers, an explosive working class in the mines, a budding banking industry, and diversified trade.

The call of the North and of the border, with its promise of better wages and opportunities, unleashed from the 1890s onward a permanent migration flow from the Center, the Bajío (lowlands), and the *altiplano* (highlands) toward the agricultural fields of La Laguna and El Yaqui, the mines of Sonora and Chihuahua, the oil camps of Tampico, and the expanding industries of Nuevo León. A decisive consequence of that mobilization was the rupture, in the North, of the traditional agricultural relations that had long dominated the Mexican countryside.

There is no better example of this transition than the development of the cotton fields of La Laguna, in Torreón, Coahuila, the center of greatest growth of all the Porfiriato. A ranch of only 200 inhabitants in 1892, Torreón was awakened in the 1890s by the railroad junction that turned it into a distributing station for all of the North. By 1895, the 200 inhabitants had become 5,000, and by 1910 there were 34,000. The highest agricultural wages in the republic were paid there, and the landowners of the region, unaccustomed to the southern systems of debt peonage or *tienda de raya* (*hacienda*-owned store debts), paid wages in money and not in vouchers, they sold goods in their stores at lower prices than in local stores, and they vied to keep their workers by offering various incentives and advantages.

That labor and social reality led to the development of a new type of migrant worker, who exercised free transit from one region to another in search of a good wage and better working conditions. Unstable and without local roots, these workers harvested the advantages of a free or semifree labor market with high wages, as well as its disadvantages: job insecurity and lack of family, community, or traditional ties in which to seek refuge in periods of bad harvests or scarce work (something that happened in La Laguna region every three years, on average). This type of free worker in the North was what furnished the northern revolutionary armies with people, allowing the availability of men for recruitment and military mobilization outside the region of recruitment—a characteristic not to be found in other armies of a more traditional agrarian background, such as the Zapatista army.

The irreducible nucleus of the Maderista rebellion was the mountainous axis of the western Sierra Madre, which traversed the states of Chihuahua, Sonora, Durango, and Sinaloa. This northern highland of small and dispersed mines was affected as no other part of the country by the mining crisis and the fall in the prices of silver toward the end of the Porfiriato. The mining crisis affected thousands of small producers, the *gambusinos* of the highlands; once Mexico adopted the gold standard in 1905, the price of Mexican silver fell to the price level of the international market.

A crisis in food production compounded the mining disorder. Bad harvests led to an increase in the price of corn and beans, the staple foods for popular subsistence. Corn practically doubled in price between 1900 and 1910, and half of the increase took place during the last year. The mining North was a territory of fragile regions where, persistently throughout the Porfiriato, there had been riots, rebellions, and roving bands. The mountainous region located between Rosario (Sinaloa) and Tamazula (Durango) had been the scene of the exploits of the famous 1880s bandit, Heraclio Bernal. The highland region between Guanaceví (Durango) and Santa Bárbara (Chihuahua) was where Ignacio Parra and Doroteo Arango wandered in the 1890s and where Francisco Villa would later appear. There had been mining riots in the 1880s and armed rebellions against municipal usurpations in the 1890s in the region of the eastern ranches of Sonora and western ranches of Chihuahua, the triangle between Cusihuiriachic, Pinos, and Ascensión. There had been periodical conflicts in other northern mining centers such as Matehuala, Charcas, and Catorce in San Luis Potosí, and Velardeña in Durango. Captain Scott, in charge of the U.S. troops on the border, had referred to those territories with prescience in August 1907: "There exists, in particular in the states of the north of Mexico, a great unrest due to the current situation. If there were a revolutionary explosion, a capable leader would have numerous followers."

New Branches, Old Tree Trunks

The leader that Captain Scott foresaw was Francisco Madero, quintessential—and, finally, explosive—personification of the last great upheaval that the Porfiriato had precipitated in Mexican society: the discontent of some of the great patriarchal families that had painfully consolidated themselves throughout the nineteenth century and had proclaimed victory with the liberal Juarista cause in the 1860s, but that had seen themselves displaced from power by the centralizing hand of Porfirismo, the alliance of the regime with foreign interests, and their sponsorship of a new oligarchic generation.

Having come to power through a military rebellion in 1876, the Porfirians took as their road toward political stability the destruction of *cacique* enclaves, which had developed after the Juarista triumph in the different regions of the country. One by one, and state by state, the old liberal *caciques* and the economic groups that had developed around them were replaced by Porfirista unconditionals or by emerging cadres of the local middle sectors, whose aspirations for upward mobility had been blocked by the oligarchic establishment of the Juarista mold. Trinidad García de la Cadena in Zacatecas, Ramón Corona in Jalisco, Ignacio Pesqueira in Sonora, and Luis Terrazas in Chihuahua: each and every one of the local strongmen and the interests they had created around themselves were subdued during the 1880s, until the end of the century. At the beginning of the twentieth century, a new guard of governing groups had taken control of most of the regions of the country. By that time, the families and patriarchs that had been displaced in the 1880s had renewed themselves in a new generation. The sons and grandsons of the Juarista *caciques*, anxious branches of renowned families, now were attempting to redraw the course of events and open their way to a new period of domination, or at least a subordinate participation in the local and national affairs.

But instead of opportunities, they found closed roads, Porfirian dynasties, and networks that were starting to perpetuate themselves in power and to serve as partners or intermediaries of foreign investors that transformed territories, cities, and markets. The consolidation of these regional oligarchies in the northern states delivered many of the standard-bearers of distinguished family names into the hands of the opposition.

Francisco I. Madero was a perfect personification of this history of affronts and rejections that the new generation of the old patriarchal trees had lived through the Porfiriato. Friedrich Katz writes:

> At the turn of the twentieth century, Francisco Madero had formed and led a coalition of hacendados in the Laguna region to oppose attempts by the Anglo-American Tlahualilo Company to monopolize the water rights of that irrigation-dependent area. When the Maderos cultivated the rubber substitute guayule, they had clashed with the Continental Rubber Company. Another conflict developed because prior to 1910 the Maderos owned the only smeltering oven in northern Mexico that was independent of the American Smelting and Refining Company.
>
> The Maderos were not alone in their fight. Many other members of the northeastern upper class were interested in water rights in the Laguna, in the cultivation of guayule, and in the operation of independent smelting ovens in northern Mexico.

The restless scions of these families acted as the purveyors of the Porfirista debacle, the riverbed through which many forces flowed toward the Mexican Revolution.

In contrast to this new state of mind, the long-drawn-out Porfirian decline was manisfested in an aging ruling class that showed no interest in retiring and had lost its sensibility when confronted by the forces that its own development had generated, as the workers' strikes demonstrated. In June 1904, Porfirio Díaz was reelected for a sixth term in office, when he was seventy-five years old, with a northern vice president, Ramón Corral, who was fifty-six years old. Luis González y González writes:

> Don Porfirio held his 75th birthday very upright and solemn, but not without the fatigue, the pains, the cracks and crevices of senility. He no longer was the oak tree he once had been. Even the acumen and the willpower became bland. The ideas escaped him, and words would not come to mind. Instead, emotions flourished. He became sentimental and tearful and, consequently, incapable of

issuing edicts. And while his managerial skills escaped him, senile distrust overwhelmed him and he did not trust even his closest collaborators.

Along with the chief in decline, the visible positions in the political showcase were dotted with other elderly men, similarly ailing. The average age of the Ministers, Senators and Governors was 70 years. The regime's young turks, merely in their sixties, were in the lower chamber of Congress. Those with the longest history, as old as the Republic, were the judges of the Supreme Court of Justice. In other words, the staff of the elderly dictator was almost as old as he, and some of his aides were even more doddering. Many of the assistants of Don Porfirio were his old comrades-in-arms, and they had no reason to be any younger than he. Others, the *científicos* ("scientists"), were born in the period between 1841 and 1856, and thus were members, without exception, of the 8 percent of their countrymen older than half a century. At the time, half of the Mexicans were older than 20 years, and 42 percent were between 21 and 49 years old. The Republic was a society of children and youngsters, governed by a handful of elderly men, who had already rendered the contribution that they were capable of making to their country and to themselves.

1908: The Sowing of the Collapse

None of the factors we have mentioned so far—the agrarian split, the labor innovations, the oligarchic obstruction, or the senility of the ruling Porfirians—would have been capable of unleashing the Maderista rebellion in 1910 if some particular confluence in politics, the economy, and the general fortune of history hadn't contributed negative effects to the fundamental imbalance that had been a by-product of progress.

The year 1908 condenses and disperses that confluence of adversities that set off the eroded foundations of the *ancien régime*. It was a terrible year for the economy because, as Luis González points out, "nature took up the cause of the poor," not that of stability:

In some parts it rained more than what was necessary, and in other parts less. There were also ominous tremors and terrible frosts. The production of corn, already insufficient, dropped even further. The scarcity of corn tortillas and beans produced a critical situation in the countryside, perhaps not so severe as that of fifteen years before, but nevertheless at a moment in which any perturbation generated great irritation. In the biennium 1908–1909, the annual value of industrial products stagnated at 419 millon pesos, the manufacturing sector fell from 206 million to 188 million. The mining and metallurgical sector increased slightly in volume but not in price. Precious metals and especially silver, depreciated . . . The same thing happened to industrial metals, with the exception of iron. The production of zinc, so important in 1906–1907, collapsed . . . Many merchandises were stockpiled for lack of buyers. Internal and external demand weakened, and the imports from abroad fell both in value and in volume. The price of exports fell by eight percent. The trade balance was negative in 1908. The economic crisis affected more severely those who already were worse off, as usual. The deterioration of the quality of life intensified the social unrest, already strong before the crisis. The country was ripe for turmoil.

1908 was also a bad year for relations with the United States, because in that year the oil company *El Aguila* was established, with a barrage of privileges and official support, an enterprise that was established as a joint venture between the Porfirista government and the Weetman Pearson Trust, later known as Lord Cowdray, in which one of the main shareholders was Díaz's own son. This was the highest expression of the project of alliance with European capital, British in this case, that the Porfiristas judged necessary in order to counter the domination of North American interests in Mexico.

The obvious governmental favoritism shown to the British company through the concession of lands in Chiapas, Tabasco, Veracruz, San Luis Potosí, and Tamaulipas amounted to a declaration of war to the powerful North American interests. This was especially true because, in those years, Mexico was beginning to turn into an oil-producing country of first rank: the production of 3,300,000 barrels of oil in 1910 increased to 14 million in 1911, an enormous jump that suddenly placed the country in third place among the oil-producing countries of the world. Thus, the importance of this conflict in the Porfirian debacle cannot be overstated. Recalls Friedrich Katz:

Some observers were convinced that the largest reserves in the world were in Mexico. In the face of such vast opportunities, Mexican business interests in Mexico were less and less prepared to put up with the Díaz government's anti-American collaboration with the Pearson Trust, and soon the opinion became rife that the only way to end that collaboration was through a change of government in Mexico.

The Porfirian regime had begun in the 1870s in the midst of virulent differences with the United States due to the intrusion of U.S. troops into Mexican territory to pursue Apaches and outlaws. Ironically, after two decades of agreements and collaboration, Díaz was ending his period in office by returning, through different circumstances, to a similar conflict that would cost him the neutrality, and in some cases even the active support, of the U.S. government toward the revolutionary bands and their agents during 1910 and 1911.

The year 1908 was also a bad one for political stability in the upper reaches of government, because Díaz himself was responsible for opening the doors to political agitation when he declared to the North American reporter James Creelman that Mexico was ready for democracy and that he would accept as heaven's blessing the creation of an opposition party. His desires were taken as orders. Once he had given his consent, the political underground of the society took center stage. The rumors became magazines, the agitation adopted book format. Querido Moheno published ¿*Hacia dónde vamos?* (Where are we going?); Manuel Calero published *Cuestiones electorales* (Electoral matters); Emilio Vázquez Gómez published *La reelección indefinida* (The indefinite reelection); Francisco de P. Sentíes, *La organización política de México* (The political organization of Mexico); Ricardo García Granados, *El problema de la organización política* (The problem of political organization); and Francisco Madero, *La sucesión presidencial* (The presidential succession). The anti-Porfirian trends came to the fore in the public arena in the form of political organizations and anti-reelection parties.

The Opposition and Its Farsightedness

From the Díaz-Creelman interview in June 1908, the horizon of the opposition was dominated by the figure of Gen. Bernardo Reyes, former secretary of war. Reyismo filtered into some of the most sensitive parts of Mexican political life: the Masonic lodges, the modest bureaucrats, the army. During 1908 and parts of 1909, in the North and the West of the country, Reyismo led to the creation of clubs, journals, and impressive speeches. Near mid-1909, however, Reyes yielded to Díaz's pressure and quelled with his silence the demands of his supporters. Toward the end of July, he announced that he would support the candidacy of Don Porfirio for president, and that of his enemy, Ramón Corral, for vice-president in the 1910 elections. As a reward for his loyalty, he was withdrawn from the military command of Nuevo León. At the beginning of November, President Díaz granted him a hearing and encouraged him to accept a trip to Europe for military studies.

At the same time that Reyes's star was fading, a Central Anti-

Reelection Club was established in mid-1909 in Mexico City that began to highlight the new shining star of the opposition—a man who, according to his own grandfather, was attempting to put out the sun with his hand: Francisco I. Madero. In 1909, Madero was, above all things, a preacher, member of a wealthy landowning family of Coahuila, author of a dense book on historical discourse, and an active organizer of opposition groups that were committed to the unheard-of strategy of traveling around the republic in order to promote his crusade—a crusade for democracy and against reelection, whose political character was adequately summed up in one of the slogans of his campaign: "The people do not want bread, but liberty."

During 1909 and 1910, Madero traversed the country in two stages. The first took him to Veracruz (recent scene of the repression against the textile workers), Yucatán (territory of violent expansion and the hemp oligarchy, recently subjected by Porfirismo to the dictates of the world market), and Nuevo León (the birthplace of Reyismo). January 1910 saw him entering Sonora in the North, after traveling through Puebla and Querétaro in the Center, and Jalisco, Colima, and Sinaloa in the West. Madero traveled with a small and faithful entourage: his wife, Sara; the stenographer Elías de los Ríos; and Roque Estrada, close collaborator and demanding witness. The tour took them to important cities, the celebration of rallies, the establishment of electoral clubs, and the prompt departure to some other point on the map. The hostility of the authorities, and the meager financial and administrative resources of the anti-reelection campaign, conferred on the tour of the "apostle" an image of ingenuity and limited efficiency. But the recent Reyista desertion and the numerous outbreaks of regional dissatisfaction were an appropriate climate for the possibilities of an independent candidate. Says Stanley Ross, "The political organization of Madero grew while Reyismo was falling apart. The independents and many of the Reyistas, abandoned by their preferred caudillo, saw the Maderista movement as their salvation."

In early June 1910, Madero once again left Mexico City, this time as the anti-reelection candidate for president of the republic. As he was leaving, the celebration of the Independence Centennial was beginning, with its chariots and parades, velvety frock coats, gazes hardened by the far-sightedness and the respectable years of so many white beards and so many past glories. Medals and formal uniforms, honor bands, swaying grandstands: Mexico 1810–1910, a grand homeland, bedecked for the exhibition of its fulfilled destiny, renewed by the laurels of its triumph over the disintegration of its internal struggles, its catastrophes, and its shabbiness.

On the perimeter of that centenary homeland, a new country was growing: a gigantic rural body made up of country roads and the smell of dung, of muleteers and peons, of sparse cities and isolated communities. As mentioned above, in thirty years, the Pax Porfiriana had imposed a drastic change on that map, separated by its mountains and its distances: the branding iron that drew the lines of the railroad (Mexico to Veracruz, to Ciudad Juárez, to Guadalajara; Tepic to Nogales, Yucatán, Tehuantepec) and the long spider's web of the telegraph. At the terminal points, the railway junctions, and the intermediate regions that the railroad touched, the other society grew: mines, gringos, white men, and modern *haciendas*; commercial houses, factories, gringos, and massive emigrations; cities that grew at a dizzying pace, consulates and foreign owners, usurpations, strikes, monopolies, adventurers, large stores, corseted women, gringos, and casinos. It included a middle class without a secure future, a budding working class, a floating population attracted as if by magnet to the border; peasant communities shaken up in their secular rhythm; modern landowners and rural patriarchs confronted by progress, withdrawn to the old houses of their *haciendas*; families that for decades had woven the regional history with their whims and their interests, and now found themselves anachronisms, postponed their rancor.

To manage these disorders, the Porfirian style had no other branding iron than that to which the country had already become accustomed in those thirty years: a gerontocratic network of chiefs, governors, *caciques*, and ministers, a political style that had developed for the control of a society prior to the gringos, progress, and capitalism. The only things that were monolithic and reiterative, from beginning to end, in the Porfirian society were its political modes, its aspirations, and, after 1900, its complacent obsolescence.

The Fissure in the Dam

Madero was a fissure, at first imperceptible, in the efficacy of those old habits. Toward his weak promise gravitated all of the symptoms that the Porfirian court was ignoring: landowners with tradition but without future, communities that resisted the usurpation of their lands, professionals without positions, teachers burned out by the misery and the heroic halo of the history of the homeland, unemployed politicians, and military officers. And that crucial provincial petite bourgeoisie: the shopkeepers, pharmacists, anxious ranchers, small farmers, and share-croppers, all dragged down by the double yoke of their local aspirations and the credit- and social-worthlessness of their modest enterprises. Toward the candidacy of Madero also flowed the North American expectations, a widespread lack of trust in the regime that was due less to the caution surrounding its physical age than to an opposition to its

last youthful impulses, which redistributed to the British concessions
that had been given to the North Americans and opened the diplomatic
doors to emerging powers such as Japan.

His tour around the country should have led Madero to the certainty
that, in effect, all of those embryonic forces were running behind his
candidacy. As a presidential candidate, Madero doubted less and less the
predictions that, in the name of the people, he made in his speeches. One
day, when he was getting off the train in San Luis Potosí, coming from
Mexico City, he shouted to the numerous partisans that had gathered to
wait for him: "There is one thing that our oppressors should understand
well: today, the Mexican people are willing to die in order to defend their
rights; and it is not that they want to incinerate the national territory
with a revolution, it is that they are no longer afraid of the sacrifice."

The disdain with which Díaz and the Porfiristas had regarded Madero
since 1908 had turned by mid-1910 into strict police control. In response
to his speech in San Luis Potosí, Madero was accused of "attempts at
rebellion and insults to the authorities," and was arrested in Monterrey
and brought back to the scene of his verbal crimes, San Luis, where he
was thrown in jail. They wanted to keep him quiet during the days in July
when the elections would be held. They accomplished that; Díaz was
reelected. A week after the new victory, the secretary of finance, José Ives
Limantour, who was leaving for Europe, passed through San Luis Potosí
and spoke with Madero—they had been personal friends for a long time.
Madero obtained conditional liberty, although he was confined to the
city of San Luis Potosí. He violated probation, crossed the border, and at
the beginning of October was in San Antonio, Texas, ready to lead an
insurrection. The basic platform of the Maderista revolution began to
circulate some fifteen days later under the title of *Plan de San Luis*. It
declared the elections null, the reelected regime illegitimate, and the
new representatives spurious; it named Madero as provisional president
of the United Mexican States, and it called for an insurrection on
November 20, 1910 at 6:00 P.M.

It did not start at 6:00 P.M. or on November 20, 1910, but by May 1911
the consequences of that call to arms had opened the doors to a new
historical period in Mexico.

The Uprising

Historian Francisco Xavier Guerra has provided us with an excellent
geographical, political, and military summary of the Maderista insurrection that begins by recognizing its spatial location in the highland mines
of the North.

The preparation for the uprising in cities such as Culiacán, Guadalajara, Chihuahua, Hermosillo, and in some localities of the State of Veracruz and of Puebla, are easily discovered, their instigators arrested before they are able to use their arms or immediately suppressed, such as Aquiles Serdán in Puebla . . . a second type of attempt had as its point of origin the United States. Political refugees, such as Madero himself, tried to cross the border and launch expeditions toward Mexico's interior with the support of local accomplices. In Piedras Negras and Ojinaga the failure of these attempts is absolute. Finally, true uprisings begin to take place. Some of the conspiracies are successful, such as that of Jesús Agustín Castro, Orestes Pereyra, Martín Triana and eighty other people in Gómez Palacio, in the region of La Laguna. There are some uprisings that are barely insurrections of a few towns of the north of the country (Cástulo Herrera and Pancho Villa in San Andrés and Santa Isabel, Toribio Ortega in Cuchillo Parado, Chihuahua; the Arrieta brothers in Canelas, Severino Ceniceros and Calixto Contreras in Ocuila and Cuencamé, Durango). In other cases, there are massive attacks that are undertaken by hundreds of men in the towns of Santa Bárbara, Belleza and Cuevas, against the great mining center of Hidalgo del Parral, attempts that are also doomed to failure, and end up as small groups of bandits that take refuge in inaccessible zones. There is only one specific region—the west of Chihuahua—where the rebellion is victorious from the beginning and is kept alive in towns and small cities: San Isidro with Pascual Orozco, Santo Tomás with José de la Luz Blanco, Temosáchic, Bachíniva, Matáchic, Moris with Nicolás Brown, Tomóchic, Caríchic . . .The month of December of 1910 confirms this initial geographic distribution. The rebellion of the western region of Chihuahua extends itself toward Janos in the north and Batopilas in the south, toward the west where some bands appear in the El Barrigón mine in Sonora, and also toward the east in direction of Satevo. The rebellion of the western mountains of Durango consolidates itself when Copalquín and the mines of Río Verde, in the district of San Dimas, join the rebellions of Canelas. A month and a half after the hostilities began, the main zone of the Maderista revolution shows a sharply defined contour. It includes essentially the mountainous axis of the Western Sierra Madre and it extends itself toward the states of Chihuahua, Sonora, Durango and Sinaloa. A singular northern Mexico, of precarious mountain and forest agriculture. Above all, it is the Mexico of the mines.

January is a difficult month for the rebellion. Despite its weak-

ness and its lack of preparation to engage the guerrillas, the federal
army launches an offensive and recovers even Ciudad Guerrero, the
center of the revolution in Chihuahua, as well as the mining
centers of Urique and Batopilas. Despite these setbacks, the
nucleus of the rebellion in the west of Chihuahua sends an expedition of more than one thousand men toward the north. It is at that
point in time that the western region of Durango, which has
similar characteristics, joins the revolution and the municipalities
of Topia and Tamazula are completely surrounded. They are
movements that contrast with the defeats of Villa and of some
dispersed groups in the center-southern region of Chihuahua, a
region of large landowners, where the revolutionaries are forced to
retreat toward the highlands at the north of Durango. It is thus that
the Maderista rebellion becomes firmly established in the mountains and mines.

In February the situation improves for the rebels. The federal
army definitely abandons the west of Chihuahua and the rebellion
extends to the mining region at the east of Sonora. There are
uprisings in the mines at the center of Chihuahua (Naica, Santa
Eulalia, in Aldama). They fail, but they are one more proof of the
multiplication of the rebel groups. Also, for the first time after
three months of fighting, a new hub appears in the south of the
country: that of Gabriel Tepepa, previous to the uprising of Zapata
in Morelos.

The decisive turning point of the revolution takes place in the
second half of March. All of the highlands of Durango are by then
in hands of the revolutionaries, and they begin to spill over into the
coastal plains (Badiraguato, Guamúchil, Mocorito) and toward the
mining region at the south of Sinaloa (Pánuco). Some dispersed
groups in Durango and in Zacatecas attack central cities: Jesús
Agustín Castro attacks Villa Hidalgo, Durango; Luis Moya begins a
long cavalcade that takes him toward the south of Durango and to
the mining region in southern Zacatecas (Juchipila, Mezquital del
Oro, Nochixtlán). In Sonora, the revolutionaries suffer defeats in
Ures and in Agua Prieta. But their failures also prove that they
have acquired sufficient strength to attack important towns.
Finally, toward the end of March, the Figueroa brothers stage an
uprising in the mining region of Huitzuco, Guerrero. On March 10,
the Zapatista insurgency begins.

In April, the rebellion extends itself like an oil stain. The troops
stationed in western Chihuahua, where only some isolated mines
in Chínipas resist, besiege the border town of Ciudad Juárez. In

Sonora, another border town, Agua Prieta, falls into rebel hands for some days. The federal army is only able to control some strategic points of the railroad. In Durango, the troops descend from the western mountains into the central plains and surround the capital city; in the east, the mining cities of Indé and Mapimí, Velardeña, Cuencamé, San Juan de Guadalupe, Juego Nazas and Gómez Palacio fall into rebel hands. All of the region of irrigated agriculture of La Laguna, between Durango and Coahuila, is besieged by the attacks of the revolutionaries. In Sinaloa, the battles flood the central plains, and in the north and the southern mining region Palmillas, Guadalupe de los Reyes, San Ignacio and Concordia fall. Toward the end of the month, the port of Mazatlán is totally surrounded. In Zacatecas, Luis Moya's men arrive at the large mining centers: Fresnillo, Nieves, Sombrerete. In the south, Figueroa's rebellion extends to Guerrero, and Zapata extends his uprising to Morelos and Puebla, where he is able to take control for some days of Izúcar de Matamoros.

Finally, in the month of May the revolution is triumphant. On the ninth, Orozco and Villa take control of the most important border city, Ciudad Juárez. The military success hastens the signing of a cease-fire on May 18, and on May 21 a peace agreement is signed, accepting the formation of a provisional government. In the days after the victory, and especially after the signing of the peace agreement, the revolutionary troops that are still mobilized attack other cities that are not yet under their control. After bloody fights, Torreón in La Laguna falls on the 15th, Iguala on the 12th, Cuautla the 19th, Culiacán the 30th, Mazatlán the 6th of June. In Chihuahua and in Sonora, thanks to the signed agreements, the Maderistas do not find resistance to occupying the cities that are still in the hands of the federal army. In the rest of the country, scattered revolutionary groups grow in a few days, and without resistance enter San Luis Potosí, Córdoba, Orizaba, Saltillo, Pachuca, etc. The military phase of the Maderista revolution reached an end at the beginning of June 1911.

Taming the Tiger

The treaties of Ciudad Juárez effected the resignation of Díaz and the end of the rebellion. Four days later, on May 25, Don Porfirio gave his resignation. The next day, he boarded the ship *Ypiranga* in Veracruz, en route to his final exile. At some point on the road to the last Mexican border he would cross, his eyes overflowed with tears, as had become increasingly common, and he summed up in one phrase the reality of

Mexico in arms that had turned its back on him: "They have set a tiger loose."

Immediately, the triumphant faction tried to tie it up again. To begin with, the treaties of Ciudad Juárez omitted any mention of the third article of the Plan de San Luis, which had promised land to rural Mexico:

> Through abuse of the law of vacant lots, many small landowners, most of them indigenous, have been deprived of their lands . . . It being just to return to the old owners the lots that have been despoiled so arbitrarily, such dispositions and findings are declared subject to review, and it will be demanded that those who acquired land through such immoral means, or their inheritors, shall return it to the original owners, who will also receive an indemnity for the losses incurred.

Next, the power of the federal army was recognized, despite the insurgents' protests, and the demobilization of the Maderista guerrillas was effected, even though they had put an end to the Porfirian era. Finally, as if the fall of the Porfirista government had been achieved through secret cabinet pressure and not as the result of a rebellion, the treaties of Ciudad Juárez established an interim government according to what was established in the law in effect: the acting secretary of foreign relations, Francisco León de la Barra, was named president.

To obliterate its own origin, demobilize its forces, and take preventive measures to avoid being scratched by the tiger's claws that it had unleashed proved to be a historic plan in Madero's rise to power. Confined by the old legality, he wanted to put to rest the agitation and expectations that had been awakened in the country he wanted to govern, in order to establish in the republic undergoing convulsive spasms a new government, not a new order. He seemed to want his movement to correspond to the impulse of a nineteenth-century political rebellion, and not the first thrusts of a twentieth-century social revolution. He soon found resistance on both sides of the road, between the unsatisfied currents that required a change and the created interests that longed for restoration.

On June 7, 1911, accompanied by a throng of more than one hundred thousand supporters, Madero entered Mexico City triumphantly. Seventeen days later, on June 24, 1911, he attempted a first interpretation of the victorious revolution in a public manifesto. Characteristically, Madero promised that he would do his utmost to alleviate the needs of the weak economic classes, but did not announce an improvement in wages; he expressed his solidarity with the dispossessed, but also his conviction that only hard work could redeem them. On the other hand, he also created uncertainty among businessmen when he admonished that they could no longer count on "the impunity that in past times was enjoyed by those privileged by fortune, for whom the law was as broad as it was narrow for the unfortunate people."

This clear example of the Maderista vocation of navigating between two rivers produced a letdown among even the closest collaborators of Madero. On June 26, 1911, only two days after the manifesto was released, Roque Estrada stated in a letter to his former leader that he and many others saw in Madero "the apostle and the *caudillo*, but never the ruler."

The Conflict Above, the Resistance Below

An important wing of the initial Maderista front, represented by Emilio and Francisco Vázquez Gómez, decided to establish a new front in order to demand the adoption of the Plan de San Luis. With the support of several revolutionary leaders, the Vazquistas began an open conspiracy to dissolve the interim government, put Madero himself in the presidency, and pave the way to the "full renovation" that the political circumstances of the country demanded.

That conflict, begun at the end of June, reached a new level on August 2, 1911, with the resignation of Emilio Vázquez Gómez as secretary of the interior and the arrest of four generals. On August 23, the Vazquista insurrectional plan was presented in Texcoco, drafted by Andrés Molina Enríquez. The plan did not recognize the government of De la Barra, handed the command of the revolution to Emilio Vázquez Gómez, reserved the right to legislate on the breaking up of the large landholdings (*latifundios*) greater than two thousand hectares, or almost five thousand acres (the claimant could select the part that he wanted), and demanded that ranches be declared corporations of social and political interest for the nation. Madero's initiative of dissolving the Anti-Reelection party, whose slogan had become irrelevant, in order to open the way to the Progressive Constitutional party, led to the split with Francisco Vázquez Gómez, who had been slated to occupy the vice-presidency with Madero. At the beginning of September, in the midst of the Vazquista uprising, the convention of the new party selected José María Pino Suárez to appear on the ticket with Madero for the upcoming elections.

The October elections found the Vazquista rebellion in full throttle, which created unrest in the northern states because the rebellion attracted several ex-Maderista *caudillos*, such as Emilio Campa and José Inés Salazar. This period also found Madero with falling levels of popular support, to the extreme that some supporters of the other conspicuous opposition figure, Gen. Bernardo Reyes, began to talk about the convenience of postponing the election. Reyes had returned to Mexico on July 9, 1911, had reorganized his partisans, had rekindled their illusions, and was predicting that in a few months the overwhelming support for Madero would diminish to the extent that he would lose the elections. But things wouldn't prove so easy. Congress refused the Reyista request for postponing the election. After a series of agreements and disagreements between Reyes and Madero, a Maderista throng harassed the old general at a rally. Mistreated and slighted, Reyes began his next-to-last political adventure and left for San Antonio to lead a new insurrection. On September 16, 1911, national independence day, he proclaimed from Texas his Plan de la Soledad, which proved to be, in effect, a solitary plan. He did not hold the sympathies of the North Americans, whose authorities arrested Reyes for violation of the neutrality laws, nor did he find many followers in Mexican territory. The expected battalions did not converge in support of the General, who finished his pathetic adventure on December 25, 1911, having surrendered of his own free will, exhausted and with his clothes in tatters, to an army garrison in Linares, Nuevo León. From there, he was transferred to the military prison of Santiago Tlatelolco, where he was imprisoned as if he were a time bomb, and from which he would emerge a year later to undertake his last adventure, on February 9, 1913. This was an insurrection initiating the "tragic week" that would stain the capital city with blood and would lead Madero's government to holocaust.

During the weak interim government, there were social movements that were not organized by the groups in power, but that also exceeded the norms of conciliation and found their own paths. A natural center of conflict was the resistance of the Maderista guerrillas to demobilization. Throughout the country, the call to demobilize brought forth riots and political turmoil, led many small bands to return to the Sierras, and gave way to revenge by the federal army against the first-time guerrillas, all done in the name of legality, of the new government, and even of Madero himself. That settlement of old accounts and the persistence of the federal army explain to a large extent the collateral persistence, until the end of 1912, of many areas of insurrection, raids, and simple banditry in many points of the country.

It was a crucial process. The resistance of some Maderista governors to the demobilizing of those forces, particularly in Sonora and Coahuila, would allow an alternative military force to begin to develop during 1911 and 1912, parallel to the still intact federal army. The so-called auxiliary corps, formed by Maderistas who had not demobilized, brought together the main insurgent leaders and their best troops in professional organized armies, paid and supported as a regular army. Considerably consolidated in the North during 1912 by the struggle against Orozquismo, until the moment of the Huerta coup d'état in 1913, those military corps could oppose an effective military network against the federal army and unleash a Constitutionalist Revolution.

Speaking of demobilization, the Zapatistas, as always, went beyond the norm: they tied any surrender of weapons to the simultaneous and equal handing over of land. Thus, protracted negotiations between Zapata and the central government began, including several unfruitful interviews with Madero. The last of them, between August 18 and 25 in Cuautla, only preceded the reinitiation of the federal army offensive against the Morelos peasants. Town by town, the new Zapatista war rearmed its partisans and spread incursions to the very doors of Mexico City. By September, in the peculiar modality of guerrilla warfare, which would dominate the political and military organization of southern Mexico during the following decade, the entire territory of Morelos was in insurrection and the federal army, as in the Porfirian era, fought once again the irreducible bands of ignorance, cruel illiteracy, and "that amorphous agrarian socialism," as Madero himself would qualify them in his report to Congress on April 1, 1912, "that for the simple minds of the peasants of Morelos could only adopt the form of sinister vandalism."

Outrage in the South

Madero was elected president on October 1, 1911, by an overwhelming 98 percent of the vote, in the freest elections that Mexico had held until then. On November 6, he assumed power and began to rule over a democratic republic, socially paralyzed, in whose conflagration he would lose his life.

He was no longer the universal and unquestioned apostle he had been when he entered the capital on June 6, acclaimed by the masses. He was a man who had turned his back on many of his supporters. He had imposed his candidate for vice-president, José María Pino Suárez, whose election required manipulation and coercion in certain states of the republic. With the policy of demobilization, he had alienated the will of and created suspicion in the hearts of many combatants, leaders, and politicians who had accompanied him in the insurrection of 1911. He had placed the army in the middle of a pacification campaign, undertaken to a large extent against the southern towns and the Maderista bands of yesteryear. He had tried to reach a settlement with the old regime by introducing conservative figures into his government, clearly linked to the Díaz dictatorship, and he had not undertaken any significant social reform, forgetting his initial agrarian promises. At the same time, despite all of his concessions to those who sought restoration, he not only had failed to achieve the confidence of foreign interests and entrepreneurial groups, and high-level Porfirian bureaucrats and financiers, but he had sealed his fate before them as a usurper, a crazy dreamer, an unscrupulous promoter of his family interests, who sooner or later would have to pay for his sins.

Madero was convinced that the country needed a political change, not a social reform. As a result, his governmental project was extraordinarily open with respect to democratic liberties—parliament, press, elections—and extraordinarily closed with respect to social reforms and the transformation of the hereditary privileges of the old order. Such was the case of the army, which he not only failed to dismantle, but rather placed at the center of his government as an active dam to the dissatisfaction of his own comrades of yesteryear; and it was also the case of the Maderista bureaucracy, which in its great majority repeated that of the Porfirian establishment. Those who sought in the revolutionary flux something more than a new government and a new social immobility parted ways from the Maderista flow.

Only twenty days after the assumption of power, following a short but harsh experience of military repression and the devastation of their towns and crops, the Zapatista towns adopted the document that established the meaning and the goals of their struggle, the Plan de Ayala, and reinitiated the war with that other world that, with subtle shades of difference, Madero and his soldiers, and his reform projects, still represented.

In that document, signed on November 25, 1911, Madero was depicted as having violated the principles of effective suffrage and no reelection that he had vowed to defend; as a man who had affronted "the faith, the cause, the justice and the liberties of the people," the man "who imposed as governmental norm his will and influenced the provisional government," leading to "reiterative bloodshed," and the "traitor to the fatherland, by humiliating by blood and fire the Mexicans who wanted liberties in order to please the *científicos*, landowners and caciques that enslave us."

The style was poor—John Womack attributed it to the rhetorical fantasy of Otilio Montaño—but the political diagnosis of the Maderista limits was accurate:

> The Chief of the Liberating Revolution of Mexico, Don Francisco I.
> Madero . . . did not carry to a happy end the revolution which
> gloriously he initiated with the help of God and the people, since
> he left standing most of the governing powers and corrupt elements
> of oppression of the dictatorial government of Porfirio Díaz, . . .

which are provoking the discomfort of the country and opening new wounds . . . [Madero] tries to avoid the fulfillment of the promises which he made to the Nation in the Plan of San Luis Potosí.

The Plan de Ayala was the clear and organic expression of the affront that the Maderista conciliation was inflicting on the social forces that had become agitated with the insurrection of 1910. It was also a significant rupture given the anti-Madero virulence, a lack of verbal control that would be characteristic of the forces that would later converge in the destruction of the apostle.

The Plan de Ayala did not address the problem of power and its reorganization. It limited itself to naming Pascual Orozco as leader of the Liberating Revolution and Zapata as backup, in case Orozco declined the offer. It was a program par excellence of a peasant rebellion and the agrarian struggle in Mexico. It stipulated that the towns and citizens that had been dispossessed of land, hills, and water would immediately regain the property of these assets, "keeping at any cost, and with arms in hand, their possession." It defined as the obligation of the "usurpers"—not of the occupying peasants—the need to demonstrate before the courts their property rights. A third part of the land, hills, and water would be expropriated, since at the time they were being used only by lazy owners who monopolized the land, and the totality of the assets of those "*científicos,* landowners and caciques" who opposed the Plan de Ayala would be nationalized.

The Loss of the Muleteer

The Zapatista rebellion was the longest-lasting of the rebellions of 1911, and would extend itself throughout Madero's term until merging with the new insurrectional wave of 1913. It was, however, the rebellion of Pascual Orozco that provided a definite sign that Madero's government was struggling to maintain a delicate and impossible balance between the two adversaries that were encircling it. On one hand were the demands of the radical strain of the revolutionary impulse; on the other, the rancor, distrust, and demands for restoration of the forces of the counterrevolution. Orozco's rebellion seemed to join these two poles in an explosive mix. It began in March of 1912, but it was slowly incubated in the errors and indecision of Maderismo, beginning with Madero's initial affront of turning his back on the forces that had brought him to power.

At the end of 1911, Pascual Orozco was, like many others, a leader who had become resentful of the ease with which Madero and his group forgot his services as soon as their path to Mexico City was clear. The Maderistas rewarded the vital military contribution of Orozco with the post of commander of the rural guards of Chihuahua, a "modest position," according to historian Michael Meyer, "remunerated with an even more modest salary: eight pesos per day."

Orozco then sought another avenue by accepting the candidacy for governor of Chihuahua, responding to pressures from local forces. But Madero's candidate was Abraham González, and the interim state government worked in his favor and against Orozco. Newspapers, street speeches, rallies, and politicians of all stripes supported González without hesitation and attached to Orozco and his followers the persistent label of reactionaries. Finally, Madero himself asked the old muleteer to forget the whole deal. Orozco relinquished his candidacy in July, but he did not forget.

Madero had his reasons for preferring Abraham González as governor, an enlightened man with whom he could reach agreements and in whose administrative ability he could trust, rather than the old muleteer whom only war and violence had brought forth from an anonymous existence in the northern countryside. But Orozco saw this preference as personal treason and as new proof that the democratic promises of the Plan de San Luis were just a joke. Insult was then added to injury. On September 1911, cautious of the possible links between Orozco and Reyismo, interim President De la Barra decided to relieve him of his command of the rural guard of Chihuahua (a state that Bernardo Reyes could set on fire from San Antonio if Orozco supported him) and transferred him to Sinaloa with the same position, although with almost double the salary. When he assumed power in November, Madero returned the muleteer to Chihuahua, now as head of the garrison of Ciudad Juárez.

Orozco did not heed the Reyista insinuations, and later he restrained some of his old collaborators, such as Antonio Rojas, who had sided with the Vazquista rebellion. But in January 1912, after an interview with Madero in Mexico City, he resigned his military post in Chihuahua and began to tread the path toward a definite split. In that interview, Madero asked Orozco two things that were unreasonable. First, that he exert pressure on the state legislature so that the interim governor (substitute for Abraham González, who had left for the capital to join the Maderista cabinet) be granted special authority in several areas, including the military. Second, that he transfer to the Zapatista front to do what the regular army had thus far been unable to do with the southerners: annihilate them. Orozco had already tasted the sour aspects of state politics, and he had no reason to strengthen the interim governor with powers that later could be used against him. And his relations with Zapata, even though they were inorganic and fluid, still maintained the deep bond of common rural origin and parallel personal history, aspects that the Chihuahuan general could not feel in the heights of the Maderista government. Formalizing that affinity, article 3 of the Plan de Ayala had recognized Orozco as the leader of the revolution that Madero was now asking him to put down. Orozco resigned. Madero did not accept his resignation, and the northern general gave him one more demonstration of his loyalty when he dealt with a second Vazquista insurrection in Chihuahua. Toward the end of February, however, that revolt spread to several places in the state, and the local legislature, recognizing the weakness of the interim governor, Aurelio González, accepted his resignation and finally named Orozco governor to contain the rebellion.

But by then Orozco no longer wanted the position. Accepting it would have meant confronting his own comrades-in-arms of former times: Emilio Campa, José Inés Salazar, and Demetrio Ponce, who had gone back to the Sierra under the Vazquista banner. And Orozco had already made the decision to break with Madero. Besides the personal reasons that the muleteer might have had, the groups of landowners, merchants, and bankers in the state had been waiting and promoting that upheaval since 1911. The Maderista government had been threatening since the beginning of the year new fiscal legislation that would restrict their profits. They needed a strongman.

For his part, Orozco needed financing, and he was receptive to the flattery and distinctions that recognized he was a clear example of Madero's ingratitude toward those who had led him to victory, the victory that Madero was now "distributing" among his friends and family. Having become conceited and irritated, as well as seduced by the voices of old lieutenants who had already raised their rifles, Orozco placed himself in the hands of those who were calling him to rebel, offering him financial aid in order to fight against those who had left him behind.

Unfortunately, his backers saw him once again as an instrument, and their interests were far removed from the general's vague premonition of his tasks of renewal in the future. The money of the Chihuahuan oligarchy flowed to finance the payroll and the arms bill of the armies of a man who, instinctively, was fighting to destroy that very thing in the Maderista government that so resembled the Chihuahuan oligarchy financing him.

A Triumphant Army

The rebellion was declared on March 3, 1912; on the twenty-fifth of that month, it found its code in the so-called Plan de la Empacadora, which included a strong condemnation of Madero and postulated a virulent anti-U.S. nationalism, a sentiment that would determine its fate in arms-trafficking and collaboration with U.S. authorities on the border, one of the reasons the Orozquista movement was unable to extend beyond a certain point.

In the political realm, the Orozquista plan demanded the elimination of the vice-presidency and the political leaders, an effective municipal autonomy, a guarantee of all forms of freedom of expression, and the extension of the presidential term from four to six years. In the economic and social realms, it demanded the immediate elimination of the *tiendas de raya* (*hacienda*-owned shop debts), the payment of workers in monetary wages, a ten-hour workday, severe restrictions on child labor, and the promise of better wages and improved working conditions. The agrarian question was approached with less radicalism, but also with more options than the Plan de Ayala: those who had lived on a lot for more than twenty years would receive property titles for the land, the lands taken away illegally from the peasants would be returned, and all of the fallow and nationalized lands would be distributed among the peasants. Landowners who failed to keep their lands under regular cultivation would have their land expropriated and would be compensated with agricultural bonds that would pay a 4 percent interest rate.

After the plan, came the bullets. The Orozquista rebellion initially began in the western highlands of Chihuahua and eastern Sonora, precisely as the Maderista rebellion had begun. In certain regions, the rebellion caught on even faster.

Most of Chihuahua fell into the hands of the Orozquistas before the government could react, and the Orozquismo advanced toward the South. On March 23, in Rellano, an intermediate point between Torreón and Chihuahua, there was the first formal battle between the rebels and the government, with a disastrous result for the federal army. Its commander, José González Salas, humiliated by the defeat, committed suicide during the retreat.

The federal defeat made evident the lack of trustworthy military cadres in the army. In the midst of the general hysteria in the capital, which already saw a triumphant new revolution descending from the North, a general named Victoriano Huerta reappeared in Madero's administration when Madero put him in charge of the military campaign. It was the same general who, disregarding Madero's instructions, had unilaterally broken a cease-fire with the Zapatistas in August 1911, leading to a split of the southerners with Maderismo. The defeat of Rellano changed the situation, and the strength of Huerta's military capacity overshadowed his political disloyalty.

Huerta assumed the campaign competently: he rebuilt the military line to Torreón, prepared his defenses during April, and resisted an Orozquista attack on Monclova in Coahuila. He once again confronted the bulk of the rebel battalions in Rellano on May 23, 1912, scoring a victory that broke the back of the regular Orozquista army. What remained was a gradual campaign of consolidating his military strength and fighting the guerrillas, which proved uncomfortable and slow, but in no way threatening to the federal military dominion over the republic, or even that of the northern states or the state of Chihuahua itself, whose capital Huerta entered with his army on July 8, 1912.

By the beginning of October, the Orozquista rebellion had ended, its battalions had been swept from Sonora, and Orozco himself had crossed over to the United States, acknowledging his defeat. In contrast, the federal army had reaped legitimacy and prestige in that campaign; its commanders appeared as true bulwarks of the established order, and they were seen as victorious for the first time against the irregular armies; the foreign interests began to see in Huerta the strongman who would be capable of fixing Madero's broken-down democracy.

In October, a nephew of Porfirio, Félix Díaz, took up arms in Veracruz, with the peculiar argument that the honor of the army had been trodden upon. His call for military solidarity for a coup d'état was unsuccessful, and toward the end of October, after a brief skirmish, the army itself retook the city and sent the nephew to a military prison in Mexico City. A court tried the rebel and condemned him to death. Deputies of the legislature interceded before Madero, and the Supreme Court decided that Díaz was not subject to military justice. Toward the end of November, given the public and political pressure in defense of the rights of the rebel despite his clear dictatorial aims, Díaz was once again imprisoned, like Bernardo Reyes, in a military prison.

Thus, by the fall of 1912, the armed movements that defied the Maderista stability had vanished. The geographic location of the Zapatista war was not threatening the government as a whole. The Vazquismo movement had dissolved, Generals Bernardo Reyes and Félix Díaz were imprisoned, and the defeat of Orozquismo had cleared the mountains and towns of the North of the armed opposition.

The Dictatorial Democracy

Things weren't going badly on other fronts, as well. After a year of strikes and tensions with the workers, particularly in the Veracruz–Puebla–Federal District industrial corridor of textile factories, the Maderista government had been able to satisfy the basic needs of the workers: reduction of the number of working hours, general increase of wages, putting an end to the impunity of punishments, wage cuts, and reprimands that made of the interior of the factories a rural *hacienda* culture. The industrialists obtained in exchange stricter regulation of the working conditions, schedules, rest periods, and responsibilities and greater possibilities for higher productivity. It was a success in bargaining precisely in the way in which Porfirio Díaz four years earlier had reaped the bloody message of Río Blanco. Toward the end of 1912, as an extension of this important agreement in the textile sector, the Department of Labor, which had been established in December of the previous year, began preparing a labor code for all industrial workers.

On the agrarian front, the same legislature and Council of Ministers was studying an original project for the restitution of the lands taken away from the peasant communities during the Porfirian regime, and had finished a survey of national lands. These measures seemed to set the stage for the initiation of an agrarian reform, as timid as one could imagine it, but the first political response of some significance to the fundamental demand that lay beneath the rough facade of the uprisings that had shaken the country and still shook in its peasant heart, the South. When 1912 ended, many factors seemed to presage a positive future. But the distrust, the divisions, and the intrigue corroded the Maderista regime. The setting for the erosion was the Congress, public opinion, the army, the diplomatic corps, and the U.S. embassy.

The chambers of deputies and senators, elected in the open elections of June 30, 1912, were the center of the institutionalized counterrevolution and the Maderista division. There, the new regime was asked to provide guarantees to the interests of the old regime, and in its seats Maderismo spent on infighting what it should have invested in consolidating itself. The press was the center of scandal. The newspapers were full of sensational and systematic reports of banditry, plundering, harvest losses, factory closures, and breakups of companies and families. Full of exaggeration and ridicule, the prevailing image was of a country characterized by chronic insecurity and governmental inability to guarantee stability. To the government's requests that the situation should not be exaggerated, the opposition responded by accusing the government of acting as an ostrich, while the press launched against Madero the most intense campaign of abuse and personal attack that anyone has been subject to in the history of Mexico. In relentless satires, caricatures, and verses, Madero was described time and time again as a physical and mental dwarf, an indecisive spirit, a cynical nepotist, a second-rate apostle, a little man without pants, and the greatest fiasco as a ruler. The most scandalous aspect of this relentless outpouring was, perhaps, that it was directed against a man who upheld the principle that it should be allowed in the name of democracy.

But the abuse, the discredit, the internal divisions, and the capital's hysterical reaction to the vandalism that the revolution had left would not have been enough to remove the Maderista government, had the U.S. ambassador, Henry Lane Wilson, not participated in open conspiracy with the army (who had been plotting for several months). Wilson represented a government that would abandon the White House in the first months of 1913, but that, regardless, had determined in its final stretch to overthrow the government of its neighboring country.

From the Embassy to the Firing Squad

Ambassador Wilson systematically had told his government a peculiar story of the new regime. The dominant note in his version was the insecurity of North American lives and properties, the inability of the government and of the dreamer that resided in the National Palace to reestablish a lasting peace, the unrest of the foreign interests, the anxiety of the European governments due to the turmoil, and the need to put an end to that carnival with a North American intervention and with the imposition of a stable and strong government.

In support of his version, Ambassador Wilson invented the exodus of desperate U.S. citizens, distributed arms to groups of resident U.S. citizens, persuaded his government of the need to station warships on the Mexican coasts, and constantly assured the White House (Republican President Taft and Secretary of State Knox) that in his campaign against North American interests in Mexico, Madero would decree confiscations and unfair laws. Following Wilson's reports, on September 15, 1912, Washington sent Madero the strongest diplomatic note thus far, accusing him of discriminating against U.S. companies and citizens, among other things because he established a tax on crude oil (twenty cents per ton).

The diplomatic note was responded to with denials. At that moment, according to German envoy to Mexico Paul Hintze, "Washington felt the need to act," and in a long conversation with President Taft and Secretary of State Knox, Wilson proposed taking over part of the territory and keeping it, or overthrowing Madero's regime. President Taft had been predisposed to doing both things, but Knox expressed his opposition to the idea of occupying Mexican territory. Then, the three agreed to subvert Madero's government. With this aim, they would use the threat of intervention, promises of positions and honors, and direct cash bribes.

Referring to Madero and the Mexican situation, President Taft wrote to his secretary of state on December 16, 1912: "I am reaching the conclusion that we should place some dynamite, with the goal of waking up that dreamer that seems incapable of solving the crisis in the country of which he is President."

The conspiracy blew up within the army on February 9, 1913, with the uprising of several sections of the capital's garrison, which set free the renowned political prisoners Félix Díaz and Bernardo Reyes, but failed to take control of the National Palace—Reyes was killed in the skirmish. The conspirators took refuge in the *ciudadela* (citadel) under Díaz's command to begin the "Tragic Ten Days" of a "false war" that threw the capital into turmoil, horrified its inhabitants, proved the inefficiency of the government, and gave way to the final coup against Madero.

On February 10, 1913, Ambassador Wilson informed the White House that negotiations were taking place between the leader of the insurgents, Félix Díaz, and General Victoriano Huerta, whom President Madero had once again put in command of the army, in a vain attempt to repeat the victorious formula of the confrontation against Orozco. Wilson immediately promised Huerta that Washington would recognize "any government capable of establishing peace and order in place of the government of Señor Madero." He then called the diplomats from England, Germany, and Spain to establish a representative diplomatic group that could intervene politically. He suggested that the White House send "firm, drastic and perhaps threatening instructions to be personally transmitted to the government of President Madero." On February 11, Wilson did in fact visit President Madero to threaten him with the intervention of North American warships to protect the foreigners and to express his sympathy for Félix Díaz, given the fact that he had always been "pro North American." On February 14, he told Pablo Lascuráin, the Maderista secretary of foreign relations, that four thousand North American soldiers were due to arrive, with whom Wilson would personally reestablish order if President Madero did not convince himself that he should abandon power through legal means. On February 15, Wilson was able to convey the same message to Madero through the Spanish representative, Cologan, emissary of the recently created diplomatic group. On February 16, Wilson boycotted a cease-fire that he himself had requested so that foreigners near the battle zone could get their belongings out, and he admitted to the German envoy that he was in constant communication with Félix Díaz and Huerta. On February 17, inside the U.S. embassy, he concluded the final negotiations among the coup forces, after a series of meetings with their representatives. The German ambassador wrote in his diary:

He [Wilson] has proposed as a basis for negotiation: a government under the command of De la Barra, Huerta and Díaz would always find support in the United States. Senator Obregón, one of the delegates, asked him formally if the United States would renounce intervention if such a government constituted itself; [Wilson] responded affirmatively. General Blanquet's troops had joined forces with [Félix] Díaz, but Blanquet is inside the Palace. He [Wilson] thinks that after the conversations that have taken place yesterday—February 17—the deal will be completed today.

It was completed at 1:30 in the afternoon of February 18, 1913, the hour in which Victoriano Huerta's troops detained President Madero. Other troops detained and tortured to death his brother, Gustavo.

By three in the afternoon, Ambassador Wilson brought together the diplomatic corps to propose a vote of confidence for Huerta and the army. Shortly after, he received Huerta and Díaz in the embassy, so that they could arrange among themselves the distribution of power, and he suggested to one of Díaz's aides that he should "cede and allow" Huerta to become interim president. Otherwise, he said, "true war" would be unleashed. On February 21, he instructed all the U.S. consuls to promote, for the "well-being of Mexico," the "submission and adhesion of all of the elements of the Republic" to the new government. Finally, when Huerta asked what would be better for Madero—sending him "outside the country or to an insane asylum"—Ambassador Wilson limited himself to responding that Huerta should do "whatever he thought best for the country." Huerta did just that: on the following day, Madero and Pino Suárez were taken out of their prison cells, placed against the walls of the penitentiary, and shot by a rural corporal and a member of the federal army.

2.
The Revolutions
Are the Revolution:
1913–1920

In the beginning, nobody moved. The inhabitants of the nation's capital—and of other provincial capitals—celebrated in the streets the end of the bombing and the terror, decorated the fronts of their houses, and read in the newspapers the reasons for their own jubilation on Madero's fall. Next, proper form was observed. Following article 81 of the constitution, Secretary of Foreign Relations Pablo Lascuráin, diligent negotiator for Ambassador Wilson with Madero, assumed the presidency of the republic. Michael Meyer and William Sherman recount:

> Sworn into office at 10:24 P.M., Lascuráin immediately appointed General Huerta as secretary of interior and at 11:20 P.M. submitted his own resignation. The Constitution of 1857 provided that in the absence of a president, a vice-president, and a secretary of foreign relations, the office passed to the secretary of interior. Huerta, clad in a formal black tuxedo, was sworn into office shortly before midnight. Madero-style democracy had ended in derision as Mexico had its third president in one day.

The judicial power congratulated the new ruler through the president of the Supreme Court, Francisco S. Carbajal, and guarantees were given to the chambers for their customary operation.

The care taken to maintain proper form was as fleeting as the presidency of Lascuráin. Before the year was over, Huerta had dissolved Congress, imprisoned several legislators, murdered Chiapaneco Deputy Belisario Domínguez for having circulated a pamphlet demanding the ouster of dictatorial government, assumed extraordinary powers in the areas of war, finance, and government, and postponed indefinitely the election of president and vice-president that had been promised for October 1913. He had also broken pacts with his fellow conspirators, whom he had displaced from their initial positions, and he was running a government by brute force that in the following months would be responsible for several notorious murders and more than one hundred proven cases of *ley fuga* (killing prisoners for supposedly attempting escape).

But Madero's death shook the republic. The country that had buried him as a ruler once again sought him as a symbol of its frustrations and hopes. In 1910, very dissimilar forces had come forth when he called for democracy. The news of his death in 1913 extinguished the hopes for change, rallied all the remaining insurrectional forces, and removed from the Huertista government any appearance of legitimacy. Huerta promptly found himself with no instrument other than the army, and no long-term alliance other than the forces for restoration: landowners and businessmen, foreign interests, the Porfirian bureaucracy, the aristocracy, and the goodwill of the U.S. embassy, even though the U.S. government had changed with the new year, and saw its initial hope of placing Félix Díaz, a "trusted pro-U.S. politician," as Madero's successor wither away in the entanglement of the Huertista intrigue. The counter-revolutionary forces had been enough to carry out the coup d'état, but proved insufficient to reestablish a lasting national pact.

The Thread of History

The pact remained broken in the South. With Madero dead, the Zapatistas continued their war and issued a proclamation calling for arms against Huerta, not to be put down until the Plan de Ayala was fulfilled. But harmony was also breaking down in the North. Before the month of May was over, the governments of Coahuila and Sonora had broken with the national government. The murder of Maderista Governor Abraham González in Chihuahua had left the field open for a formidable popular insurrection, whose legendary intensity can be summed up with the name Francisco Villa. The northern sierras of Durango and Sinaloa, Zacatecas and San Luis Potosí were once again populated with rebel bands. And there was the armed harvest of literally hundreds of insurrections in small cities, towns, and ranches that would lend to the war against Huerta the multitudinous aspect that the Maderista uprising achieved only in some regions in the North.

For the governor of Coahuila, Venustiano Carranza, old landlord and ex–Porfirista senator, the ascent of Huerta to power simply meant the breaking down of the constitutional order that prevailed in the republic. As a legitimate authority, Carranza found the narrow thread of history in the decision to break with Huerta in order to establish himself, by that simple act, as the representative of the assailed constitutionality—an act that would enable him to call the nation to overthrow the "usurping government" of Mexico City. The narrow thread of history: it was the historical certainty of being the only legitimate representative left in the country as long as he was the only one who refused to recognize the dictatorial authorities of the federation. And there was the practical certainty of not having any other road open, because the consolidation of Huertista power would represent for Maderista governors such as Carranza definite political destruction and perhaps even death.

Carranza took the funds deposited in the banks of his state on loan, assured the military chiefs and the central government that he would support the coup, regrouped the few loyal forces he had left—ex-Maderista battalions that had not been demobilized under the command of his brother Jesús Carranza and Pablo González—and, finally, he orchestrated a resolution by the local congress disavowing the central government. He then left Saltillo, the administrative capital, on March 1, 1913; six days later, he was involved in a skirmish in Anhelo; fourteen days later, he attempted unsuccessfully to retake Saltillo; and, at the end of March he took refuge with his seven hundred soldiers in the *hacienda* of Guadalupe.

There, the errant governor—without funds, administrative apparatus, or a regular army—prepared, debated, and signed with his officers the so-called Plan de Guadalupe, which disavowed the power of the federation and of the state governments that thirty days after the announcement of the plan had still not pledged to break with the Huertista regime. The document recognized Governor Carranza as the First Chief of the Constitutionalist Revolution, despite the fact that he had been unable to take over a garrison with a thousand men in Saltillo a few days earlier. Although the document lacked articles to address the required social reforms—which created some reservations among signing officers such as Francisco J. Múgica and Lucio Blanco—the plan of the *hacienda* of Guadalupe presaged the victory of the cause and the organization of a new government. It was March 26, 1913.

Sonora's Reasons

In the border cities and the governmental offices of the nearby northern state of Sonora, the conditions for victory that Carranza and his men anticipated in Coahuila were already falling into place. At the end of February, the Maderista governor of the state, José María Maytorena, political and social twin of Madero, inheritor of a patriarchal family of displaced landowners, had decided to withdraw from the scene, as a victim of the same peculiar political split that had characterized Maderismo: he couldn't close his eyes to the atrocities of the coup in Mexico City and the assassination of Madero, but he couldn't put himself in charge of an uncertain rebellion that would demand expropriations and, if successful, would suck into its whirlpool the family, social, and political interests to which governor Maytorena was inextricably linked.

He asked for sick leave and went into exile, leaving the state in the hands of a new generation of politicians and military leaders that Maderismo had extracted from their Porfirian incubation.

The prerevolutionary history of those Sonorense leaders reveals a group of men committed to survival, not out of material desperation, hunger, or unemployment, but rather because of the lack of opportunities due to the accumulated privileges of the local oligarchies and the lack of access to decision-making and political positions, as well as to large businesses. Manuel M. Diéguez was the accounting assistant of the superintendent of Cananea mines, because he knew English and a bit of business administration. Esteban Baca Calderón was a schoolteacher who had studied the Jacobin and Liberal slogans, had arrived at Cananea searching for a suitable environment for his Magonista political work, and who, in his own words, had formed his character on "the anvil of intellectual work, in the difficult struggle to dissipate the darkness of ignorance and fanaticism." Benjamín Hill was the legal representative of the emerging municipality of Navojoa, owner of two properties that added up to 2,500 hectares (6,175 acres) without irrigation, a flour mill, and a family name whose local history was immersed in legend and prestige. Adolfo de la Huerta was manager of "one of the most important companies of Guaymas" (the *hacienda* and tannery of Don Francisco Fourcade) and also a bachelor in great demand, due to his tenor voice, at the parties of the port high society, whose upper crust families still regarded him, nevertheless, as a *zapetudo* (social climber). Francisco Serrano was a smallholder of Huatabampo, who had started out as an opposition journalist in the independent campaign of Ferrel against the Cañedista domination of Sinaloa and had been able to secure the position of private secretary to Governor Maytorena in 1911. Alvaro Obregón was also a small landowner who harvested chickpeas for export in Huatabampo, a man who at the age of twenty was already an expert in agricultural machinery, and by 1911 had invented a harvester whose iron mold had already been requested from a smelter in Culiacán; he was a poor but profitable relative of the Salido landowners, the most modern of the Mayo region. Plutarco Elías Calles had been a schoolteacher and bureaucrat in the Guaymas treasury, but above all he had been manager of a flour mill in the North of the state (with a monthly wage of 300 pesos), administrator of the *haciendas* of his father, Plutarco Elías Lucero, and, as he defined himself in a 1909 letter to the authorities, "a proper man dedicated to work, and an unconditional friend of the government." Salvador Alvarado was a small merchant who had tried his luck as a pharmacist in Guaymas, and as a villager had been suffocated by municipal corruption in his hometown of Potam, Río Yaqui. Juan Cabral's parents did not lack the resources to board their son at Sonora High School—the best in the state—nor did their son lack the will to launch himself at the age of 19 as an orator in opposition to Mexican *caciquismo*, during his vacations in La Colorada, the most important mining center in the District of Hermosillo.

If the revolution hadn't come along, all of these men would have been half-successful as managers, merchants, and farmers, but they wouldn't have had a means to achieve—beyond political prominence—the social and economic status of the Porfirian oligarchy, to whose displacement and, at the same time, emulation they devoted themselves from the positions and with the resources that the revolution placed in their hands. With time, both in their spoils and in their enterprises, the only consistent social project of these middle sectors would be the expulsion of the old oligarchy of landowners and businessmen.

In the context of the Sonora rebellion, these small farmers, middle managers, merchants, teachers, and modest ranchers achieved political and military supremacy by displacing the Maderista leadership of landowners. In particular, due to the bitter fight against the state government and the class initiatives of José María Maytorena—a patriarchal heir who aligned himself with Maderismo through the Reyista faction as a representative of the great pre-Porfirian families who saw themselves cornered in their "feudal estates" by U.S. investments, capitalist agriculture, colonization deals, and the strict political control of an aging triumvirate (Rafael Izábal, Luis Torres, and Ramón Corral).

That legion of newcomers had consolidated prestige and positions during the successful campaign of the previous year against the Orozquista armies that flooded the eastern part of the state, and that had built a small state army exceeding three thousand soldiers, with its own officer corps and an organization that derived its line of loyalty from the contempt and distrust of the federal army. Following Maytorena's resignation at the end of February, the local legislature, evoking the powerful Sonorense motivation of state sovereignty threatened by pressures from the center, rejected, on March 5, 1913, Huerta's claims to legality, and the interim governor, Ignacio Pesqueira, called one and all to insurrection. From the top of the constituted government, the Sonorense leaders sent their armies against the federal forces, as if they were battalions of an occupation army.

A recent hero of the battles against Orozquismo, Alvaro Obregón, was placed in command of the local armies, which first advanced toward the North on the garrisons of the large mines and the strategic frontier from which arms, munitions, uniforms, and even airplanes would come. The government of Hermosillo devoted itself to encouraging the recently developed habit of self-defense—it had fought this way during the 1912 Orozquista rebellion in the state—by mobilizing municipal presidents, prefects, commissioners, and neighbors to form small volunteer groups that would later concentrate in larger bodies.

By the end of March, the rebels had enough power to guarantee an insurrection directed from the government palace of Hermosillo: two border ports, Nogales and Agua Prieta; the most important mining city of the state, Cananea; and agreements with the main mining, trading, and cattle-raising firms to pay their taxes to the rebel authorities. Before March was over, the initial three thousand armed men had doubled, and all of Sonora, except the port of Guaymas and the southern garrisons, were under rebel control.

Villa's Motives

What in Sonora was only a professional process of reuniting the militias and ex-Maderista leaders who had been displaced by the demobilization to rural corps and auxiliary battalions—these corps received the name of "irregulars"—was in the rest of the country a hailstorm of fragmented uprisings, connected also by the iron thread of the past: Maderista leaders and troops reinitiated in February 1913 the war that had been artificially stopped in 1911, and promptly mobilized to continue their duel against the federal army, which Madero's conciliation had left at a standstill.

At the gateway to Mexico City, Jesús Agustín Castro started an uprising and began to move North, with the 21st Rural Corps under his command. Near Mazatlán, Juan Carrasco and his irregular troops tested the impulse for insurrection, and on March 6 began their own revolt to "overthrow Huerta." In Tepic, Rafael Buelna began his adventure, a scholar who had only just left his adolescence behind and would soon become the young hero par excellence of the Revolution. The Maderista colonels from Durango, Calixto Contreras and Orestes Pereyra, took over a segment of the 22nd Rural Corps to begin their forays from town to town, and would build in the following five months an army of 2,500 men. With the elements of the 48th and 21st Rural Corps, Gertrudis Sánchez rebelled in Michoacán, promoting himself to general over six hundred men, and together with the self-appointed colonel, Joaquín Amaro, took over Tacámbaro on April 14. A corporal of the irregular battalions of Zacatecas, Fortunato Maycotte, took off with two hundred men to join the anti-Huerta adventure. José Baños in Pochutla, Pablo

Pineda in Juchitán, and Rómulo Figueroa—of a traditional anti-reelection family—in Guerrero returned to the war that Madero had interrupted with his victory, which had resumed with his death.

None of these renewed guerrillas had the popular intensity and mass following of the new *caudillo* of the western sierra of Chihuahua and Durango, the old bandit Doroteo Arango, now known as Francisco Villa. A Maderista soldier, recently escaped from the military prison of Santiago Tlatelolco, where he had been incarcerated for insubordination during the Orozquista campaign of the previous year, Villa had been rescued by Madero himself from the firing squad after Victoriano Huerta condemned him to death in that campaign. Now, with Madero dead, he came back from his exile seeking revenge, without knowing that he was starting to build one of the most effective popular armies of modern times.

In Chihuahua, Huerta had been able to attract the grieved soul of Pascual Orozco to the cause of the coup, together with numerous creditors of the same affront that had become affixed in the Chihuahua bureaucracy, Congress, and oligarchy. The first victim of that settling of accounts was the governor of the state, Abraham González, who was kidnapped and later murdered at the beginning of March by Huerta's minions. Thus, the most moderate political group was eliminated, which would have been capable of directing in Chihuahua, as well as in Sonora and in Coahuila, an organized rebellion from above, or at least would have muted the raw popular fury at its procedures and demands. Through the crack left open by that abolished leadership, the tumult of the Villista insurrection took center stage in Chihuahua, with its irrepressible fury, tributary more of violent excess than of Carranza's pondering on legitimacy or the antioligarchic sentiment of the rising leaders of Sonora.

Francisco Villa was the glowing actualization of an agrarian and warrior utopia that in the North of Mexico took the form of military colonies. Sharecropper of a *hacienda*, outlaw educated in the cowboy wisdom of the sierra, a wanderer, Villa was the natural son of community life, armed and in the open, that the Apaches and cattle rustling had imposed as a way of life on the isolated towns and the border territories of nineteenth-century Chihuahua. He was one of the natural sons of these towns, always willing to defend by their own hands their land, homes, and family when confronted by external hostility, towns without an economic surplus for seigneurial distinctions, educated in hard work, the horse, and the rifle, a warrior discipline, and the egalitarianism of a society without hierarchies.

Doroteo Arango wanted to return to that society, to a simple, rough, and stimulating world, highlighted by threats and raids, which he had left to become a bandit. It was the world that he aspired to establish and re-create in the republics of military colonies inhabited by the veterans of the revolution, whose general characteristics he described to John Reed in 1914. In those colonies, which would receive land from the state, the men would work three days per week, and on the other three would receive military training and would teach the people how to fight. Thus, when the entire country found itself threatened, as had the military colonies of the isolated North fifty years before, "a telephone call from the national palace would be enough, and in half a day all of the Mexican people would rise up in the countryside and the factories, completely armed and well organized, to defend their children and their homes. My greatest ambition is to live my life in one of these military colonies, among the comrades that I cherish, who have suffered so much and so deeply with me."

It is the history of a nineteenth-century guerrilla who did not want change, and, in order to accomplish that, developed an awe-inspiring professional war machine. The incarnation of that spirit, Francisco Villa, without intermediaries, attracted the popular rebellion of Chihuahua and Durango and entered the country seeking revenge on March 6, 1913, with eight armed men on horseback riding beside him; a month later, he would have five hundred men, and weeks later, twelve hundred men.

The Tide and the Gringos

At the end of March 1913, the outline of a new rebellion had become clear, which this time would destroy the Porfirista army: the constant Zapatista front in the South and center of Mexico; the columns loyal to the First Chief Carranza that would establish an army of the Northeast under the unimaginative command of Pablo González; the organized forces of the rebel government of Sonora that would carry forth the campaign on the Pacific Coast until establishing the military genius of Alvaro Obregón; and the great Villista tide, which was destined to break the back of the federal resistance and eventually would ride down to the center of the republic in the trains of the Division of the North.

On April 18, 1913, in Monclova, representatives of all of the Northern forces recognized the Plan de Guadalupe as a common guide, and then, in a period of fifteen months, the "Constitutionalist Revolution" unfolded. Between March and April, the federal army was wiped out of the state of Sonora, except the port of Guaymas, which would remain under siege until the final defeat of Huerta. Villa passed from Chihuahua to La Laguna, and soon he had an army of ten thousand men, which he christened on September 29 as the Division of the North; he took Torreón on October 3, Ciudad Juárez in mid-November, Chihuahua on

December 8, and the entire state of Chihuahua on January 11, when he defeated the Huertista troops in the battle of Ojinaga.

In May, Zapata disavowed Orozco, assumed the command of the Liberating Army of the South, and organized a military offensive that by the beginning of 1914 had gained enormous strength in Morelos, Puebla, Tlaxcala, and Guerrero, and had captured Chilpancingo and Taxco; by mid-1914, he had completely expelled the Huertista forces from Morelos, and he was within sight of Mexico City with the capture of Milpa Alta on July 20.

Obregón occupied Culiacán on November 20, 1913, and by the beginning of 1914 he started a march westward, on Nayarit and Jalisco. He achieved important victories over the federal army in Orendáin and El Castillo, and on July 18 he triumphantly entered Guadalajara. Villa achieved successive victories during 1914 over the select troops of Huertismo, starting with the reoccupation of Torreón in April of 1914 and his victories in San Pedro de las Colonias, Paredón, Ramos Arizpe, and Saltillo. He crowned his campaign with the occupation of Zacatecas on July 23, 1914, in command of an army of sixteen thousand men, including the newly enlisted strategist Felipe Angeles. It was a professional war machine, with supply lines connected to the border cities, and a professional structure of ranks, wages, and the military organization of a regular army. Parallel to its military debacle in 1913 and 1914, Huertismo suffered a political debacle, which had at its center, ironically, the same source that had supported his assault on power: North American interventionism. The new U.S. president, Woodrow Wilson, took office on March 4, 1913, scarcely two weeks after the assassination of Madero, and he immediately started a new policy toward Mexico. He wanted as a neighboring country a stable nation, based on free enterprise and parliamentary democracy. This new pastoral conviction—the previous president had wanted to wake up the dreaming president of Mexico, now dead, with dynamite—soon translated into a confrontation with Huerta's dictatorship. And it displayed itself, as Berta Ulloa has written, in "four stages of progressive insertion in Mexico's internal affairs":

Between March and May of 1913, he observed the situation; from May to August, he tried to mediate between Huerta and the Constitutionalists; from August 1913 to February 1914, he stated that his policy would be one of "vigilant waiting" and he convinced the U.S. Congress and public opinion, as well as the European powers, to support his threats against Huerta, to try to force him to resign. In the fourth and last stage, that began on February 1914, the interventionist conviction became stronger, and he used an incident in Tampico to order the armed occupation of the port of Veracruz.

On April 21, 1914, without a declaration of war and with five hundred casualties among the defenders, the U.S. Marine Corps infantry disembarked from four warships stationed at San Juan de Ulúa and occupied Veracruz. They wanted to put Huerta's government in a bind—and they achieved it—but they also unleashed the anger of the Constitutionalist rebels laying siege to the regime from the battlefields. Also, they had just established a government (on November 1913), headed by First Chief Carranza, that would rule for many years and that was unyielding to any foreign "mediation" or intervention in Mexico's internal affairs. The Constitutionalist government suppressed the demands of some leaders, such as Alvaro Obregón, whose first impulse was to declare war on the United States. It did send a strong protest, demanding the unconditional evacuation of the occupied port. In order to "establish peace among the Mexican factions," in the words of President Wilson, the U.S. government convened in Niagara Falls a conference known as ABC, due to the participation of Argentina, Brazil, Chile, and the Mexican representatives, whose prolonged and useless discussions finally found an end and a solution on the battlefields of Mexico: on August 14, 1914, the Constitutionalist armies achieved the unconditional surrender of the Huertista regime, and established themselves on the scene as the only possible party for negotiation. Huerta left Mexico, only to die a few years later of natural causes in a Texas jail, after trying to lead a rebellion against Carranza. The Constitutionalist armies triumphantly entered Mexico City. In death, Madero won the battle that he had lost in life: the destruction of the federal army, but still not the taming of the tiger that the country had unleashed.

Internal Injuries

Not all of the victors triumphantly entered the capital, nor did all of them uphold the same cause. In their own spinal column, the northern armies already showed a fracture. They were suffering from it from the beginning of 1914. Time and time again, the simple confiscations of Villa (of lives, cattle, minerals, and money) had created international repercussions that had proved particularly irritating to the scrupulous administration of those matters that the First Chief advocated. These repercussions also underscored the profound differences in plan and style of both leaders. Carranza had a notion of the state; he acted and organized his government in the spirit of being the effective representative of the Mexicans, and he subordinated to that nation—well nourished with his nationalist stubbornness and his keeping the proper judicial, political, and bureaucratic forms—all of the other aspects of war, its bloody logic, and the irrationality of violence. Villa, on the other hand, was the uncontrollable impulse of a popular army in motion, increasingly self-sufficient and organized. His narrower purpose was to achieve victory, and beyond that impulse there was no explicit plan for a government, as in the case of Carrancismo, or of fundamental reforms in the property system or economic relations, as in the case of Zapatismo. His radical instinct and his raw utopianism led one U.S. representative to say that the Villistas were "socialists without knowing so," but were covered by the military wave that knew only the command of advance and was defying in its increasing autonomy the condition of supreme authority that Carranza jealously demanded for himself.

Villa occupied Zacatecas against Carranza's orders. Carranza cut off the supply of coal from Monclova for Villa's trains and retained a shipment of arms and munitions coming from Tampico with the same destination. Obregón and González, commanders of the armies of the Northwest and Northeast, not of the Division of the North, crowned their war effort by being the first to enter Mexico City. When the moment of victory arrived, there was also a settling of accounts, with respect to the revolutionary troops of the South. The Treaties of Teoloyucan that ratified the Constitutionalist victory stipulated the demobilization and the handing over of arms from all of the battalions of the federal army, except those that served on the Zapatista front. For the Obregonista troops of the Northwest, as well as for the Gonzalistas of the Northeast, which had joined forces in Querétaro, the southern guerrillas and the commander of Anenecuilco were as distrustful as they had been since their first uprising against the federal army. The radical agrarian heart of Zapatismo, with its colonial and indigenous load and its stamp of old Mexico, had little or nothing to say to the lay and entrepreneurial North, white, productive, wheat consuming, to whom the communal demands called to memory only the war against the Yaqui and Mayo Indians. It had even less to say to the *caudillo* officer corps of the northern armies, sons of the semirural and semiurban middle classes that the boom in the North created in the final decades of the Pax Porfiriana. That officer corps, derived from schoolteachers, merchants and small farmers, and frustrated minority partners of large landowners and Porfirian oligarchies needed to get rid of the obstacles to their advancement, not turn back, like the Zapatistas, to restore communities of peasant towns in the suspended time zone of the old Mexican rural society. John Womack sums up that conflict:

> Carranza was adamant. He wanted peace, but he would not compromise. Fearing for Mexico's very existence as a nation if Villa's party took power, he saw in Zapata only an accomplice to Villa's subversive work of disorder. Anything Zapata did was bad, even if Carranza had proposed similar action. "This business of dividing up

the land is ridiculous," he told envoys from de la O, when he himself had already declared that land reform was inevitable. What counted for Carranza was that reform have an official source, that it literally issue from a metropolitan office. And to him the Zapatistas were only country renegades, upstart field hands who knew nothing of government. If they had fought Huerta, so also they had backed Orozco against Madero. He warned one Zapatista commission that unless the southerners laid down their arms he would order attacks against them "as bandits."

Zapata was no less stubborn. For him also the sore point was the constitution of an interim government, which would control the elections of the new federal and state regimes. If Carranza became president, Zapata believed with good reason, he would stifle the southern movement and disable the agrarian cause. In Zapata's eyes only a regime constituted according to his Ayala plan could guarantee the eventual enactment and enforcement of agrarian reform. This was not because of the plan's reformed Article 3, which declared him the revolution's Jefe Supremo, but because of Article 12, which provided the machinery to replace him—a grand junta of the chiefs of the nation's great popular armies, which itself would name an interim president. And like Carranza, Zapata would admit no compromise before recognition of his plan. The information his secretaries continually gave him about Carranza confirmed him in his notions: the northern First Chief, so went reports, was a thieving, ambitious old *cabrón*, surrounded by conniving lawyers indifferent to the miseries of common people.

It was not a minor point. By the time Obregón occupied Mexico City, the liberating army of the South had occupied Cuernavaca and controlled the state of Morelos, Chilpancingo, and a considerable part of Puebla; and his advance posts were on the southern limits of Mexico City itself: San Angel, Tlalpan, Xochimilco. Once the dispute was settled, in August 1914, the southern rebels reiterated in a manifesto their decision to keep on struggling for the three great principles of the Plan de Ayala: expropriation of lands in the public interest, confiscation of assets of the enemies of the people, and restitution of lands to the individuals and communities that had been dispossessed.

End of an Era: The Convention

The moment of triumph, then, was also the hour of upheaval and settling of accounts. And there exists beneath the din of the discord that crucial hour of revolutions in which the past is closed off by the collapse of the old regime, and the future appears in pieces in the endless mix of currents, plans, and alliances that once again knock on the doors of civil war. Adolfo Gilly writes:

> All of the declarations and actions of the leaders of the revolutionary factions . . . that had defeated Victoriano Huerta and destroyed the federal army, converged in stating a need: the reorganization of the State. On this point the crisis of the victors is set in motion, because each fraction had a different idea on the reorganization, according to the class interests that were predominant in their interior. Villa and the direction of the Division of the North had become more radical with the progress of the Civil War, their rupture with Carranza had transpired and they coincided increasingly with the positions of the Zapatistas. They controlled, from Torreón to the North, all of the state of Chihuahua, where there was a Villista government, and part of Durango. The governor of Sonora, José Maytorena, had broken up with Carranza and had an unstable alliance with Villismo. Pablo González controlled the port of Tampico, and the Constitutionalists controlled the capital of the country, part of Sinaloa, part of Jalisco, Veracruz and the peninsula of Yucatán, whose exports of henequen would become—like the oil in the Gulf Coast—a source of considerable resources to arm and provision their troops, as the cattle of the Chihuahua *haciendas* was a source of funds for Villa. The Zapatistas controlled Morelos, Guerrero, part of Tlaxcala and of Puebla.
>
> The situation of Carranza in Mexico City was, thus, very precarious. No stable power could transcend that territorial division of armed power. The relative balance of military and political forces in the month of September of 1914 was pressing for the search for a solution by agreement.

The search for that agreement was also its closing period. Between October 10 and November 10, 1914, the divided revolutionaries assembled in the city of Aguascalientes a convention that declared itself sovereign and independent of all previously constituted authority, adopted the main articles of the Plan de Ayala, disavowed Carranza as interim leader responsible for executive power and Villa as chief of the Division of the North, and named Eulalio Gutiérrez, a revolutionary leader of San Luis Potosí, as interim president. There, in the exhausting, and often irrelevant, sessions of speakers, proposals, and discussions, the social problems that had not been settled by the war cropped up. The revolutionary tide acquired ideological density; the pragmatic questions that had dominated the northern armies gave way to social definitions.

And from the victors, the urgency of change and a radical spirit developed, which united armies and regions all over the country. But the political division and the *caudillo* allegiances imposed their own law, and division prospered.

Eulalio Gutiérrez was a perfect representative of the mid-level leaders who were attempting to get the convention to establish a political agreement to break up the current alignments—Villa, Zapata, Carranza—and establish a new front that would put an end to the civil war. That broad group of chiefs, Friedrich Katz explains,

> was characterized by no firm political, geographical, or organizational unity. The common objective of its members was the elimination of Villa, Carranza, and, if possible, Zapata from the leadership of the revolution. Beyond that, the members of this group held widely divergent views on what the next step should be. In ideological and social terms, they occupied an intermediate position between Carranza and Villa. Most of its members, particularly its spokesmen, came from the middle class: Alvaro Obregón, the former rancher and public official who commanded the Army of the Northwest; Eulalio Gutiérrez, the most important revolutionary leader in the state of San Luis Potosí; Lucio Blanco, the revolutionary leader from northeastern Mexico. For most of them, Carranza was too conservative. Villa and Zapata too radical. They wished to reduce the power of the old ruling group far more than did Carranza, but, with few exceptions, they were opposed to the kind of radical social transformation Zapata and, to a lesser extent, Villa advocated. Some envisioned a system of parliamentary democracy, which neither Carranza nor the Villa and Zapata groups could establish. Others had set up what amounted to independent fiefdoms in their home states and feared Mexico's return to a strong central authority. By eliminating the three leaders, they hoped to attain these often heterogeneous goals. They actually succeeded in having Gutiérrez elected provisional president, with the support of all parties at the convention, calling simultaneously for the removal of Villa and Carranza.

> This compromise quickly proved to be untenable. The fourth group was too weak, too heterogeneous, and too divided to impose its will.

The military conditions of those weeks decreased the little power that the original Conventionist attempt had, to begin with. In November, the partisans of Carranza and of Villa's ally, José María Maytorena, were in a death struggle at the famous site of Naco, Sonora. Maytorena had returned in July of that year to claim his rights as constitutional governor of the state. The situation divided the "fourth group." One part, with Gutiérrez at the fore, had aligned itself with the cause of Villa and Zapata. And given the ferocity with which Villa was disputing the hegemony of their own native state, by supporting Maytorena, Obregón and the Sonorenses, with their strong network of loyal troops developed in the extended campaign of the Northwest, aligned themselves with Carranza, also reckoning that they could exert some influence over him, which they would not be able to attain through Villismo or Zapatismo.

The Carrancista delegates withdrew from the convention, the convention declared Carranza in contempt and recognized the impossibility of finding a third road, and named Villa as the chief of its armies. The country, armed, headed for a violent resolution of its fate, in the most decisive year of its revolutionary turmoil, 1915.

1915

There are intense years, of peculiar historical concentration, years in which everything seems to happen, as if in those years the threads of society become tied up, and one is able to see without obstruction the design on the whole garment, on the front and the back, what is hidden and what is visible, the quick pulse and the imperceptible sediment. The year 1915 is one of those that condensed in a concentrated beam the features of the Mexico that was departing and glimpses of the Mexico that was beginning to exist.

It is the year of the definition of the civil war with the defeat of the Villista and Zapatista armies, the peasant armies of the revolution. It is the year of the establishment of a new national political hegemony, whose fundamental continuity would not be lost in the years to come. It is the year of the foundation of the revolutionary Mexican state, of the consolidation of a government recognized nationally and internationally, which would develop the modern agrarian legislation of the country with the law of January 6 and establish the first organic pact of the revolution with the organized workers of the House of the Workers of the World (Casa del Obrero Mundial), in February of 1915, a pact that anticipated the character of the fundamental relation that both actors would have in the following seven decades.

It is also the year of the popular experience of the revolution, the year of the *chinga* (turmoil), of the battles that would confront armies of eighty and one hundred thousand men, and of the total military mobilization in the great armies or in small local groups devoted to aggression or self-defense, to cattle-rustling or revolution. It is the year of precariousness and destruction. Authority is as unstable as the currency. Small transactions in Mexico City were done with tram tickets. Within the sea of paper money issued by the different armies, "the poorest people," recalls Alejandra Moreno Toscano, went back to "barter transactions, without using paper money: good for good, service for service."

The confusion, the regional isolation, the violence, and the abolition of norms are the norm. It is the year of massive emigrations: to the armies or the borders, from the convulsive countryside to the relatively protected cities, in a process that swells and dislocates Mexico City, Veracruz, Guadalajara, Monterrey. It is the year in which battles, epidemics, and migrations profoundly alter the demography of the nation, which in total will register the disappearance of a million Mexicans in the decade of revolutionary war. In the tranquil line of the Porfirian towns, massive groups of vagrant Mexicans suddenly arise. The revolutionary armies occupy all of the visual sphere. On top of their crowded trains, in large cavalry columns or small infantry groups, they come and go from towns and cities, occupy the Porfirian houses, blow up trains, collect cattle and harvests, move around the country. They kill and are killed, they are a landscape that takes up arms, full of vigor and misery, unruliness and destructive power. Thousands of men leave their homes and their towns, to which otherwise they would have been tied, and learn by themselves what they have only heard before, that the country to which they belong is a vast geographical and human entity and that they can travel throughout the country and make it their own.

Following them, together with them, the women trail along, immobile and sedentary centers of the towns and the families, now converted into an anonymous mass of *soldaderas* (women who accompany troops), who go through a fulminating revolution of the social and sexual mores, women in the open countryside whose liberation in an act of war would later be compiled in literary and film archetypes (from Mariano Azuela to Indio Fernández), as the new outspoken Adelita, promiscuous and tomboyish, sexually active, free to the point of abandon, garrulous to the point of impudence.

It is the year of unwarranted violence, with its devastating sequel of looting, destruction, uncertainty, mourning and epidemics, dissolution of the family nucleus, sons of the Revolution and wives of the regiment. And it is a culture of risk, impunity, and living day by day, which breaks down the walls of dominant morality, the morality of economy, restraint, and religious resignation. That terminal experience of the brutality of war is summed up in the autobiography of José Clemente Orozco:

Tragedy destroyed everything around us. The troops went on the railroad to the killing grounds. The trains were blown up. The helpless Zapatistaswho fell prisoners of the Carrancistas were executed in the atrium of the parish churches. People got used to the slaughter, to the merciless egotism, to satiating their senses. The factions subdivided infinitely, and expressed their irrepressible desire for revenge. Underground intrigues were carried out between friends of today, enemies of tomorrow, willing to mutually exterminate each other once the time arrived.

The year 1915 is also the year of the triumph of northern Jacobinism, a new and vigorous wave of abolition and derision of the old Catholic Mexico. It is the year of a string of foreign priests whom Obregón expels from the country after informing the public that they suffer unspeakable venereal diseases, the year of Carrancismo that is also anticlericalism: temples used as barracks, atriums with tents, convents assaulted, and the ostentatious desecration of the objects used in worship. It is the northern flooding of the lay Mexico whose roots go back to the reforms of the previous century, whose cumulative affront to the Catholic majority would explode in the 1920s with the Cristero War, but whose uncompromising stance, first on the constitution and then with the state action, would deepen the secularization of civil life and public education in contemporary Mexico.

José Clemente Orozco emigrated to Orizaba at the end of 1914 with the battalions of the House of the Workers of the World. He recalls:

> When we arrived at Orizaba, the first thing we did was to assault and loot the local temples. The Temple of Los Dolores was depleted, and we installed in the nave two flatbed printing presses, several linotypes and the engraving machines. We wanted to publish a revolutionary paper called *La Vanguardia*, and we installed the editorial staff in the priest's house.
>
> The temple of El Carmen was also assaulted and given to the workers of La Mundial so that they could live there. The saints, the confessionals and the altars were chopped up to provide firewood for the women, so they could cook, and we took the altar ornaments and priestly vestments. We all left decorated with rosaries, medals and scapulars.

The Emergence of Mexico

The year 1915 was also one of isolation of the country from the rest of the world, of the regions bordering Mexico City, and of the successive invasions of the capital city by the revolutionary armies, a traumatizing encounter between the center and the country it ruled.

Alejandra Moreno Toscano describes the situation:

The crisis in the city was not dissimilar to what had occurred on previous occasions. Then, the city had been affected as a result of the agricultural catastrophe. On this occasion, it was more a matter of hegemony than economy. The origin of the problems was political; the city was being gambled to decide the revolution, although the visible effects were economic: shortages, inflation, monetary disorder.

Days before the first entrance of the Zapatistas into Mexico [City], all shops closed their doors. The urban population began to buy foodstuffs in excess to store them in their houses. There was fear of looting. When Villa entered with his troops, the same scene repeated itself, but he was accompanied by twenty thousand soldiers who required food. When Obregón came back and the Zapatistas withdrew to Padierna, electrical power was cut off (because the Zapatistas closed the power sources at Xochimilco) and, as there was no coal either, the city's inhabitants had to come out at night, hidden by darkness, to cut the trees of the streets and avenues, for fuel.

All of the factories of the Federal District had closed (the trains were not bringing in the commodities required for production). The city was full of unemployed people and beggars, who wandered the streets without a fixed destination, and slept in the streets. Typhus began to wreak havoc. The city government recognized its inability to maintain control of the city under these conditions, and left it on its own. It declared that it could no longer maintain the orphans and elderly people in the institutions, nor the people in the insane asylum of Castañeda, and opened the doors of those establishments so their dwellers could leave freely to seek their own subsistence.

Despite the precarious nature of the situation and its isolation, or precisely because of it, the urbane consciousness of the country was confronted with the elemental and powerful "novelty of Mexico." The country and its misery, its customs and anonymous passions, its ambitions and hopes, its aspect, its form of speech, its tangible immediacy, appeared as a revelation for that consciousness.

In 1926, a city man, Manuel Gómez Morín, by then already the founder of the Bank of Mexico, summed up his experience as follows:

With optimistic stupor we found out about unsuspected truths. Mexico existed. Mexico as a country with great capabilities, with aspirations, with life, with its own problems. Not only was this a fortuitous human gathering come from afar to exploit certain riches or observe certain curiosities, only to leave after a while. It was not only a transitory or permanent geographical displacement of the body, with the spirit remaining abroad.

Mexico existed, and so did the Mexicans.

The colonial policy of Porfirismo had made us forget this fundamental truth.

In the heart of the cultural and intellectual life of the capital city, affecting French manners, shaken by the modernist audacity and the metaphysical rebellions that alternated bohemian decadence with positivist history, the naturalism of the old novelists with the consecration of classical Hellenism in the new generations, the apparition of the rough and raw Mexico of the Revolution had the effect of a catharsis of national discovery and affirmation. López Velarde sang to the "soft fatherland," Mariano Azuela published *Los de abajo* (The underdogs), José Clemente Orozco painted "anticlerical posters and rabid caricatures," as he calls them, but also masterly pencil drawings of revolutionary "hospitals," battles, executions, dandies who were forced to dance by pistol shots, Zapatistas, Carrancistas, "the people in arms," using arms, suffering them.

Empty Baskets

Finally, 1915 was the "year of hunger," the year of the dislocation of production and supply, the most certain indicator that the destructive gale of the revolution had lost momentum. In the case of Mexico City, Alejandra Moreno Toscano describes it as follows:

> The railroads, controlled by the armies in conflict, were used exclusively for military purposes—movement of troops and supplies—and stopped transporting basic grains and merchandise. Afterward, all of the horses and mules were confiscated, for the same purpose, which explains the drastic interruption of the urban supply. The oscillations of the political conflict also explained why the shortages in goods for the capital alternated. When the Conventionists controlled Mexico [City], there usually were vegetables, tropical fruits, Toluca corn, but not coal. But when the Constitutionalists controlled the city, the opposite occurred.
>
> When the Convention met to discuss what should be done to control prices, a crowd of women intruded in the Chamber of Deputies carrying empty baskets and demanding justice. A delegate

took the floor and suggested that a collection be held at that moment to distribute some money. The women responded "we don't want money, we want bread" and abandoned the chamber . . .

By June 1915, the scenes of disorder multiplied themselves: women with empty baskets walked around the city's markets, only to find them closed; they walked all day, from San Juan to La Merced, from Lagunilla to Martínez de la Torre. Everywhere, people appeared who seemed ready to break down the doors with axes and knives, and ransack the stores. The merchants, hiding behind parapets on their rooftops, defended their properties.

The Civil War: For a Government without Sidewalks

At the beginning of November of 1914, a majority of the country was Conventionist. The Villista and Zapatista armies occupied almost all of the Center and South of the country, all of the Pacific except Acapulco and Mazatlán, and all of the North except Agua Prieta in Sonora and Nuevo Laredo and Tampico in Tamaulipas. With their files and their troops, Obregón and Carranza moved in mid-November from Mexico City toward the Gulf and Tabasco, Campeche and Yucatán, and established the Constitutionalist headquarters in the port of Veracruz, which the North American occupants left in the hands of the First Chief, Venustiano Carranza, at the end of November 1914.

On December 6, from the balcony of the National Palace, Villa and Zapata reviewed the troops of the Division of the North and of the Liberating Army of the South, which were marching triumphantly into the capital of the Republic. The government of the Convention, presided over by Eulalio Gutiérrez, which was entering Mexico City together with these armies, was, in the military sense, a government without an army and, in the political sense, the remains of a pact. Having developed as an attempt at conciliation between Villistas and Zapatistas and the left wing of Carrancismo, it had lost a fundamental ally in the figure of Obregón. What remained of that pact was also conflictive.

The concentrated Zapatista agrarianism attracted the left wing of Villismo, and seemed capable of providing a programmatic and governmental center to the Conventionist alliance, but it was blind to the presence of other national forces, and it also entered into conflict, in the agrarian policies, with the conservative wing of Villismo, where people like José María Maytorena had great power, which took advantage of its force in Sonora to return the *haciendas* and other expropriated assets to their Porfirian owners. The Villista strategist Felipe Angeles was also an obstacle to the Conventionist radicalism; he believed in gradual reforms, after the armed struggle, and saw in foreign influence an important source of capital, science, and the example that underdeveloped countries such as Mexico required. Thus, the agrarian law of October 28, 1915, established by Manuel Palafox, secretary of agriculture of the Conventionist government and administrative soul of Zapatismo, was signed only by some of his radical colleagues, who were members of the same cabinet: Otilio Montaño, Genaro Amezcua, and Miguel Mendoza.

Besides these ideological differences, the plans of the Conventionist government were also frustrated by the explosive unruliness of Villa himself and his savage faction, where people like Rodolfo Fierro and Tomás Urbina incarnated the unlawful impulse, alien to any institutional notion, any idea of political conciliation or administrative construction.

Finally, there was a central constraint: the true powerbrokers in the Conventionist alliance, Villa and Zapata, did not want to and could not organize a government at the service of their interests. They lacked what Carranza had in excess: the notion of state, as it becomes clear in this conversation held during their first meeting in Xochimilco, on December 4 of 1912:

Villa: I do not need public positions because I do not know how to deal with them. We will have to see where those people are [the members of the Conventionist government], we will only let them be in charge, as long as they don't create problems for us.

Zapata: That is why I warn all the friends that they should be careful, or otherwise, the *machete* will fall on them . . . I trust that we shall not be betrayed. We have limited ourselves to prodding them, taking care of them, taking care, taking care, on one side, on the other, to keep them in the pasture.

Villa: I understand very well that we ignorant men make the war, and the cabinets have to take advantage of them; but they should not cause any more problems.

Zapata: The men who have done most of the work are those who enjoy those sidewalks less. Only sidewalks. And I say it for myself: the moment I get on one of those sidewalks, I start to fall down.

Villa: That ranch is too big for us. It is better to be out there. As soon as this is all fixed up, I want to leave for the campaign of the North. Over there, I have a lot to do. Over there, they are still going to fight a lot.

The Civil War: Stepping-Stone to Hegemony

Neither the Villistas nor the Zapatistas thought of their struggles (as they were mainly peasant armies) as a contention for national hegemony. For Villa, the country ended at the point where his extremely long supply lines that ran from the border started to become vulnerable; the North beckoned him and did not let him go. For Zapata, the world ended where the popular organization of his army would lose the peculiar agrarian and military roots that characterized him. Zapata's country included the states of Morelos, Guerrero, and parts of Puebla, Hidalgo, Tlaxcala, Mexico state, and the Federal District. Villa's nation was demarcated by the railroad tracks and the great financial and military placenta that the U.S. border represented. Within the limits of this Conventionist weakness began the advantages of Carrancismo, even though it found itself cornered.

For Carranza, the country was a conceptual, political, and administrative totality, of which he believed he was the only legitimate representative, without giving much importance to the fact that he did not at the moment control much of that territory. He did not need third-party "enlightened men" or "cabinets" to shepherd—he had his own men— nor did he feel that the ranch was too big. From Veracruz, before occupying it, he had negotiated, as undisputed leader of Mexico, the withdrawal of the U.S. Marines. His general and ally, Alvaro Obregón, who had broken with the Conventionist pact, had a sufficiently flexible and global idea of his military tasks to be able to plan, in the imminence of the military collapse at the end of 1914, the need to board his troops at Salina Cruz and, after an uncertain coastal trip up the Pacific, to land in the western part of Mexico to join the troops of Diéguez in Jalisco and start his new campaign on familiar terrain. For the Zapatistas, guerrilla warfare was not only the origin, but also the natural military condition. At the suggestion made by Carranza to fragment his army and resist the Villistas in this manner in a difficult moment of the campaign, Obregón responded: "I did not leave Sonora as a bandit to go around fleeing and hiding. I am the commander of the Constitutionalist Army, and if necessary I will die in that capacity."

The arrogance of that attitude in such a precarious political and military situation is perhaps the most precise psychological expression of a revolutionary faction that correctly understood its historical position. There was no other group in the country that held the notion of representing a national government and that had the will and the means to set up itself as such. The glimpses in that direction that the Conventionist government provided, as has been said, were nullified by its heterogeneity and by the autarchical spirit, foreign to the secrets of legitimacy and institutionality, of the Villista and Zapatista leaders.

The practical consequences of those ideas of origin were decisive. At the end of 1914, the Zapatistas did not attack the armies of Carranza, which had retreated to the Gulf and the Southeast, because they felt that was outside their territorial domain; the Villistas also didn't attack, because they didn't want to make their supply lines vulnerable. Also, they did not want to create friction in their relations with the Zapatistas, whose territory they would have had to cross for a campaign in the Gulf. Carranza and Obregón obtained from that Conventionist military immobility the first crucial resource they needed—time. The second was their control over apparently peripheral regions, but which in reality were quite strategic: the oil fields of Veracruz and Tamaulipas, the active ports of Tampico and Veracruz, and the hemp exports from Yucatán. They received abundant quantities of foreign exchange and taxes from these, which allowed them to provision the Carrancista army and government, among other things because World War I led to a boom in the production of henequen and because the oil exports increased from 200 thousand pesos in 1910 to 516 million pesos in 1920.

The Civil War: Sidewalks of the Future

To the military preparations, Carranza added the political preparations. To begin with, he made additions to the Plan de Guadalupe on December 12, 1914, promising to decree "during the struggle" laws to favor the establishment of small properties, eliminate *latifundios* (large landholdings), and return the land that had unjustly been taken away from the communities. Carrancismo also promised to establish fair taxes and better wages and to improve the conditions of the "proletarian classes"; it guaranteed the freedom and the fulfillment of the reform laws, the independence of the judicial power, and the regulation of the exports of wood, oil, water, and, in general, all natural resources.

And Carranza kept his word. He began at the beginning, with the agrarian law of January 6, 1915, the first of a new period on the subject, destined to appropriate the Zapatista banner. The timely law mandated the returning of lands to the communities and the right of all peasants to own a plot of land. (Unfortunately, only the right was decreed, because during the following five years of Carrancista power, only 427,000 acres would be distributed to 44,000 peasants.) At the same time, Carranza established an alliance with the *hacendados* to follow a practice contrary to the law, and he made the compromise to return the *haciendas* that had been taken over during the revolutionary wave. This was an agreement he also kept, defining in this fashion one of the conservative alliances that would, at the same time, sustain and erode his regime.

Later on, galvanized by the sensibility and the measures of the Obregonista wing, the Constitutionalists sought and found support in the cities among the workers. By the end of 1914, once he had reorganized and provisioned his army, Obregón began the advance on the center of the country. He took Puebla at the beginning of January 1915, among other reasons because the Zapatistas prepared such a poor defense of the city that it was almost as if they had offered it up as a gift. By the end of January, Obregón entered Mexico City, whose occupants had evacuated it without a fight. Once back in the capital, he imposed emergency measures to relieve the populace's hunger. He also confiscated the Mexican Telephone and Telegraph Company and placed it in the hands of the leaders of the Mexican Union of Electricians, whose leader, Luis Napoleón Morones, was designated manager by the workers' assembly. Through the House of the Workers of the World, the Constitutionalists established a mechanism for the distribution of food and clothes, and they successfully petitioned the First Chief for the establishment of a political alliance with that new clientele.

In 1915, despite its rich iconography of martyrs in Río Blanco and Cananea, the Mexican working class was socially a very narrow caste, without cohesion or consciousness of its interests. It came to the Revolution with very limited experience as a modern proletariat, marked by its habits of mutualism better suited to guilds and artisans: it had neither a tradition of struggle nor a proletarian ideology. The first coherent images of these ideologies had arrived through foreign activists, Italian and Spanish anarcho-syndicalists, and during a period that coincided with the movements of Cananea and Río Blanco, by the radical slogans of the Mexican Liberal party and the Flores Magón brothers.

As workers in a fundamentally North American and British industry—railroads, mines, oil—they tended to identify the exploiters with foreigners. This is why the stubborn and inflexible nationalism of Carranza touched the political consciousness of these workers who, in fact, when the U.S. Marines occupied Veracruz, had told the Huerta government that they would repel the invaders. The peculiar northern Jacobinism, especially of Obregonismo, also touched similar chords in the anarcho-syndicalist and Masonic culture that dominated the mutual-aid societies and the guilds. The Carrancistas felt in that organization and in the urban workers a key group in the network of alliances that it needed to extend its social base during the Civil War. In mid-February, after a hesitant meeting, the House of the Workers of the World signed a collaboration pact with Carranza that united some three thousand urban supporters of Constitutionalism—tailors, carpenters, typographers—guaranteed the official sponsorship of the worker movement, and created the mold into which all of the alliances between the state and

Mexican unions in the following seventy years would fit, with slight variations. The House of the Workers of the World abandoned its traditional line of direct action, independent from all government participation, and offered its participation in the armed struggle. In exchange, the workers received the official support to unionize all of the workers in the territories where Carrancismo established control, and they were granted an optimal and symbolic headquarters in Mexico City: the House of the Tiles, the old Jockey Club, center of Porfirian wealth and elegance.

By the end of February 1915, the political and judicial strategy of Carrancismo was well established. Only the military definition was missing.

The Civil War: Battles

Leading his army, Obregón left the capital on March 10, 1915, secured his supply lines from Veracruz, forgot about the Zapatistas in the South, and, at the beginning of April, was in the Bajío (lowlands) ready for his first clash with Villa. Four great battles, won by the Obregonista forces, defined on those battlefields who would hold military dominance in the Revolution: the two Celaya battles in April, the battle for positions in Trinidad during the month of May, and the battle of Aguascalientes at the beginning of June, in which a desperate situation created by food shortages forced Obregón to launch a sudden offensive that caught the Villista lines off guard.

After the battle of Aguascalientes, in mid-1915, the Villista withdrawal to the North was the scene of a caravan in flight, without morale, which in the future would continue to lose, without even fighting, what a year before it had achieved with brilliance. Slow trains exhibited the sumptuous cars that the leaders should have occupied; now, they went about empty, with their windowpanes broken, and scarred with bullet holes in the sides. The demoralization was the dominant note, fights broke out for provisions, and desertions and surrenders multiplied.

On July 16, Obregón took San Luis Potosí; a day later, he occupied Zacatecas. The Zapatista front, which in March had advanced on Mexico City when Obregón left, was also repelled. In the North, Pánfilo Natera surrendered to Obregón and occupied, with part of his troops, the city of Durango. On September 4, the Constitutionalists entered Saltillo, on the 13th, Monclova; and a few days later, Piedras Negras. On the 27th, San Pedro de las Colonias fell without a fight, and, in the following days, Torreón and Gómez Palacio. On October 17, the United States recognized Carrancismo as a de facto government. At the beginning of the same month, the Villista armies gathered in Casas Grandes, at the bottom of the sierra of Chihuahua, to invade Sonora. In the arid fields of Hermosillo and in the trenches of Agua Prieta, Villismo would lose the last of its formal battles. The defeat would take them back to their original place and condition: the state of Chihuahua, the sierra, and the raids. The effective pacification of those regions would not be possible until 1920, a period that shows the deep popular and regional roots of Villismo, an origin that its long adventure and its vast numbers during 1914 and 1915 did not manage to dissipate in the long run.

While the armies of Obregón and Villa were deciding their fate, the Zapatistas occupied, ruled, and transformed their southern world, distributing the lands and the *haciendas* of Morelos, establishing their own power and their own laws, and defending rifle in hand, the armed battalions of the people. But their fate was also sealed by Villa's defeats in the Bajío. On August 2, 1915, Pablo González recovered the capital from the hands of the Zapatistas, who had occupied it since March, when Obregón left for the North. After the Obregonista campaign in the North, at the beginning of 1916, the central war returned to Morelos. Now undertaken by the Carrancistas and under Pablo González's command, the invading troops—as under Huerta's command in Madero's administration and under Juvencio Robles in Huerta's administration—looted, stole, set fires, killed, and exiled entire towns to the mountains. On May 2, they took Cuernavaca and, in mid-June, the town that had acted as Zapata's headquarters, Tlaltizapán, was punished for this by the execution of 132 men, 112 women, and 42 children.

Year Zero: The Constitutional Dispute

At the end of 1916, the agrarian rebellions of the South and the North had reverted to their original condition. They were stubborn and resistant local rebellions, but they did not defy the new political, military, and administrative hegemony of the country. The Carrancistas devoted themselves, as a result, to the fundamental task of the hour, consolidating their power and anticipating the foundation of the new order. On September 19, 1916, Venustiano Carranza, still acting as the First Chief in charge of executive power during the pre-Constitutional period (1915–1916), called for a Constitutional Congress to codify the new political pact that was emerging in Mexico as a result of the Revolution. On October 22, the elections to name the deputies to the Constitutional Assembly were held. The single prerequisite for admission was to have remained faithful throughout the vicissitudes of the Civil War to the Plan de Guadalupe and to the leadership of the First Chief, Carranza. It was a very exclusive Congress: for Carrancistas only.

By that time, Carrancismo was far from a homogeneous and united bloc. It was, in reality, an intricate labyrinth of conflicting currents, tendencies, and *caudillos*. The Constitutional Assembly was the appropriate scene for a new political and ideological delimitation of the victors. The internal conflict between the "radical" and "conservative" deputies changed the open division and competition, which had been established a long time before, between the nationalist, liberal, and restorationist tendencies of Carranza and the pragmatic, multiclass, anticlerical, statist, and probusiness positions of the Sonorense Constitutionalists, whose avowed leader was Alvaro Obregón.

The conflict didn't take long to break out. On December 1, 1916, the Constitutional Assembly received in Querétaro the Carrancista project of a new national code. It was the project that could be expected of a true statesman such as Carranza, who remained on the liberal horizon of the nineteenth century, which the Porfirian dictatorship had denied in reality without abolishing it in the laws. At the end of the tunnel of the Civil War, Carranza saw the dire need for a political reorganization and a constitutional restoration, as the state had done in the era of Juárez—obsession and shadow in the Carrancista memory—at the end of foreign intervention fifty years before.

Deaf and blind, due to education and age, to the powerful social demands of the conflict from which he had just emerged victorious, Carranza held a perception of a fundamentally political nature. His constitutional project repeated almost verbatim the constitution of 1857, with only one significant reform. The Liberal constitution had foreseen the existence of a weak executive branch. That condition had been, according to the prevailing conventional wisdom in the political culture of the time, what had led to dictatorship; feeling cornered by the enormous constititutional limits that prevented them from acting, Juárez, first, and Porfirio Díaz, later, had found a way of escaping that straitjacket, and ended up violating the constitution in spirit without violating its forms. Using that stratagem, Díaz in particular started to transform the constitutional order into an external simulation; the Congress, into a farce of national representation; the federal republic, into a fictitious collection of sovereign states; the judicial branch, into an administrative and political extension of the executive branch; all of democratic life, into a charade of empty legal norms and inflexible operational goals.

The only reform proposed by Carranza was the establishment of a strong executive power, which would be able to deal with the emergencies that cropped up and also guarantee, as a consequence of its secure hold on power, the real existence of the other branches of government, municipal autonomy, and the sovereignty of the states. The Jacobin wing of the Congress wanted to go even further; it wanted to recognize as well the fresh imprint of the underlying social demands of the Civil War (there still were, after all, fifty thousand armed men around the Republic). It was the reformist wing that virtually created the Mexican Constitution of 1917. Its intervention added, amid arduous debate, compromises on labor legislation (article 123); a mandatory and lay education (article 3); an agrarian legislation, which gave the nation control over the underground and natural resources and subjected property to the modes that public interest demanded (article 27): it was not only a political constitution, but also a social constitution, which recorded from the perspective of the new state the structural realities that violence had forced out of the basement of the Porfiriato.

The dispute on the constitution was also a perfect political expression of the discord that the years of preconstitutional Carrancista government (1915–1917) had brought upon the postrevolutionary republic. It came about in the midst of the rebirth of the North American hostility, stimulated on this occasion by the bloody occupation by Villa of a small U.S. border town, Columbus, at the beginning of March 1916. The immediate response of the administration of Woodrow Wilson to that attack was the creation of a ten-thousand-man column, under the command of General Pershing, which adopted the title of Punitive Expedition and entered Chihuahua in search of the guerrilla. Eight months of fruitless pursuit of Villa put relations between Mexico and the United States on the verge of a diplomatic break and armed conflict between the two countries, leaving "behind such a degree of hostility and distrust," as historian Friedrich Katz has written, "that in the period that followed no Mexican leader could attempt a rapprochement with the United States."

The friction with the United States encouraged the internal opposition, to a large extent still armed. In anticipation of a conflict with the U.S. army in Chihuahua, the Carrancista government reinforced its troops in the northern region of the country, which, toward the end of 1916 and beginning of 1917, aided the return of Zapatista control over the entire state of Morelos, except for the major cities. The eternal conspirator, Félix Díaz, once again found support in the United States, on this occasion to "obtain the control of the henequen and oil industry of Mexico," and he entered Veracruz with troops, although, as always, without much success. Manuel Peláez, a regional *caudillo* of the Gulf oil zone, had been able to consolidate his control by buying arms in the United States, defying the Carrancista government with his autonomy. Esteban Cantú in Baja California had accomplished the same thing, to a large extent thanks to his good relations with the U.S. authorities on the other side of the border.

To these forces that were undermining the peace, one could add the proliferation of small and large regional *caciques,* with their own troops and arms, which imposed their law on the defenseless towns by offering protection of all kinds against, among other things, the irreducible banditry that the Civil War had left in its wake. All of this was in addition to the strong popular dissatisfaction with the Carranza government, not simply because its agrarian promises had remained only on paper (as we mentioned before, between 1915 and 1920, only 427,000 acres were distributed to 44,000 peasants), but also because Mexico experienced in those years a dramatic drop in the quality of life. This was underscored by the desperation generated by the general insecurity, the monetary catastrophe that the country had inherited from the circulation of the more than twenty types of currencies that each army printed and recognized as the only valid legal tender, and the generalized corruption of Carrancista authorities and military men, for whose greed the people used the verb *carrancear,* as a synonym for stealing. On top of all this, the bad weather and the bad harvests, the unemployment due to the drop in commercial and industrial activities, made 1917—the year of the creation of the new regime—another year of hunger and shortages, of great suffering and punishment for the Mexicans, which initiated in this fashion the pact for a new era.

The Carrancista Restoration

After the military triumph, Carranza's policies were oriented toward restoration. First, he dealt with the composition of the bureaucracy and his advisers. Carranza knew that the government and its judicial and administrative refinements required and valued the proximity of men who were experienced in bureaucratic and diplomatic intricacies, legal astuteness, and parliamentary procedure. His closest adviser, author of the agrarian law of January 6, Secretary of Finance Luis Cabrera, was the clear incarnation and epitome of the Carrancista civilian politician. But the privileged roll call of the First Chief was long and controversial. Instead of the military officers of the moment, who knew about war and had ambition for power, Carranza preferred to honor people like Félix Palavicini, Alfonso Cravioto, Luis Manuel Rojas, lawyers and managers of a conservative vein who not only did not come out of the revolutionary rank and file, of little education and no experience in government, but usually came from the professional and bureaucratic circles of the old regime.

The intimate circle of those Carrancista civilians was the source of political intrigue against Obregón and of irritation for hundreds of ignorant, rude, illiterate chiefs, as well as for other leaders who thought they had won their place in the government on the battlefields and not in the offices that surrounded the First Chief's office. That fence separated Carranza from his old army subordinates and filled them with the annoying feeling that they were being displaced. Commenting on the situation, Gen. Francisco J. Múgica, a rebel Carrancista officer since the signing of the Plan de Guadalupe in 1913, a Jacobin supporter of the social reforms of the 1917 Constitution, wrote in mid-August 1917 to his ideological twin, Salvador Alvarado:

> Having been in February and March in Mexico, I saw more rancor against the Villistas, the Zapatistas and the Conventionists than against the Huertistas. The journalists of the revolution are those of the dictatorship and the military coup. In the Ministry of Finance there is 80 percent Huertistas, in other Ministries they are in a minority, but they are still there.

On the agrarian front, the policies of the Carrancista state were not directed toward the fulfillment of its own law of January 1915, but rather toward the alliance with the *hacendados* to guarantee that the *haciendas* would be returned. Carranza wanted to rejuvenate economic activity this way, by restoring the productive units that existed before the Revolution, thinking that the rejuvenation would provide a quicker response to the widespread situation of hunger and high prices that was affecting his government.

In an open letter in 1917, Zapata himself was critical: "The *haciendas* are being given or rented to the favorite generals; the old *latifundios* replaced in many cases by modern landowners that use epaulets, military caps and a gun in their belts; the people are being mocked for their hopes." The accusation was directed against one of the lasting effects of the Revolution, which would also impinge in the prestige and legitimacy of the Carrancista military officers: the transfer of old Porfirian properties to the hands of a new class of owners that had come out of the ranks of the Constitutionalist army, the predatory origin of the enriched and bourgeois revolutionary family that would become well known in the decades to come.

The Carrancista restoration on the agrarian front also included the military objective of pacification and putting down of the Zapatista rebellion. In 1918, for the second time since 1915, Pablo González, following Carranza's instructions, began his task of cleaning up Morelos, a historical task that concluded, in typical fashion, with treachery and betrayal: Emiliano Zapata was asked to come to the *hacienda* of Chinameca on the morning of April 10, 1919, where the Gonzalista troops riddled him with bullets after saluting him.

The workers also tasted the bitter fruit of the restoration. After the fight with Villa and in the midst of the monetary chaos and the drop in real wages, the organization of the workers sponsored by Carrancismo through the House of the Workers of the World served to channel, homogenize, and in a certain way generalize the protests.

At the end of December 1915, the tram workers and the electricians of Guadalajara stopped work to demand higher wages. In the El Oro mine of the state of Mexico, the strikers replaced the bosses and took over the installations. All over the country, labor petitions, strikes, and strike threats occurred, demanding higher wages and payment in gold and silver, and not in the *bilimbiques* issued as paper money by the Carrancista armies. The response was implacable: on November 30, 1915, one of the most combative unions of the Revolution, the railroad workers' union, was incorporated into the army and subjected to military discipline. At the beginning of 1916, the red battalions were dissolved. The hero of Morelos and Chinameca, Pablo González, issued a proclamation against labor unrest that was prevailing at the end of January 1916, in one of the first manifestos in which the government demanded superior status over class conflict: "If the revolution has fought against the Capitalist tyranny," said González, "it cannot sanction the proletarian tyranny." Immediately after, González and his troops invaded the Jockey Club, evicted the unions, and closed down the House newspaper, *Ariete*. His example spread through the states. The local military officials arrested the leaders of the House who insisted on promoting the payment of wages in gold, and gathered them in Querétaro on instructions from the First Chief.

The definitive confrontation took place on July 31, 1916, when the unions of the Federal District declared themselves on general strike, about ninety thousand workers headed by the electricians' union. Carranza's response was extreme: on August 1, he declared martial law, dissolved the union meetings with the army, and decreed the death penalty for the workers associated with any proposition or attempt at striking, even if they had only heard about it.

Together with this settling of accounts with the workers and peasants, Carranza sought a new relationship with the foreign companies, derived from his active nationalism. He practiced a decisive governmental intervention in their affairs, stipulating higher taxes, and punishing them with fees and expropriations if they did not immediately restart production, particularly in the sphere of mining, where many companies had stopped their production. This also had a cost.

The discontent of the military officials who had been passed over, the persistence of regional rebellions and belligerent autonomy, the repression against the peasants, the split in the alliance with the workers, and the hostile relations with the foreign companies and the U.S. government were all sufficient conditions for the erosion of the Carrancista government. As Friedrich Katz has written:

> There was nothing very revolutionary about Carranza's domestic economic policies. What he basically attempted to do was to reestablish Porfirian conditions for the benefit of large segments of Mexico's traditional upper class as well as for its new bourgeoisie. These groups were to be cultivated at the expense of both foreign business interests and the lower classes of society on whom the burden of paying for the expenses of revolution were to fall. For obvious reasons Carranza had far less difficulties in imposing these burdens on the poor than on the foreign interests.

In the hazardous political atmosphere of the restoration, Carranza left behind the legitimacy of his regime, the impulse that had led him to the triumph in the Civil War and, finally, to the power and the glory.

The leader who was to tie up the loose ends escaping Carrancismo, the recognized head of the Jacobin wing that introduced the key articles in the constitution (class conciliation, the development of the postrevolutionary state, the national appropriation of the strategic resources, and the secularization of education and culture), was Alvaro Obregón, leader of the new political alliance that was emerging from the rubble of the Carrancista era.

The Hour of the *Caudillo*

Born in Huatabampo, Sonora, thirty years before Madero called for the rebellion of 1910, Alvaro Obregón was already the symbol of success and a bright military star by the time Carranza assumed power as Constitutional president of Mexico, in the first months of 1917. Of all the virtues of Obregón as a military leader, perhaps the most important was the one that also exalted him as a politician: his extraordinary sense of opportunity, the lucid balance of his resources and of the moment or the conditions in which they could best be used.

In the months of May and June 1913, the Sonorense revolutionary forces fought two decisive battles with the federal army, the battles of Santa Rosa and Santa María, on the train tracks from Guaymas to Hermosillo. On both occasions, before firing a single shot or using a single man, Obregón had placed his enemy at a clear disadvantage, simply by holding back and waiting. When the supply line of the federal army to Guaymas was itself in crisis, Obregón went on the offensive, eliminating key logistic positions in the federal rear guard and flanks—such as the water holes, essential in the frying pan of the Sonorense summers—and discharged all his intact military might on an enemy that was already vulnerable due to thirst, fatigue, immobility, and tension. Using another mode of combat, the battles of Celaya again showed a commander who resisted the Villista attack from the trenches, until the adversary wore out, allowing him to take the offensive with the input of fresh cavalry troops that had not yet joined the battle. At the end of those battles, which decided the victory of the Revolution, Obregón confided to Carranza that the Constitutionalist armies had the enormous luck of having Villa as the enemy commander. It was an implicit comment on his own military talent, the conviction that, if he had been in Villa's place, Obregón would have dismantled the Carrancista armies by the simple recourse of avoiding frontal combat and waiting instead until the natural wear and tear of his advance would place him in the appropriate condition and terrain. He had accomplished this before in Sonora, and he would do it again in 1923 with the De la Huerta rebellion, whose armies advanced at a good clip and triumphantly from their leader's base of operations in Veracruz, only to encounter in the center of the country the calculated resistance that destroyed him in a few formal battles.

And, as in war, so it was in politics: first, in the elections that would place Obregón as municipal president of Huatabampo in 1912, then in his incorporation into the campaign against Orozco. Later, in the intricate chess game for state supremacy during 1913 and 1914, Obregón always found the appropriate breach and calculated the rhythm required to take advantage of it. The same strategic impulse guided his decisions leading to the split with Carranza. Later, at the end of 1917, after the Constitutional Assembly sanctioned the new fundamental code of the country, the haughty and irate secretary of war, the recognized political compass of the radical wing of that assembly, presented his resignation to the Carrancista cabinet to publicize its many internal contradictions and withdrew to his birthplace. At the time of his resignation, only five years after his first formal taking up of arms against Orozquismo in Sonora, Obregón was already many things: victorious commander when he was outnumbered by the Villista armies; mutilated hero when he lost his right arm to a mortar in Trinidad; author of the first strategic alliance between the working class and the governments of the Revolution; the northern Jacobin married by the church in 1916; a politician fed up with the intrigue and flagrant dishonesty in the Carrancista circles; and the ambitious man who saw on the horizon the silhouette of the presidential chair.

He had foreseen that possibility long before, and, in certain ways, he had worked to obtain it. In his unique and uncommon self-deprecating humor, he once answered someone who was asking him if he had good eyesight: "Yes, I have very good eyesight. Imagine that I was able to see the presidency from Huatabampo." He had been able to see it again, even closer at the convention of Aguascalientes in August 1914, with the accord that he promoted and that later went unfulfilled, for Carranza and Villa to retire to their private lives, which would have allowed the country to avoid a new bloodbath. He was able to see again after the victory over Villa, when he tried to induce Carranza to assume the position of provisional president, which would have prevented his reelection for the following constitutional term. And he decided to take it by force after 1917, when he separated from the Carrancista caravan and its errors, to establish new alliances and dispute the position at the next opportunity.

He went to Sonora, disavowed Carrancismo implicitly but clearly, bought a *hacienda* called El Náinari, and began to develop an agricultural center. He traveled to Canada, Cuba, and the United States, had an interview with Woodrow Wilson, and watched as Carranza got mired in the entanglement of his restorationist vocation, the corruption of his collaborators, and the murder of Zapata. On June 1, 1919, escaping the political factionalism that had so eroded Carrancismo, Obregón established himself personally as the point of reference for national politics. He accepted the ideological shell of the Juarista Liberal party, and he announced himself to the nation as a candidate for president of the republic without making compromises with any party or faction. Free from any previous commitments, he devoted himself to the task of tying up the loose ends that Carranza's scheme of government had left out in its intolerance, and he set out to create a government of conciliation with all the excluded parties, over which he would govern, by negotiation or force, the ever-changing nature of the alliances of a fragile equilibrium always on the brink of catastrophe, with the pragmatic and unchallengeable hand of the *caudillo*.

On the Road to Tlaxcalantongo

In 1919, a year before his presidential term was over, Carranza presented his own candidate for the position, a "civilian" candidate who was also Sonorense: Ignacio Bonillas. Obregón traversed the country triumphantly promoting his cause. Foreseeing that there would be no solution without a military confrontation, Carranza tried to subvert the Sonorense state powers, the operational base of Obregón, and guarantee the loyalty of the military garrisons of the region, by changing the command to Carrancista generals. He then accused Obregón of conspiring with the rebels and subjected him to a lawsuit for sedition in Mexico City. Obregón escaped from the capital trap, and the Sonorense government and military officers announced in April 1920 the Plan de Agua Prieta, which disavowed the Carrancista government. After the plan came what Luis Cabrera, the main ideologue of the First Chief, called a "strike of the Generals" as evidence of the support that Obregón had gained among the army and of the sympathy that his cause evoked among the active politicians of the nation. One after another, they joined the ranks of the Plan de Agua Prieta: military commanders and revolutionary leaders, rebels and workers, Zapatistas and political parties. Pablo González, who owed everything to Carranza, abstained from participating. The military command of Guerrero surprised Obregón in flight, proclaimed him as their commander, and organized the assault on the capital city.

Carranza, surprised by the turn of events, sought the voice of the past and tried to repeat it. He decided to retreat to Veracruz, recondition his forces, and return victorious to retake the rest of the country. He arranged for the evacuation of Mexico City, loaded the government files and treasury on a long train convoy, established a strong personal guard with loyal troops, and set out on a long and difficult trek toward the Gulf, under constant attack by the Zapatista forces, a high desertion rate, and fatalities. Before he arrived in Puebla, he had abandoned the convoy and, with a small retinue, was riding a horse on the sierra, trying to reach Veracruz, where he could count on the loyalty of the local strongman, Gen. Cándido Aguilar, who would provide him with a refuge. He was not able to cross the sierra. On the night of May 21, 1920, he was assassinated in Tlaxcalantongo, a small town on the sierra, where he was asleep, protected only by the solidarity of a handful of steadfast followers.

He was buried four days later in Mexico City, in a third-rate grave, on the morning of the day on which Congress would elect Adolfo de la Huerta as substitute president, the civilian head of the Agua Prieta rebellion, and the first in a series of four Sonorense presidents that postrevolutionary Mexico would have in the following fourteen years.

3.
From the *Caudillo* to the Maximato: 1920–1934

Ten Years Later

By the time the memorable Sonorenses occupied the presidential chair for the first time, the war and its effects—epidemics and migration—had eliminated 825,000 people from the Mexican territory. The population had been tallied at 15,160,000 inhabitants at the end of the Porfirian period in 1910; the November 1921 census found a population of only 14,355,000 Mexicans.

Death came with bullets and battles, but also with epidemics of typhus and yellow fever (1915–1916), and with the so-called Spanish influenza (1918–1919). The northern frontier attracted conspirators, revolutionaries, and arms dealers and buyers, but also workers, refugees, and people who wanted to abstain from the Revolution. Emigration was so attractive that the 200,000 Mexicans who lived in the United States in 1910 had multiplied fourfold by 1930.

The economic cost of the Mexican Revolution, its "opportunity cost," has been estimated by the experts at 37 percent in terms of GDP not produced. During the decade of violence, all of the sectors of the economy, with the sole exception of oil, suffered a significant decline. The global agricultural production of the country had grown at an annual rate of 4.4 percent between 1895 and 1910, and it fell at an average rate of 5.25 percent between 1910 and 1921, until it became half of what the maximum Porfirian production had been; the agricultural exports, which made up 31.6 percent of the total exports in 1910, fell to only 3.3 percent in 1921. Mining production also fell dramatically at an annual rate of 4 percent, from 1,309 million pesos in 1910 (calculated at 1950 peso rates) to 620 million pesos in 1921.

The manufacturing industry followed a similar course and was capable of recovering the 1910 levels only by 1922: ten years of stagnation. The violence destroyed a significant amount of infrastructure, in particular railroads, with entire sections of the tracks disappearing, and losses of 3,873 railroad cars, 50 locomotives, and 34 passenger cars. Close to 1,250 miles of telegraph lines were also destroyed. A good part of the government's efforts between 1916 and 1919 was directed toward restoring the lost railroad equipment, with such a high impact on the railroad company's public debt that it became unsustainable, and toward a partial reconstruction of the telegraph lines, which in 1921 offered only a small loss in relation to the total lines inherited from the Porfiriato (23,235 miles).

Of all the prerevolutionary economy, only the oil industry maintained its growth rate, and even sped it up. Its incredible growth rate of 43 percent between 1910 and 1921 allowed Mexico to increase its net exports from 200,000 barrels of oil in 1910 to 516,800,000 barrels in 1921. A large part of the political negotiation during the decades to come would have to do with the prosperity of this enclave, the only truly dynamic source of production in the depressed revolutionary economy, and a true islet of control by the foreign companies, whose resistance would develop, in a meandering to and fro of confrontations and negotiations, the emergent revolutionary nationalism.

By 1921, the working force had been reduced by almost 400,000 people, from 5,263,000 employed Mexicans in 1910 to 4,883,000 in 1921. There were 100,000 fewer Mexicans working in the countryside, 50,000 fewer in the mines, 60,000 fewer in the free professions and private employment, and, of the 90,000 registered landowners in 1910, only 1,700 remained, an undeniable demonstration of the degree to which the quiescent life of Porfirian high society had been destroyed by the revolutionary whirlwind. The number of housewives, on the other hand, had increased significantly, by more than 130,000.

According to the labor profile of the postrevolutionary society, only 324 of every 1,000 Mexicans worked (330 in 1910) and, of them, 224 worked in the countryside (237 in 1910), 40 worked in industry, 19 in commerce and finance, 10 in services, 5 in transport and communications, 4 in the government, and 3 in mining, especially in the oil industry (6 per 1,000 in 1910). Another substantial slice of the pie, 330 of every 1,000 Mexicans in 1921, were housewives (304 in 1910) and 331 of every 1,000 were minors (358 in 1910). In sum, we could say that one-fifth of the Mexican population of 1921 was devoted to agricultural activities, one-third to homes and domestic work, another third to the task of growing up, and only the remainder, in minimum numbers, were distributed in declining order to industry, commerce, finance, services, communications, the government, and mining.

The rates of natural population growth reached 6.1 percent in 1921, although they were considerably reduced by the deaths of 222 of every 1,000 newborns. The memories of the epidemics, the repercussions of hunger and destruction, the paralysis of the budding sanitary system introduced during the Porfiriato, all left a deep imprint on the revolutionary experience concerning the issue of health care, which was guaranteed as a right to the population by the 1917 constitution.

After this whirlwind, the Mexican manner of passing away remained basically the same: an overwhelming quantity of deaths were due to stomach illnesses (349 of every 1,000 deceased), a similar number to lung and respiratory diseases (influenza, pneumonia, tuberculosis, and bronchitis), a high proportion to malaria (148 per 1,000), and only a handful to heart disease (31 per 1,000), accidents (47 per 1,000), or criminal actions (24 homicides per 1,000). In sum, Mexico was still dying according to the patterns of a predominantly rural society, one that was still in the throes of endemic and epidemic diseases, without generalized systems of public health, clean drinking water, hygienic food, or hospital attention; it was a society affected by high percentages of curable diseases and without the modern mortality characteristics of a mechanized, urban life, and the pathology of progress.

The first indicators of the future began weakly to insinuate themselves in such things as the growth of the urban population, which rose from 11.7 percent in 1910 to 14.7 percent in 1921. Mexico City began in those years to have the heartbeat of the future, because the marks of violence and the expulsion of people from the countryside due to the insecurity had made its population jump from 470,000 Porfirian inhabitants to 659,000 postrevolutionary inhabitants.

The society that the Sonorenses inherited after the civil war was still fundamentally rural, but depressed in its agricultural and cattle-raising production capacity, demographically reduced by 800,000 people eliminated by the war, the epidemics, and emigration; severely damaged in its infrastructure and in its monetary system due to the destructive and financial excesses of the battling armies; unsafe outside the cities, which began to grow in those years; and with only one prosperous enclave—itself a defiance of the revitalized nationalism of those years—the oil companies, whose expansion in the midst of war clearly spoke of the decisive connections they had with the force of the world markets, even more than with the turmoil of the country, even if that turmoil was a revolution.

The Leaders

The Agua Prieta rebellion, led by the Sonorenses, would be the last victorious rebellion in the history of contemporary Mexico. Future victories would belong, invariably, to the constituted powers, stability, and institutions. Adolfo de la Huerta, civilian head of Aguaprietismo, was the interim president of Mexico from June 10 to December 1, 1920, enough time for the efficient task of pacifying the most diverse rebel groups, and to call for presidential elections for September 5 of that year, which Alvaro Obregón won by 1,131,751 votes to 47,442 votes for his closest runner-up.

Obregón ruled as constitutional president during the period 1921–1924, handed over power to his countryman Plutarco Elías Calles for the following period (1925–1928), and he succumbed to the Porfirian temptation of having himself reelected as president of Mexico for the next term (1928–1932). As president-reelect, death surprised him when a Catholic fanatic, José de León Toral, shot him to death during a political breakfast in the La Bombilla restaurant on Tuesday, July 17, 1928. The acting president, Plutarco Elías Calles, heard the news of Toral's bullets and not only decided not to run for reelection, but announced in his last presidential address to the nation the end of the era of the *caudillos* and the beginning of an era of institutions. In full agreement with the army, the chambers of Congress named Emilio Portes Gil as provisional president for two years, who then called for special elections for the period 1930–1934. The elections were won by the engineer Pascual Ortiz Rubio, the first official presidential candidate of the National Revolutionary party (PNR), established the previous year. Ortiz Rubio soon understood that the new institutional concert had an old orchestra conductor, and he was forced to resign after his differences with the strongman of the period, Plutarco Elías Calles, made his government untenable. He had begun on a bad footing: the very first day of his administration, after assuming power, he survived a murder attempt by Daniel Flores that destroyed his jaw, on the patio of the National Palace itself. The resignation of Ortiz Rubio before Congress, on September 2, 1932, gave way to the last interim president in Mexico's contemporary history, the Sonorense businessman and general, Abelardo Rodríguez, who was designated unanimously by Congress to govern from September 3, 1932, to December 1, 1934.

Literature, through Martín Luis Guzmán, has memorably christened the tragic and fratricidal years of Obregonista domination (1921–1928) as the period of the "shadow of the *caudillo*." The six years that follow the death of that shadow in La Bombilla correspond to the presidencies of Portes Gil, Ortiz Rubio, and Abelardo Rodríguez, who are known in Mexican history as the Maximato. This is in reference to the undeniable weight of the next *caudillo*'s shadow, that of Plutarco Elías Calles, recognized in his time by his admirers as the Jefe Máximo of the Revolution. Those two historical presences dominate the course of events of fifteen years of postrevolutionary politics, between the victory of the Plan de Agua Prieta and the year of the election of Lázaro Cárdenas to rule the country, in 1934. They are years of pacification and institutionalization of the forces that were unleashed by the violence of the previous decade, the road of Mexican society toward stability and of political organization toward Mexico's greatest accomplishment of the century: the peaceful and institutional transferral of power. The paradox of that transition to the rule of institutions and the end of the *caudillos* is that it would not have been possible had it not been for the presence of two fundamentally *caudillo*-like and personalistic individuals. It was a twentieth-century political modernization conducted by *caudillos* reminiscent of the nineteenth century.

When 1934 ended, the period that the paradox covers, Mexican society had established the foundations of its main institutions. Stability brought about economic reactivation. The wealth produced in the country grew at an annual rate under 1 percent between 1920 and 1925, but in the following five-year period, under Calles, it made a significant leap to 5.8 percent per year, and the country saw the beginning of its most decisive territorial transformation since the Porfirian trains, with the development of a network of highways and of ambitious irrigation projects that would expand the possibilities of an economically active state, capable of filling the holes in infrastructure that the absence of investment and private initiative had left. The economic depression in the United States and the worldwide panic of 1929 affected that growth and translated, in the first years of the 1930s, into a new period of negative growth rates, with a strong adverse impact on oil and mineral exports, traditional sources of foreign exchange for the Mexican economy.

Fifteen years after armed struggle, just before the ascent to power of Lázaro Cárdenas in 1934, the basic economic profile of Mexican society had barely changed: seven out of every ten employed Mexicans were still working in planting, cattle-raising, or related industries; those who had jobs in the cities, trade, and the professions were only fifteen of every hundred; and 14 percent were employed by the manufacturing industry.

It was a stabilized society that had changed little in its material structures. But it was also a restored society, which had postponed the fundamental impulses and demands of the social war that had shaken it up. Its active economic nationalism had become more moderated, and it had established with the United States a kind of conservative agreement, after several attempts at increasing the national control of foreign investments and enterprises. In 1929, Calles had given the command to halt agrarian distribution, because he believed that it was affecting the economy, despite the fact that since the Carrancista agrarian law of January 1915 until the end of the Abelardo Rodríguez administration in December 1934, the revolution in power had distributed only 18.7 million acres to 800,000 peasants in a country that was still overwhelmingly rural—3,600,000 persons still lived off the land in 1930 (70 percent of the 5,165,000 Mexicans who made up the total economically active population).

Power and money had softened the egalitarian and antioligarchic spirit of the 1913 rebellions to open the way to the consolidation of a new oligarchy, which acquired wealth through illegal businesses, commercial speculation, taking over the *haciendas* of the old Porfirian landowning class, personal enterprises that were subsidized and fattened up with public funds, and the development of a new entrepreneurial class of ex-revolutionaries. The president who would place the presidential sash on Cárdenas in 1934 was the incarnation of that new, softened revolutionary family: Abelardo Rodríguez, promoter of gambling in Mexico and prostitution for border export, who transformed Tijuana into the recreation zone for the U.S. naval base of San Diego.

Fast Forward

Those fifteen years of Sonorense domination brought to the country an avalanche of innovations whose succession in fast forward must include, in the first place, the almost absolute pacification of the entire country and the beginning of a feverish reconstruction, the public aim of the Obregonista government of putting an end to the "revolution" to inaugurate a new, constructive, and promising phase for the country. It was that spirit that was imbued with unusual force in the Vasconcelos project to redeem and enliven federal public education that would be able to disseminate the gospel of learning and national identity to all corners of Mexico and for which the old Department of Education was transformed into the Ministry of Education (1921). Ramón López Velarde synthesized the new national sensibility in his poem "Suave patria" (Soft homeland, 1921) and José Vasconcelos, his universalist chauvinism, in *La raza cósmica* (The cosmic race, 1925). Those were the years of the beginning of Mexican muralism (Diego Rivera and José Clemente Orozco), with the "decoration"—as Obregón himself said in his report—of the walls of the National Preparatory School and the definite birth of Mexico and "Mexicanism" as the ultimate substrate of the revolutionary experience. They were also the years of a difficult and meandering search for negotiation with the United States, which considered the 1917 constitution confiscatory and extended long claims for the external debt and damage to U.S. properties during the Revolution. The tasks of the government and the administration absorbed all of the almost-juvenile energy of the generation born in the last decade of the nineteenth century, and the average age of the governing group was barely over thirty years of age. This demographic change in the ruling elite of government was accompanied by technological modernization. At the

beginning of the 1920s, radiotelegraphy was introduced in the communications system, as well as the first direct commercial flights in
transportation, the use of the telephone and cinema became generalized,
and the automobile displaced the horse-drawn carriages and mule-
driven trams, bringing the first traffic jams to Mexico City. In 1921,
agricultural trade tripled, and Mexico became the number two world
producer of oil. The year 1923 also marked the De la Huertista rebellion
that affected half of the army, and the recognition of the Obregonista
government by the United States. Rafael F. Muñoz published *Memorias
de Pancho Villa* (Memories of Pancho Villa); Alfonso Reyes, *Ifigenia
cruel* (Cruel Iphigenia); and Mariano Azuela, *La malhora* (The evil hour).
From the debris of the rebellion, the government of Plutarco Elías Calles
started the development of a new type of active state that would promote
and intervene in the economy, and whose major initiatives were the
establishment of the central bank in 1925, the Banco de México, and of
an official rural development bank, the Banco de Crédito Ejidal, in 1927.
High school education was started, as well as the development of a
national highway network and an ambitious irrigation agriculture. In
1925, the first collective labor contract in the labor history of the country
was signed, and the Regional Confederation of Mexican Labor (CROM)
experienced a boom, as a model of the unionism advocating class
conciliation and that would administer the government's pact with the
organized workers, according to the historical program outlined in
article 123 of the constitution. The search for the Mexican national
identity was achieved in the heart of the Callista rural schools, and in the
passing of the first oil law (1925), which put relations with the United
States on the verge of intervention. The year 1926 marked the Cristero
War and the first significant inflow of tourists. The terminology of the
ruling elite began to include the word "development," and the showgirls
in the dance halls, with the provocative exhibition of their bodies and
gestures, gave glimpses of a new public sensuality, in sharp contrast to
the Catholic Mexico that was fighting in the western sierras and the
Bajío for the empire of Christ the King.

The year 1929 brought the Wall Street crash and the world crisis, the
creation of the National Revolutionary party (PNR), the establishment
of university autonomy, negotiations that ended the Cristero War, and
the last military rebellion of contemporary Mexico, which signaled the
definite transition of the army to the institutional realm. In that key year
of Mexican history, Martín Luis Guzmán published *La sombra del
caudillo* (The shadow of the *caudillo*); the first commercial radio station
of Mexico, XEW, was established; the interim president, Emilio Portes
Gil, carried out the largest land distribution of the postrevolutionary
governments; and, with the independent candidacy of the former secre-

tary of education, José Vasconcelos, the country experienced the first civilian dissidence of the educated middle classes against the *caudillo* political domination that had emerged from the postrevolutionary restoration. The first years of the 1930s brought the introduction of talking pictures to Mexico and of Rufino Tamayo as a public muralist; the Vatican conversion of the Virgen de Guadalupe into patron saint of Latin America; the introduction of the "socialist school" and the lofty intention of the government to win the hearts and minds of Mexico's children. The first philosophical product of the dominant Mexicanism of the 1920s came to light with the publication of Samuel Ramos's book *El perfil del hombre y la cultura en México* (A profile of man and culture in Mexico). The deep restructuring of the political forces in the different regions and cities of the country gave birth to a new agrarian organization, a new workers' movement to replace the CROM, and a new corporate structure that was able to organize within the PNR the massive militancy of the main classes of society and the army. Finally, in 1934, from the fallout of the Maximato, which had demolished *caudillo* inheritances and tenuously built the institutions that would replace them, the first institutionally presidentialist government of the postrevolutionary period was installed. This government would end the hegemony of the Jefe Máximo and of the Sonorense dynasty, to place at the center of government those traditions that had long been postponed in the popular and nationalist meaning of the Revolution.

The Catastrophic Equilibrium

Two trends led to restoring stability in the 1920s. The first, which we could call the catastrophic equilibrium, included the settling of accounts between revolutionary factions, the subordination of the warlords who had been inherited from the civil war, and the institutionalization of the armed forces. The second combined the issues of the construction of the state and included a confrontation with the traditions and beliefs of the "old society"; the Cristero War of 1926–1929; the conflict with the United States for control of the strategic resources of the country; the first bold attempts at developing the state as an instrument of economic, educational, and cultural action and regulation; and the incorporation of the social movements into the state system through an organized representation from above of sectors. The ideal location for that massive incorporation was also the negotiation apparatus of the elite, the National Revolutionary party (PNR), created in 1929.

The civil war of 1910–1917, as well as the reforms and interventions of the past century, left the country with a significant number of strongmen, military leaders, and regional *caciques* with their own power, arms, and interests. At the time he assumed the presidency, Alvaro Obregón appeared as the natural head of that constellation of ambitions and reputations, the first among such equals as Benjamín Hill and Salvador Alvarado, and the focus of agreement and unification of a long list of revolutionaries with undeniable predominance in several states of the country: Angel Flores and Rafael Buelna in Sinaloa; Plutarco Elías Calles in Sonora; Genovevo de la O and the Zapatista generals in Morelos; Fortunato Maycotte in Guerrero; Guadalupe Sánchez, Lázaro Cárdenas, and Manuel Peláez in Veracruz and Tamaulipas; Saturnino Cedillo in San Luis Potosí; Manuel García Vigil in Oaxaca; and the Carrancista officers who were in decline, but still retained, as many others in the whirlwind of the Revolution, influence over their troops and their own military lineage: Francisco Munguía and Manuel M. Diéguez. After the Agua Prieta rebellion was victorious, and Adolfo de la Huerta was installed as interim president, the first task of the Sonorense era was to pacify: to attract, compromise, eliminate. Francisco Villa was offered the exact incarnation of his agricultural utopia, the *hacienda* of Canutillo in Durango, to which he had to withdraw with an armed guard of fifty men, paid for by the Ministry of War, which would also absorb into the army the rebel Villistas who wanted to remain in the armed services. The rest of the Villistas, who refused to go to Canutillo or to enter the army, would receive a great deal of land in other parts of the republic. Villa accepted the offer and signed the Pacification Act in Sabinas on July 28, 1920, in an agreement that followed by only days a previous settlement of accounts with Pablo González, the Carrancista general who abstained, with his twenty-two thousand men, from intervening in the conflict between Agua Prieta and Carranza, the man to whom they all owed their ranks. González was accused of fomenting a rebellion, was arrested in Monterrey, judged in a city theater, condemned to death, and finally set free to go to a border town, from which he would periodically prepare statements against Obregón, before disappearing into the night of time.

These were only the "big fish" in an extended stretch of negotiations and agreements that included the demobilization of fifty thousand men (a similar number remained in the regular army), political commitments for agrarian reform with the Zapatista officers who laid down their arms, the bribing of Félix Díaz, who had led an "insurrection" in Veracruz when the Agua Prieta rebellion was successful, and the execution of Jesús Guajardo, the murderer of Carranza. Knowledgeable of the weaknesses of their allies and enemies, the triumphant Sonorenses also distributed benefits; they showed tolerance toward businesses, at the expense of the public treasury; they allowed land appropriations and other peremptory forms of improving their assets. Obregón summed up this extended list of cases with the famous aphorism: "There is no general capable of resisting a cannonball of 50 thousand pesos."

Legitimized in the ballot boxes and recognized as the first among equals at the end of 1921, Obregón occupied the presidential chair and steered his government toward a difficult but effective equilibrium, with party politics in Congress, moderate economic growth, a legendary educational administration, an extended dispute with the United States, and the first visible incorporation of the agrarian and worker demands foreseen in the 1917 constitution, which had been ignored by Carranza: three years of an internal peace that the country had not enjoyed in the last decade.

The Shadow of Washington

The Mexican Revolution had a decisive impact on the internal situation and also altered the external relations of Mexico. Of course, the most notable and dangerous effects were the relations with the great powers, in particular, with the United States, and in Mexico's alliances with the Latin American countries.

When Carranza was eliminated by the Sonora group, Mexico had been partially invaded on two occasions by U.S. forces, and it had been threatened countless times. Contacts with the principal European countries had diminished, and they started to normalize only in 1920. The citizens of the United States, England, France, and Spain had enormous claims against Mexico for damages inflicted during ten years of civil war, and by the lack of payment of the significant external debt that had been accumulated during the Porfiriato and was increased by Madero and Huerta. The 1917 constitution—in particular, article 27—was hanging like a sword over the agricultural and oil properties of foreigners, because it opened up the possibilities of their being expropriated or nationalized.

A product of his nationalist position, Carranza fell when he was trying to reduce some of the most visible disputes with foreign governments. Once Carranza was out of the way, the government in Washington decided that an excellent opportunity had been opened to restate all of its demands against Mexico and to try to reach a favorable solution. The first step was to declare that Adolfo de la Huerta had obtained power in an unconstitutional manner and to withdraw the diplomatic recognition that had been reluctantly granted to Carranza's government. The official relations between the governments of Washington and Mexico City were suspended once more. Other European and Latin American nations imitated the conduct of the United States. None of the members of the international community could afford to ignore the indications from Washington on what should be done in the case of Mexico. England and Germany had disregarded Washington in the recent past without any result other than affecting their own interests. In May 1920, Mexico was once more formally isolated from the main centers of world decision making.

Shortly before Carranza's fall, U.S. Sen. Albert B. Fall had chaired a committee that was investigating the Mexican situation. Fall was a Republican, a blatant representative of the oil interests, and, therefore, a declared enemy of the Mexican Revolution. The senator had devoted himself to demonstrating that it was necessary to show strength to Carranza, and, when Carranza disappeared from the scene, he recommended against recognizing any new government in Mexico as long as it did not agree, among other things, to exclude U.S. interests and firms from the stipulations of articles 3, 27, 33, and 130 of the 1917 constitution. If the Mexican government refused, it would be informed that if it could not demonstrate that it was capable of keeping peace and order in its territory, the U.S. Armed Forces would take care of the situation. President Wilson's government wasn't as ruthless as Fall desired, but it did adopt a strong-armed policy. When De la Huerta initiated recognition procedures, the State Department informed him that it would be granted only after negotiating full guarantees to the property rights of U.S. citizens in Mexico. De la Huerta decided to forgo formal relations with the United States.

In May 1921, the U.S. government proposed to Obregón a Treaty of "Friendship and Trade" that was tantamount to formally accepting Fall's recommendations of the previous year. The project included guarantees against nationalization, a ban on the retroactive application of the measures established in the 1917 constitution, recognition of the mining and oil rights acquired by U.S. citizens according to the laws of 1884, 1892, and 1909, as well as the payment or retribution for all U.S. properties taken over after 1910.

Washington's position was politically unacceptable for Obregón, because signing such a treaty would place national sovereignty and the very essence of the Revolution in question. But disregarding the United States was also dangerous, since the White House could support an armed movement against his government with unforeseeable consequences. Obregón decided to accept the U.S. demands to the extent possible, and insisted that he would negotiate a formal agreement such as the U.S. proposed only if he was first granted unconditional recognition. The U.S. government refused to grant recognition: the deck was stacked in its favor, and it did not see any reason to play its cards.

The Conciliating Rebellion

The impasse in the relations between both countries continued until 1923. Neither of the parties would budge from its original position, despite the fact that some European powers lost patience with the United States, because by blocking their diplomatic relations with Mexico, they were prevented from having adequate representation in the country to look after their interests. To prevent a major crisis, Obregón was able to get the Supreme Court to determine that the legislation that nationalized the oil industry could not be applied to the properties acquired by the big foreign companies before 1917. In 1922 he sent his secretary of finance, Adolfo de la Huerta, to New York to negotiate an agreement with the bankers outlining the terms by which Mexico would pay its external debt. The agreement was signed, and Mexico recognized an external debt of $508,830,321. It was an astonishing amount given the difficult position of the federal budget, but it put the financial circles, such as the renowned firm of J. P. Morgan, in a favorable state of mind with regard to Obregón.

By 1923, the U.S. intransigence had diminished, and Obregón wanted to achieve recognition before the agitation of the coming presidential campaign created fissures in his government that could be used against him. An agreement was then reached to hold talks in Mexico between personal representatives of the presidents of both countries, with the purpose of addressing the points of disagreement. The famous "Bucareli Conferences" took place between May and August of 1923, and their result was not a treaty, but something less formal: an agreement between the presidential representatives. Mexico committed itself to paying in cash all agrarian expropriations greater than 4,335 acres that affected U.S. citizens, which made any expropriation of large landholdings very unlikely; in exchange, the United States accepted a payment in agrarian bonds of all expropriations less than that area. Mexico also recognized that it would not affect the oil properties from which foreign companies could demonstrate that they had begun to extract crude oil before 1917 (the so-called doctrine of positive act). Mexico also agreed to sign a special pact, and a general agreement on claims, to examine the damage done to U.S. properties after 1868. In September 1923, both countries named ambassadors and finally renewed formal relations. In a short time, several European nations—with the notable exception of England—began negotiations to reopen their embassies in Mexico.

Obregón was able to reestablish communications with Washington just in time, because a few months later he had to confront a rebellion of a substantial part of the army. He then needed U.S. support, both to purchase arms as well as to prevent his adversaries from obtaining provisions on the other side of the border. The rebel leader, De la Huerta, was very conscious of the importance of U.S. influence, and he took great pains to prevent any actions that might affect the material or political interests of the United States. He sent a personal representative to Washington to seek the support, or at least the neutrality, of Washington by conveying his sympathy with U.S. demands. The efforts of De la Huerta were in vain, as Washington was not predisposed to reopening its controversy with Mexico and supported Obregón. In the end, when the situation of the rebellion was desperate, De la Huerta took anti-imperialism as his banner and accused Obregón of having mortally affected Mexican sovereignty with the Bucareli agreements. But this policy change was of little use to him, and he could not prevent his defeat.

Martín Luis Guzmán has reconstructed in *La sombra del caudillo* (The shadow of the caudillo) the atmosphere of tragic fatality that induced Adolfo de la Huerta to this break in the alliance with the elite of the Sonorense group. Caught up in the whirlpool of the presidential succession of 1923, carried to and fro by forces he could barely understand, in disagreement with the Bucareli Conference, dragged down by the majority revolt of the National Cooperativist party in Congress, involved in his own declarations that he would not run for president, and irate due to the campaign to discredit him that followed his resignation as secretary of finance, De la Huerta decided to announce his candidacy against his countryman and rival, Plutarco Elías Calles, the secretary of the interior who was supported by the *caudillo*. Before De la Huerta was able to understand fully what he was doing, half of the army had aligned itself behind his cause, and the rebellion prospered. Knowing full well that this division would unleash an unpredictable reaction on his part, Obregón warned:

"I will not be responsible for anything that might happen from now on." And what happened was the emergence of the nocturnal side of the *caudillo*. Foreseeing his possible alliance with De la Huerta, Villa was murdered in 1923 in an ambush, and the murderer did not even spend one year in jail. The Cooperatist deputies that supported De la Huerta's cause were expelled from the Congress. The leader of the powerful Regional Worker Confederation of Mexico, Luis N. Morones, an unrepentant Callista, assumed the offensive against the Senators that obstructed the approval of the Treaties of Bucareli, which would guarantee U.S. support and recognition of Obregón's government to face the imminent rebellion. He publicly declared: "The senile and rusty old men that attempt to parade their miserable ridicule in front of the Senate will suffer the effects of direct action . . . Our enemies should hurry to sharpen their daggers and aim their murderous rifles, because we are in a ruthless war, a tooth for a tooth, a life for a life."

And he was as good as his word. A week later, Sen. Field Jurado, a partisan of De la Huerta, was shot to death near his home, and three other Cooperatist senators disappeared after being kidnapped. Thus terrorized, the Senate ratified the Bucareli agreements; the United States sold the Obregonista government the arms it required to shore up its army, and it refused to speculate politically with the De la Huertista cause, whose rebellion began on December 4, 1923, and ended in March of the following year, and implied the elimination, by death, exile, or dismissal, of fifty-four generals and seven thousand soldiers.

The Cristero War

Once the De la Huerta opposition was eliminated and the army was disciplined, Gen. Plutarco Elías Calles started his campaign for the presidency. He was declared the winner, and he assumed the position on December 1, 1924. But, following the wave of catastrophic equilibrium, Calles couldn't rule in peace either. He had to confront the Cristero rebellion—which he had helped to provoke—that exploded in 1926, as a sequel to the virulent dispute between the federal government and the high authorities of the Catholic church.

On July 31, 1926, the practice of Catholicism was suspended in the Mexican Republic. Mass could not be celebrated, nor could the holy sacraments, including baptism, be administered or religious marriages be conducted. It was the final stage in the growing conflict between northern Jacobinism and the national religious traditions and their administrators, the priests. The 1917 constitution ratified in its articles 3, 25, 27, and 130 the anticlerical dispositions of the 1857 constitution, and consequently it was denounced by the Catholic hierarchy as detrimental to the church and its followers. During the administration of Alvaro Obregón, the militant, irreducible, and extensive Catholic Association of Mexican Youth (ACJM) was created, and the hostility between the revolutionary regime and the hierarchy grew. In 1915, in an act that was characteristic of northern Jacobinism, Obregón expelled a group of Spanish priests from Mexico City, having previously widely publicized the presence of venereal diseases among them. The Jacobin became a statesman, but nonetheless, at the beginning of 1923, he was concerned about the presence of forty thousand pilgrims in a ceremony to lay the foundation stone of an enormous statue of Christ in Mount Cubilete, Guanajuato, where the bishop of San Luis Potosí had proclaimed Jesus Christ as the King of Mexico. The papal ambassador, Monsignor Ernesto

Filippi, present at the ceremony, was immediately expelled from this new kingdom. The hostility extended into the following year, until the celebration in October 1924 of the also successful Eucharistic Congress, whose main public ceremonies were canceled because they violated the constitutional prohibitions. At the beginning of 1925, at the instigation of CROM leader Luis Morones, natural enemy of Catholic trade-unionism, which had obtained some advances since the Porfiriato, a schismatic Mexican church was established. It was placed under the leadership of the patriarch José Joaquín Pérez, who disavowed the authority of Rome and declared religious celibacy as immoral. In Tabasco, the Callista governor Tomás Garrido Canabal obtained from his legislature a decree by which no priest could celebrate Mass unless he was married, an ironic coercion that forced the Jesuit bishop of the locality, Pascual Díaz, to abandon the state, insulted and ridiculed by the outrageous Garridista Jacobinism.

At the beginning of 1926, Archbishop Mora y del Río publicly reiterated in the daily newspaper *El Universal* some declarations he had made nine years earlier that the church would resist any attempt to apply the anticlerical articles of the 1917 constitution. The reaction of President Calles, defied in his earthly hegemony, was devastating: he ordered the closing of several convents and churches, and he expelled two hundred foreign priests from the country. The number of priests allowed in certain states of the republic was reduced (16 for Yucatán, 25 for Durango, 12 for Tamaulipas), and the Bishop of Huejutla was arrested, tried, and condemned for having opposed the laws of the country and having publicly denounced the "crimes and assaults committed by the government" (March 26, 1926). The new Vatican envoy, Monsignor Caruana, was also expelled under the charge of having made "false declarations regarding his birth, profession and religion."

The response of the church hierarchy and of lay Catholics was to create the National League of Religious Defense, an organization that channeled the irritation of urban Catholics and repeated in its manifestos, declarations, and slogans what the hierarchy stated in its pastoral letters, diocesan messages, and in pulpits all over the country. Calles's counterattack was to introduce a new penal code that included the typification of religious crimes: penalties from one to five years for priests and clerics who criticized the laws, the authorities, or the government; punishments for religious acts celebrated outside the churches; and prohibition of wearing clothes or insignias that identified the owner as a member of the church (June 24, 1926).

The League then promoted a boycott against the government among Catholics to create an economic crisis; people should limit their purchases to the minimum necessary, they should not buy newspapers opposed to the League, or lottery tickets, nor should they attend theaters, dances, or lay schools. The persons who signed the leaflet that proposed the boycott were incarcerated due to the seditious character of their initiative, among them René Capistrán Garza, founder of the ACJM; Archbishop Mora y del Río; and the expelled Bishop of Tabasco, Pascual Ortiz Díaz. The bishops responded on July 25 with a joint pastoral letter, endorsed by Pope Pius XI, announcing their decision to suspend the practice of Catholicism in the churches of Mexico, given that the governmental hostility made it impossible to maintain. Forty thousand organized workers saluted the policies of Calles on August 1, 1926, in the Plaza of the Constitution, where architects, engineers, and masons had added a new floor level to the National Palace in an unintentional symbolic coincidence with the consolidation of the governmental hegemony that Calles was trying to impose over the church.

Congress or Arms

For the first time in several centuries, there were no religious services in Mexico. Calles accepted the situation as a welcome outcome, favorable to reducing the level of fanaticism. And when a commission of bishops asked to be granted a hearing to express their displeasure with the severity of the antireligious laws, the president answered that in his judgment the prelates had only two options left: "Congress or arms." They went to the Congress with a petition to rescind the laws, signed by more than two million Mexican Catholics. On September 21, 1926, the petition was rejected by Congress. The other option, arms, was then all that was left for dozens of radical priests and their peasant and urban followers.

Mexico then experienced the second rebellion since 1910 of a deeply and intrinsically peasant character, a rebellion that at one point included 50,000 men ready to fight; lasted three years (1926–1929); ignited the states of Jalisco, Michoacán, Durango, Guerrero, Colima, Nayarit, and Zacatecas; cost 90,000 lives (12 generals, 1,800 officers, 55,000 soldiers and *agraristas*, 35,000 Cristeros); and, finally, could not be solved by arms or snuffed out by the army, but rather by negotiation and reaching a modus vivendi that the religious hierarchy established with the provisional government of Portes Gil in 1929. It was the uprising of old, peasant, and Catholic Mexico, still tied to its traditions and the religious balm of its town life, being defied by the revolutionary Jacobinism. But it was also the resistance of the church bureaucracy and hierarchy, the traditional power of colonial Mexico, overcome but not defeated in the Liberal wars of the nineteenth century, and restored in all its splendor during the Porfiriato.

The Cristeros revolted because they believed that the government was making the life of their church impossible: they could not receive Holy Communion, hear Mass, or confess. The historical origin of the conflict was, however, more remote, as it went back to the old conflicts with monarchism, the issue of secular power in conflict with ecclesiastic power, the separation of church and state that the majority of the European countries were able to settle during the Enlightenment and their political revolutions of the eighteenth century, while in Mexico it had its last throes in the second decade of the twentieth century, after a war in the 1860s and a popular revolution fifty years later. The deep roots of the City of God in Mexican society were profound and entangled.

The Cristero War of revolutionary Mexico expressed in a more violent way the struggle for revolutionary leadership developed in the liberal tradition and in the lay customs of the North of Mexico, in contrast to the old traditions of the Catholic regions of the West, the Bajío, and the center of the country, regions where the Spanish colonization had left a deep and indelible imprint, a vision of the world, an agrarian culture and religion that the dispersed colonization of the northern zones had not consolidated. It was a confrontation between two world visions and two plans for the country. The first one, which Calles represented, included the educated middle classes and the direct beneficiaries of the revolutionary political establishment; the second one included the faithful peasant masses that followed their saints and their multisecular customs, the regions and the towns where they lived, the local priests, the small landholdings, and the subsistence agriculture.

In the midst of that conflict, directing it, was the Catholic church, a church that had entered the terrain of social action, that during the Pax Porfiriana had improved its structure to recover the positions lost during the liberal wars of the Reform, and that was counting on a vast network of representatives—a priest in every town—plus the enormous ideological weight of preaching to a devoutly Catholic country. Calles, Amaro, and Morones fought against this church; they wanted to see it subject to a world that they were capable of directing, and that guaranteed their historical continuity; they wanted a Mexican church, an entity that could be controlled by a lay national state. They wanted to subordinate that other alternative power, convert it into an appendix or even a significant part of the political pyramid they considered indispensable. They ended up confronting the church directly, and especially the Catholic peasants, whose actions transgressed in more than one instance the limits of both bureaucratic bodies. The revolutionaries seemed to have more points in common with that church—that institution that recognized the sources of its authority not in the revolutionary political world or in the 1917 constitution, but rather in the Vatican—

than with the Cristero peasants. Calles could talk, negotiate, understand the motivations and interests of the church and its representatives, even though he exhibited an almost physical repugnance toward them. On the other hand, he could not understand the Catholic peasants of the West, nor was he capable of estimating even approximately the true dimension of their struggle. But, to him, religion was a thing for women, and Jalisco was the "henhouse" of the republic; he imagined that he could simply order the suspension of religious practice, and that the people would gradually forget about religion and become nonreligious. In response, he had a war on his hands whose magnitude he refused to accept or believe, despite the fact that its presence was felt every day, for three years, in the number of casualties and in the inability of the 100,000-man federal army to contain it.

The anticlericalism that the Carrancista chiefs had displayed since the first days of the 1913–1914 insurrection was an exalted aftermath of the liberal tradition of the era of reform, an instance of ideological struggle for the hegemony of civilian power over the ecclesiastical colonial society. As an ideological principle of the struggle for the creation of the state, it had one purpose: to sweep antagonists from the road and eliminate any religious uprising. As a political praxis to eliminate Catholicism among the Mexican peasants, it had another purpose: the repression of a broad cross section of the Catholic people that had not fallen into the value system of an educated society, a society of citizens concerned with earthly matters and ruled by the ultimate administrator of those earthly problems: the political state.

The government was not capable of suppressing the Cristero Rebellion by force, but the Cristeros also weren't capable of breaking the government's hegemony. Thus, a sort of bloody stalemate was reached, which they were able to overcome only after protracted negotiations with the church—in which the U.S. embassy intervened— which led to the agreement of June 21, 1929. The church and the government committed themselves to respecting their respective realms of this and the other world, the temporal and spiritual spheres: the church wouldn't incite its followers to take power, nor would the state attempt to interfere with the internal order of the ecclesiastic institution.

The Shadow of Washington, Part 2

The De la Huerta–Lamont agreement of 1922, the Treaty of Bucareli of 1923, and an additional agreement between Obregón and the representatives of the oil companies in October 1924—by virtue of which a provisional understanding was reached on taxes and other issues—led to the creation for the first time in many years of a climate of relative cordiality between Mexico and United States. Calles assumed the presidency without having to worry excessively about international problems; Obregón had solved them for him. To complete this political rapprochement, the only additional requirement was to give form to the body of claims with the United States and perhaps also with the European nations that had already granted recognition to Mexico's government. The fact that diplomatic relations with England were still suspended did not greatly trouble the government, because Great Britain could not harm Mexico too much.

The first problem in what appeared to be the beginning of a new relationship with the United States presented itself before Obregón left power, because Mexico was unable to resume payments on its external debt. The fight against the De la Huertistas had absorbed the funds that had been earmarked for that purpose. It was thought that the problem was temporary and that Calles would be able to resume the payments. But, for the time being, the 1922 agreement on the external debt was suspended, although Mexico did not deny its determination to make good on it as soon as possible.

The situation began to deteriorate seriously in 1925, when the White House received notice that Mexico's government was preparing the first oil laws according to the 1917 constitution. The law draft was not well received, and there was frank disapproval when Mexico's Congress approved it in December 1925. Washington and the oil companies rejected in the law the so-called positive act because it did not correspond to what had been agreed to in Bucareli. The doctrine of positive act maintained that the landholdings of the foreign oil companies could remain unaffected by the prevailing legislation only if the companies had invested in those lands a positive act of oil exploration or exploitation before the laws were passed. The 1925 legislation appeared to the companies to be restrictive and unacceptable; it protected less land from the application of the clause that returned to the nation's control the underground resources of the nation, and it imposed a limit of fifty years on the rights that had been acquired in perpetuity by the oil companies during the Porfirian regime. At the same time, another Callista law reiterated the constitutional prohibition to foreigners of holding properties along a 31-mile stretch of coastline and 62 miles from the border: many foreign mines, ranches, and oil fields found themselves within the "prohibited zone."

At the end of 1925, U.S. Ambassador James R. Sheffield, convinced that Calles was a radical, argued that the United States should not allow the new legislation to be enforced, due to its retroactive and confiscatory nature. Calles responded with vigor and intelligence to an avalanche of U.S. diplomatic notes against the new legislation, but he abstained from taking any drastic action against the oil companies that refused to be subject to the new legislation. This disobedience put Mexican sovereignty in a quandary, but an armed conflict with the United States would have been even worse.

The oil problem was compounded by other issues, among them the Cristero conflict and the Mexican position on the struggle in Nicaragua. When the conflict between the church and state erupted, Mexican Catholics sought help from the United States, whose church unleashed a vast propaganda campaign against the Mexican government in general, and against Calles in particular, demanding from Washington a firm attitude with respect to Mexico.

In the case of Nicaragua, where a civil war was taking place, the United States supported the conservative group of Adolfo Díaz, while Calles declared himself in favor of the liberal leader, Juan B. Sacasa. The Mexican support for Sacasa not only was moral, but also included the transfer of certain war matériel. The open intervention on Mexico's part in what the United States considered its exclusive area of influence enraged Secretary of State Frank Kellogg, who presented before the U.S. Senate a memorandum entitled, "Bolshevik Objectives and Policies in Mexico and Latin America." Kellogg wanted to portray Calles as a Soviet instrument, and that image was reinforced when, at the end of 1924, Mexico established diplomatic relations with the Kremlin.

In order not to fan the flames of discord, Calles tried to neutralize the pressures from the U.S. government and oil companies by insisting on keeping good relations with the bankers. The 1922 agreement had not been kept, but in October of 1925 a new agreement was negotiated, and in 1926 the Mexican government sent to New York a first payment of $10.6 million as part of a liquidation of the direct debt, and $3.8 million to pay the railroad debt. The following year, a new payment of $11 million was sent. It was a financial sacrifice that was directed at trying to prevent the bankers from joining forces with the oil companies, and with the Catholic church, in demanding a U.S. intervention against Mexico.

If an open conflict did not ultimately take place, it was to a large degree because both the bankers and a group of U.S. congressmen refused to support the aggressive policy of Ambassador Sheffield, considering that armed actions in Latin America should be a thing of the past and that the possibilities of negotiation with Mexico had not been exhausted, because Calles was offering to take his differences with Washington before an international arbitrage tribunal. President Coolidge and his secretary of state showed themselves very sensitive to the existence of antiintervention forces.

The British, who for some time had been reticent about reaching an agreement with Mexico, negotiated their differences with Calles and reestablished diplomatic relations. They transformed themselves into the very voice of moderation: instead of threatening, they said, Washington should try to reach a mutually beneficial agreement and help the Mexican government to consolidate the peace and internal order.

Enemy Brothers, 1927

The internal order seemed to be just on the verge of breaking down in mid-1927, on this occasion due not to the Cristero rebellion or the U.S. belligerence, but rather to fratricidal conspiracy. In 1927, the initial stages of seeking Calles's successor were creating a division in the Sonorense crowd. This time the rebels were Secretary of War Francisco R. Serrano and Gen. Arnulfo R. Gómez, lieutenants and true younger-brothers-in-arms of Obregón and Calles.

A fundamental consequence of the De la Huerta rebellion was that it dragged behind it almost everything that was left of the first generation of Constitutionalist military chiefs, the last warlords with national prestige and autonomous command of troops: Salvador Alvarado and Manuel Diéguez, Rafael Buelna, Enrique Estrada, and Fortunato Maycotte. The years and the bullets had taken away the rest. In 1919, Zapata had been murdered in Chinameca, and on a morning in 1920 Lucio Blanco was executed. In Tlaxcalantongo, First Chief Venustiano Carranza had fallen, cancer had carried away Benjamín Hill in 1921, and an ambush had eliminated Villa two years later. At the beginning of 1924, with the Obregonista victory and the exile of De la Huerta—who survived as a singing teacher in San Francisco—there was no major military leader left on the horizon, except the *caudillo* of Huatabampo and his successor, Plutarco Elías Calles, both giants at the center of a leadership vacuum that was as infamous as the list of those whom the whirlwind had dispersed.

It seems logical that, within that vacuum, and confronted with the succession of Calles, presidential aspirations would arise in such people as Luis Morones, by then the powerful leader of the CROM, secretary of labor, and exalted orator of the Callista worker movement. In the very ambitions of the Cromista leader, Alvaro Obregón must have read the historical necessity of his own candidacy, the happy marriage of the needs of a country without leaders and the ambition of a *caudillo* without rivals. The main body of the revolutionary establishment also saw in Obregón its winning card and the providential man, whose eminence was magnified in contrast to the lack of leaders, and whose authority was deepened by the consolidation of his prestige.

But Obregón's new road to the presidency also created an anti-reelection fervor that was concentrated in the presidential candidacy of Arnulfo R. Gómez (Anti-Reelection party) and Francisco Serrano, who started their campaign in July 1927. The electoral hopes quickly evolved into military certainties. Obregón and Calles—asserted Serrano and Gómez to their opposition followers—would not allow fair elections. It thus became necessary—they told their comrades—to strike first and expel them from power with the same violent means that they used to keep themselves in power.

The conspiracy settled on a date: October 2, 1927, during some military maneuvers in the Balbuena military field, which President Calles, the candidate Alvaro Obregón, and the new secretary of war, Joaquín Amaro, would all attend. The troops of a Sonorense general, Eugenio Martínez, would apprehend them and call the army and the country to inaugurate a new period under a provisional government. But Obregón and Calles did not attend the military maneuvers that day; Eugenio Martínez, an old comrade in arms of Obregón, was relieved from his command of the Balbuena maneuvers and sent to Europe that same afternoon; and the conspiring military units were easily neutralized, and their leaders were shot. On October 3, Francisco Serrano was arrested with his entourage in Cuernavaca. On the road back to Mexico City, he was taken from the car on the highway and executed, together with his companions, near Huiztilac. The following day, the press morbidly displayed the photographs of the bullet-riddled bodies. A few weeks later, Arnulfo R. Gómez was captured in the sierra of Veracruz and executed on December 5 of the same year. The spectacle was cathartic; Calles and Obregón, in executing Serrano and Gómez, eliminated not only two countrymen, comrades-in-arms since the beginning, but also their most faithful and constant lieutenants, united by years of common risks, shared war, fidelity at all costs, and even family ties. Nobody was exempt from the influence of that example of terror. Under the impact of the execution of Serrano, Manuel Gómez Morín, who would later found the National Action party (PAN) and was one of the technical experts in the creation of such institutions as the Bank of Mexico and the Bank of Rural Credit in the 1920s, challenged his generation to "combat the pain."

Obregón's goal was to announce his candidacy for president for the second time. He had been able to get Calles to ask Congress for a constitutional amendment to allow reelection after a term, which in a sense was equivalent to revoking one of the central principles of the Revolution: no reelection. In reality, although he was formally retired from political activity when his term ended, Obregón had remained as the true center of power. When the elections were finally held in 1928, he won without any problem, as everyone had foreseen—with the exception of a fanatic Catholic, José de León Toral, who on July 17, 1928, murdered the president-elect, naively thinking that he was thus advancing the cause of the Cristeros.

From La Bombilla to Institutions

What Toral actually accomplished was to allow the system he hated so much to take a historical step forward toward a long-term institutionalization. The surprising disappearance of the Sonorense *caudillo* underscored the chronic imbalance of the system. To begin with, only Calles's political ability prevented the frustrated Obregonistas from immediately taking up arms to regain the power they already considered rightfully theirs. They accused President Calles of having instigated the murder. The accused placed the investigation of the murder in the hands of the accusers. He reached an agreement with the main generals in command of the troops, and he was able to get Congress to name Emilio Portes Gil—someone acceptable to both Calles and the Obregonistas—as provisional president, in charge of calling for new elections to elect a constitutional president to conclude the six-year term that Obregón had not been able to complete. In this fashion, it was possible for Calles to hand over power formally to Portes Gil on November 30, 1928. Portes Gil was a civilian who until then had been a dominant figure only in local Tamaulipas politics.

To fill the vacuum left by the death of the *caudillo*, Calles proposed in his last presidential address "to pass once and for all from the historical condition of being a country of one man to being a nation of institutions and laws." In place of the "indispensable man," a modern institution should be created: a great party to unite "the revolutionaries of the country" and provide continuity to the group and its accomplishments. On December 1, 1928, Calles and a handful of his associates presented to the country a manifesto proposing the creation of the National Revolutionary party (PNR), an organization that should become from then on the disciplined place in which the "revolutionary family" would settle its differences and select its candidates.

In March 1929, the first national convention of the new party was held in Querétaro. According to its program, it would devote its greatest efforts to the establishment of democracy, the "improvement of the social environment," and the "national reconstruction." When the moment arrived to name the first presidential candidate of the brand new PNR, the revolutionary family there assembled selected the engineer Pascual Ortiz Rubio—ex-governor of Michoacán, lacking any personal power—and not the prominent Obregonista Aarón Sáenz, a young industrialist who was the prototype of the budding concessionary bourgeoisie that would typify with its businesses and enterprises linked to the state the years of barbarous Mexican capitalism.

The decision in favor of Ortiz Rubio irritated an important segment of the army, which had supported the candidacy of Obregón, in hopes of gaining promotions and influence. The measures to professionalize the army itself, imposed by Calles's government through Secretary of War Joaquín Amaro, had affected the local autonomy and the dreams of independence of the military leaders who still belonged to the civil war generation.

Before the Querétaro Convention was over, on March 3, 1924, a group of Obregonista generals and civilians started a rebellion in the North under the so-called Plan de Hermosillo, accusing Plutarco Elías Calles, "the Judas of the Mexican Revolution," of using the PNR to keep himself in power through the nomination of Ortiz Rubio.

In support of the Plan de Hermosillo were thirty thousand men and a third of the active officer corps of the army, headed by Jesús M. Aguirre, chief of military operations in Veracruz; Gonzalo Escobar, of Coahuila; Fausto Topete, governor of Sonora; Marcelo Caraveo, of Chihuahua; Francisco R. Manzo, chief of operations in Sonora; Roberto Cruz, of Sinaloa; Francisco Urbalejo, chief of Durango; and the entire navy. The government retained the loyalty of the air force, which played a decisive role, and five thousand men of the armed battalions of workers and *agraristas*, which Saturnino Cedillo once again placed at the command of the government, as he had done in the De la Huerta rebellion. The uprising took root in ten states: Sonora, Sinaloa, Durango, Coahuila, Nayarit, Zacatecas, Jalisco, Veracruz, Oaxaca, and Chihuahua, but it lacked durability and true popular following.

At the end of March in Jiménez, Chihuahua, some 105 miles to the northwest of Torreón, the federal army under the command of Juan Andrew Almazán started the successful retaking of Chihuahua and flushing out of the rebels from the sierra, which included the use of the first massive aerial bombardments in the history of Mexico, with U.S. bombs and advising. During March, General Lázaro Cárdenas advanced with his army on the West by Jalisco and Nayarit to Sinaloa, recovering those territories for the government with relative ease. At the end of April, the rebel leaders of Sonora had abandoned the state and were issuing their proclamations from U.S. border towns, asserting that they had been betrayed. Surrenders and desertions followed in quick succession. Soon, the government could announce the cost balance of the last military rebellion of modern Mexico: 14 million pesos spent on the campaign, 25 million lost in destroyed railroad tracks and looted banks, two thousand dead. What had been gained: a headless army once again, the consolidation of the political pact that stressed the negotiations within the revolutionary family, not the conspiracies or coup mentality of the military chiefs. Recognizing with irony the terminal character of the Escobar revolt, Luis Cabrera wrote:

> This rebellion, which is known as the *train and bank rebellion,* was easier to put down than that of 1923, because it was limited to having the rebels take money from the banks and withdraw to the United States, through the Central and the South Pacific railroads, respectively, destroying the railroad communications.

In that almost-comic adventure, one of the historical bases of the contemporary social pact of Mexico adopted a naturalization card: the rebellion was used by the government to introduce new policies toward the army that were the beginning of its institutionalization and subjection to civil authority. In the end, when the dust settled, there were fewer veteran generals and more discipline within the army.

The Shadow of Morrow

By mid-1927, the International Committee of Bankers, with its headquarters in New York, realized the moment had arrived to intervene more actively in order to persuade the U.S. president that active negotiation, and not confrontation, was the appropriate response to the Mexican problem. At the end of 1927, Coolidge had already accepted the banker's proposition and had named a new ambassador to Mexico, Dwight Morrow, a lawyer and member of the banking firm J. P. Morgan and Company. His task as a new ambassador, he was told, was to achieve a modus vivendi with Calles, especially with relation to the oil problem. And this was precisely the policy that Morrow wanted to set in motion, because only in this way could Mexico continue to pay its huge external debt, in which J. P. Morgan had a direct interest. For Morrow, there were two immediate tasks: to make it clear to the Mexican government that negotiations should substitute for the defense of unyielding positions, and convince the oil companies and the Cristeros of the same thing.

Morrow presented himself as a new type of ambassador, disposed to understand and even accept some of the Mexican positions. He immediately established contact with the main figures in Mexican politics and tried to win their personal trust. This change of tactic was received first with surprise and then with relief and delight. At an informal breakfast with Calles, after having supported his policy of public works, Morrow proposed solving the crisis by modifying the controversial oil legislation. The response of the president was immediate: in November 1927, the Supreme Court declared the oil law of 1925 unconstitutional—because it was retroactive. It was the first step toward the solution of the problem, at least from the U.S. point of view. The second step was to draft a new law that would be acceptable in the oilmen's eyes. The U.S. ambassador followed this process closely, and even made concrete suggestions with regard to its contents. At the same time, he tried to convince the large oil companies that if a specific time limit was not set on their acquired rights and the "positive act" was not interpreted broadly, they should in exchange make a symbolic concession: to agree that the original land titles be transformed into "concessions." The companies objected, but Morrow insisted on this point. With Washington's endorsement, but against the wishes of the oil companies, Ambassador Morrow approved the new legislation that was passed by Congress in 1928. Grudgingly, the oil companies started to prepare themselves to exchange their old titles for the new ones. With this symbolic victory for Mexico—because, in essence, the created interests of the oil companies were upheld—one of the most critical chapters of relations with the United States seemed to close.

With the oil problem solved, an urgent solution to the Cristero conflict was needed, because as long as it continued, the government would not have sufficient resources to continue its payments to the foreign creditors. Internal calm was also necessary for the economy to function adequately and be revitalized.

Ambassador Morrow turned out to be an excellent intermediary between the Vatican, the Mexican Catholic hierarchy, and the Calles government. Unfortunately, when an agreement was almost at hand in 1928, Obregón's murder took place and the negotiations were suspended. Morrow did not despair, but rather he kept insisting until Portes Gil and the church accepted a renewal of the negotiations. In the end, it was the ambassador once again who approved the terms of the agreement that had been reached in June 1929 between President Portes Gil and Archbishop Leopoldo Ruiz y Flores. The end of the Cristero War was seen as a personal triumph for the U.S. ambassador, and as the way to preserve what had already been accomplished by Washington.

Morrow's help to the established order was equally important when the Escobarista rebellion broke out in March 1929. The government of Portes Gil needed two things urgently from the United States: on the one hand, arms and munitions; on the other, strict vigilance of the border to prevent the rebels from receiving supplies. The ambassador tried to satisfy both needs. The U.S. Department of War sold arms and munitions directly to Mexico, and at the same time it authorized several producers to provide the Mexican government with whatever the U.S. army was not able to provide. The Department of Justice also kept close surveillance on the Escobar agents, together with the army intelligence service, and on several occasions confiscated clandestine arms shipments.

The Anzures Shop

Provisional President Portes Gil handed over to his successor a reasonably peaceful country, although it was affected by the great World Depression, which affected Mexican exports very negatively and reduced the income for the federal government. In the elections of November 17, 1929, Ortiz Rubio had only one significant foe, Obregón's former secretary of public education, José Vasconcelos, nominated by the National Anti-Reelection party. Vasconcelos's fame as an intellectual had by then surpassed national boundaries.

Vasconcelos and his group, made up basically of urban and middle-class elements, enthusiastic but inexperienced, were directly affected by the first overwhelming political victory of the unified revolutionary family. Once Ortiz Rubio was declared the winner, they accused the government of fraud and refused to recognize their defeat; in December 1930, before leaving for voluntary exile, Vasconcelos made an emotional appeal to arms, but his words had no effect: the army was solidly behind the federal government.

Ortiz Rubio's victory had demonstrated the authoritarian nature of the new party, but it did not provide the winner with the powers corresponding to his high office. He had been named candidate and declared the winner, not by his own power, but rather by the support from the true power behind the throne, Calles, who had built a platform from the mixed interests and revolutionary factions. The first PNR president would soon find himself incapable of ruling. Following his inauguration on February 5, 1930, he survived an assassination attempt but was injured, and he was forced to go into seclusion during the first weeks of his government. Once he resumed the normal functions of his position, he realized that his degree of control over his cabinet was minimal, and he soon lost all control over the Congress, the PNR, and the state governors. An important instrument in reducing his power was ex-president Emilio Portes Gil, who still remained in the Ortiz Rubio cabinet due to the influence of Calles. Apparently separated from formal power, Calles was becoming the great political referee, the Jefe Máximo de la Revolución (main leader of the Revolution). The crises within the cabinet, the party, the Congress, and the local governments followed one another in quick succession, and most of the time were due to Calles and his supporters' desire to undermine the position of the president for Calles's benefit. Tbey were able to do it completely.

Despite his poor health, Calles directed the political life of the country from his house in the Anzures neighborhood or from one of the ranches to which he frequently traveled to improve his health. Whenever a critical situation demanded (the Escobar rebellion, the reorganization of the railroads, or the crisis in finances), he assumed the key public position for a few months, after which he left, leaving behind a trusted person in charge. The situation, which was difficult in itself, became unsustainable for Ortiz Rubio when Calles decided to "recommend" to his followers that they not accept any of the vacant administrative positions in the federal government, even when they were offered by the president himself. On September 2, 1932, after having notified Calles, Ortiz Rubio presented his resignation as president to the Congress, a resignation that was promptly accepted without any discussion. Calles's power reached its climax at that time, and the so-called Maximato its highest point.

By Calles's instruction, the Congress decided to name Gen. Abelardo Rodríguez as substitute president to finish Ortiz Rubio's term. The new president, an officer whom Calles could trust, was also Sonorense; in 1931, he had been named undersecretary of war and the navy, when Calles himself had resigned the position after solving one of numerous cabinet crises; Rodríguez then went on to become secretary of industry, trade, and labor and, later, secretary of war and the navy, without ever stopping to prosper as a businessman.

In contrast with Ortiz Rubio, Rodríguez didn't have to confront severe crisis due to differences with Calles. There was from the beginning a tacit agreement between the two: the president was in charge of supervising the correct operation of the public administration, while the Jefe Máximo reserved for himself the main political decisions. The friction was thus minimized and was more in style than in essence.

Among the problems that the substitute president had to deal with were two main ones: the resurgence of the tensions between the government and the church, and the designation of the PNR candidate for the period 1934–1940.

The new conflict with the church and with the Catholics in general had its origin in Calles's decision to impose so-called socialist education, whose explicit goal was nothing less than changing the traditional mentality of the majority of Mexicans in order to give the coup de grâce to the secular prestige of the church. The designation of the PNR candidate became problematic because the "revolutionary family" itself suggested two strong contenders: Gen. Manuel Pérez Treviño, president of the PNR and a man with very close ties to Calles, and Gen. Lázaro Cárdenas, more of a military man, ex-governor of Michoacán, and secretary of war and the navy. Besides counting considerable support within the army, Cárdenas had become a leader of a revitalized *agrarista* movement and was also favored by some leaders of the fragmented workers' movement. After weighing for some months the strengths of the two contenders, and considering that in any case his predominance wouldn't be affected, Calles decided in favor of Cárdenas in June 1933. Immediately after, in a second display of partisanship (Aarón Sáenz was the first one, in 1929), Pérez Treviño withdrew from the struggle and returned to the PNR to direct Cárdenas's political campaign.

The PNR ratified Calles's decision and drafted and approved a six-year plan that would guide the program of the new government. The plan—originally inspired by Calles—had a markedly nationalist, *agrarista*, and laborist character. In his long and vigorous presidential campaign all over the republic, Cárdenas presented himself to the electorate as a representative of the radical wing of the Revolution, in clear contrast to the relative conservatism of Calles. Few believed at the time that Cárdenas would be able to put the program into practice, at least as long as the Jefe Máximo continued acting from his Anzures shop.

The Material Reconstruction

When the Revolution broke out in 1910, Mexico was going through an economic boom without equal since the beginning of the nineteenth century. Mining, the railroads, and export agriculture were the basis of such a prosperity, solid for some, precarious and superficial for others.

The Revolution did away with the atmosphere of calm that was required for that type of economy, and during the period of Civil War, several Mexican and foreign observers believed that the country had plunged irreversibly into moral and material ruin. More than one despaired of ever seeing a prosperous Mexico within a reasonable time-frame. The destructive power of the Revolution was highly visible, but it was less extensive than many of its detractors supposed. As has been said, the large oil, mining, and manufacturing companies were hardly affected, and not all of the *haciendas* were sacked and burned. As soon as the Sonorense clique achieved power, it began creating the basis for a recovery that would be slow and painful.

The new rulers were practical and modern people, small landowners and businessmen from the North who were anxious to set the economic machine in motion and to benefit themselves and the country. They wanted to eliminate some of the obstacles to growth that had arisen during the Porfiriato in order to lead Mexico to a path of extensive capitalist and nationalist development. They wanted to eliminate the *latifundios*, but only those that were not productive, and they accepted the idea of developing the *ejido*, but only as a marginal and transitory form of property. In their opinion, the best agricultural producer was the medium producer: the rancher, from whose ranks so many of the revolutionary leaders had emerged. They hoped to eradicate the monopoly of foreign capital on the exploitation of the natural oil and mining resources, but they invited foreigners to invest in the areas that interested the new group in power. They wanted, in essence, to modernize Mexico, and, in order to do so, they could only follow, with certain modifications, the successful model that they had seen up close, that of the United States.

As we have described before, by 1920 there were only a few bright spots in the economic panorama, especially in contrast to the many dark spots: the precarious personal safety outside the cities; damage to the communication and transportation systems, in particular, the railroads; the unrestrained issuance of paper money, and the confiscation of part of the gold and silver reserves, which had unhinged the monetary system and carried it to the verge of ruin and resulted in the closing of several banks. The insecurity and difficulty in obtaining financing had made agricultural production decline, many of the small mines were closed, and external credit had simply vanished.

In some nonoil areas, there was stability and even some modest advances, such as in the generation of electricity and construction, but within the global context these weren't very important. The typical Mexican still lived in a rural community and earned his subsistence in agricultural activities, where the Revolution had caused severe damage and its reconstructive work had yet not begun.

During Obregón's administration, the income produced grew at a relatively slow rate, slightly above 10 percent in four years. Neither the state nor private enterprise had adopted initiatives that had immediate positive effects on economic activity. The great Obregonista efforts were concentrated on trying to establish an agreement with foreign powers, basically with the oil companies and the bankers, through renewed payments on the external debt, which had been suspended since 1914. He wanted to stimulate the investment of capital from abroad. The agreement seemingly was fruitful when the De la Huerta rebellion started in 1923, and turned the tables. The government wasn't able to meet the terms of its own agreement on the payment of the debt, and external capital was not forthcoming. When Obregón left office in December 1924, the situation seemed, nonetheless, more stable than in 1921. Calles had a plan of greater impact, even though in general it was similar to Obregón's plan. It set as a goal putting the monetary system in order, balancing the budget of the federal government, and restructuring bank credit. First, Alberto J. Pani and then Luis Montes de Oca were the secretaries of finance, in charge of putting the Callista plan into practice.

The reorganization of the budget began to produce the desired effects immediately. In 1925, at the end of the first year of Callista government, the federal budget yielded a surplus of 21 million pesos, thanks to the elimination of some subsidies, reduction of the public sector purchases, and diversification of the sources of income. An important part of that strategy was returning to private hands several of the railroad lines that the government had confiscated for military reasons during the civil war. There was the hope—which would prove to be vain—that the railroads would become profitable once more if the private companies reorganized them under strict economic criteria, which required, among other things, cutting back on personnel.

Banks, Roads, and Dams

With respect to the monetary and credit policy, the Callista government took a less spectacular step, but one that would have a longer-lasting effect: it established the first central bank of the country, the Banco de México, a project that Obregón wasn't able to carry out. Until its creation in 1925, the Mexican banking system was completely dominated by private institutions, many of them foreign, and there were few possibilities of controlling their activity to conform to the economic plans of the government.

The Banco de México was established with a capital stock of 50 million gold pesos, a respectable quantity for the period, and it had to struggle against the enormous distrust that had been engendered in the population against paper money and against the lack of cooperation of the private banking system. The Banco de México acted first as a central bank, and at the same time as an additional private bank. In a short period of time, it lost this last quality—and the losses associated with loaning money to influential politicians—and its powers were increased to guarantee the control of the rest of the banking system.

Fully involved in this reform, the government also created the National Banking Commission to reinforce its control of the banking system, and it developed new state banks to supplement the areas that were not being served by the private banks. In this fashion, the Bank of Agricultural Credit was established in 1926, to create and control rural credit associations. Its success was limited. To begin with, the bank never could raise the initial capital stock of 50 million pesos that was mentioned in the original project. Furthermore, some of its loans were political (among them, a loan to Obregón) and were never reimbursed. Finally, the number of rural credit associations that benefited was relatively small, given the needs of the Mexican countryside. By 1930, the bank registered losses, but it had established a precedent. In that same year, the Cooperative Agricultural Bank was created, with capital of only one hundred thousand pesos, and from the beginning it was placed under the influence of the CROM, as a consequence of which its effectiveness was practically null. Thus, the new banking system had its successes, but also its failures, as a product of corruption, inefficiency, and the lack of resources.

Confronted with the demands of reconstruction, the absence of foreign capital, and the weakness of the local bourgeoisie, the state had to shoulder responsibilities that until then it had not known. The most staggering were the reconstruction of highways and the opening of new zones of irrigation.

The highway project had a long history from the Obregonista government, but it was Calles who gave it final form when he created the National Highway Commission in 1925. Two years later, an ambitious project of building 6,200 miles of highways in a period of seven years was under way. By then, the highways that connected Mexico City with Pachuca and with Puebla had been built, the initial stages of the Panamerican Highway and the Acapulco-Veracruz Highway, respectively: the two great highway axes that would unite the Gulf of Mexico with the Pacific and the northern border with the southern, both passing through the capital of the country.

The main road-building company belonged to a prominent general and politician, Juan Andrew Almazán, and the resources to finance the construction were obtained to a large extent through a special tax on gasoline. The project took more time than was planned, but when it was finished, it was one of Callismo's greatest accomplishments.

The development of irrigation works was similar to the highway project, as Obregón had ordered studies to be drawn to increase the limited irrigated area of the country, but the lack of funds prevented him from pursuing this project. Two years later, the Federal Law of Irrigation of 1926 created the National Irrigation Commission, which began its chores immediately by establishing consulting and building contracts with several North American countries. By 1927, President Calles was able to announce that seven dams had been built to irrigate almost 494,000 acres. Between 1926 and 1928, the government assigned 40 million pesos to irrigation works, but the government wasn't able to achieve a success similar to the highway network. One of the largest dams, of Guatimapé in Durango, was a failure, and other projects also suffered from severe planning errors. From then on, however, the government would not leave the task of irrigation in private hands, as had been the case under the Porfiriato; the 1920s inaugurated what would be a prolific tradition of construction of hydraulic and hydroelectric infrastructure by the Mexican state.

The Impossible Debt

To these innovations, some unresolved issues were added, the major one being the chronic problem of the external debt. In 1922, the Obregonista minister of finance, Adolfo de la Huerta, had reached an agreement with the creditor banks, by virtue of which Mexico recognized a debt in the enormous amount of $700 million. The agreement, known as the Lamont–De la Huerta Treaty, represented an excessive weight on the national budget, it got mixed up initially with the De la Huerta rebellion, and it couldn't be fulfilled. In 1925, the new secretary of finance, Alberto Pani, renegotiated the agreement and obtained a reduction of $220 million in the Mexican obligations, by separating the railroad debt from the total amount. He agreed, in exchange, that Mexico would pay $21 million directly to a fund for the payment of the interest and would start to pay the principal of the debt in 1928.

That small breather that Pani negotiated presupposed, in any case, an enormous effort, and it did not include the granting of an immediate loan to Mexico as had been speculated in official circles. The secretary of finance received criticism for having agreed to pay the debt bonds at their nominal value, when in fact in the external market they had been devalued significantly. Regardless, everything seemed to indicate once again that the country, by agreeing to pay a significant debt of close to $480 million, was on the road to normalizing its economic relations with the great capital markets, which at the time were loaning left and right to practically all of the Latin American countries, with the exception of Mexico. The illusion promptly vanished. In 1928, the Mexican government could not afford to meet its scheduled payment, and history repeated itself.

From a general perspective, the greatest interest of Ambassador Morrow was being able to get Mexico to pay its external debt. Ironically, it was only at this point where he met failure. As mentioned before, after an amendment to the 1922 agreement, Mexico made two payments to the International Committee of Bankers, but it could not meet its third payment. By the end of 1927 it was obvious to Calles and his secretary of finance that Mexico did not have the funds to cover the next year's payment. To get out of the difficulty, they asked the bankers to send a commission to study the finances of the country and make realistic recommendations on how they could pay the debt. The recommendation of that commission was very simple: to reduce public expenditure enough to be able to pay $30 million that year and $70 million three years later. The bankers were not as realistic as they supposed; to stop the highway-building programs or the irrigation works would have endangered one of the bases of legitimacy of the new system. In 1928, the negotiations continued but Mexico didn't make any payment. In 1929, the situation repeated itself, the federal government had to spend large amounts to continue with the Cristero rebellion and to put down the Escobarista rebellion. In 1930, the situation didn't improve, because the effects of a lower income due to the reduction in foreign trade caused by the world crisis began to be felt. Despite everything, Mexico agreed that year to renegotiate the agreements of 1922 and 1925 and signed the Montes de Oca–Lamont agreement, in which it was able to cancel $211 million from the debt for unpaid interest since 1914. The amount to be paid was still impressive: $267.5 million plus $50.7 million of the railroad debt.

The world crisis aggravated the problem of the Mexican budget, and other countries were also forced to stop paying their debts. The government of Ortiz Rubio suspended negotiations with the International Committee of Bankers and, without denying its obligations, it simply forgot about the problem. As the problem had extended to other countries that faced bankruptcy, the U.S. government wasn't able to apply much pressure unilaterally against Mexico.

The Claimants

Another international problem that the Revolution had to face from its beginning was the constant claims by the great powers regarding the damages that the civil war had caused to foreign persons and property. This type of claim was added to direct claims against the actions of the government, such as expropriations, confiscations, forced loans, and so on. The sum of the claims reached astronomic proportions.

The governmental responsibility for those damages was difficult to avoid, and it was accepted, even though Mexico would always argue that, according to international law, the country was not forced to compensate anyone for damages caused to foreigners by rebel elements that were impossible to control. The revolutionaries were one of the risks that foreigners who wanted to invest in Mexico had to face from the beginning. The great powers never accepted this argument, despite its solid legal basis, and as a result of the agreements of Bucareli, two commissions were formed to examine the mutual claims between Mexico and the United States: a general one that would deal with all of the cases that had accumulated since the previous century, and another special one to deal with those claims that had arisen during the Revolution. Having established this precedent, the other affected powers—England, France, Spain, Germany, and Italy—received an invitation to form their respective special commissions.

Mexico had little interest in or resources to solve this troublesome matter, and the negotiations with the United States continued until 1925, the year in which the conventions were signed and the arbitrators (a Panamanian and a Brazilian) were elected to preside over both commissions. The special convention stopped its work promptly, because the United States refused to present its claims after the Brazilian arbitrator supported the Mexican position against the sixteen Americans murdered by Villa in Santa Isabel. From then on, the claims were dealt with bilaterally, outside the convention, and were solved little by little. With respect to the general convention, the United States had more than 2,800 claims against Mexico, and the Mexicans presented more than 800 against the United States, a sea of claims from which only a small fraction would be examined. In 1934, the General Convention of Claims was eliminated, because Washington agreed that the most practical solution was that Mexico pay a fraction of the total number of claims presented, avoiding an annoying examination of each one. This fraction was only 2.67 percent of the total, but the form and amount of payment would be settled only in 1941, with the payment of $10 million. In the end, it could be said that Mexico came out from under this problem relatively successfully. If the United States decided to accept only the 2.67 percent of claims, it was because Mexico had previously been able to get the European countries to accept a similar percentage.

The 1929 Crash

It was Calles who could finally start the process of economic reconstruction of the country, although it was an erratic process, with its ups and downs. The best years of the period were 1925 and 1926. Afterward, the silver market entered into crisis, directly affecting the main export that produced income for the federal government. The industrial metals didn't accompany silver in its downfall, and the total value of mining production didn't fall; the second export product, oil, continued the fall that had started in 1922, and the value of its production in 1928 was half of the 1925 production. Given the enclave character of these activities, mainly linked with the foreign market, the negative effects of their decline on the rest of the economy were relatively small, as far as simple numbers would seem to indicate. The productive dislocation of certain agricultural goods and regions, induced by the Cristero rebellion, had a greater impact on the daily life of the country than the downturn in the external trade balance or the fall in exports. In any case, the problems of 1927 and 1928 weren't serious if compared with the crisis that began to incubate at the end of 1929, and which had its climax with the great crash in the United States triggered by the collapse of the stock market in October 1929. That crash translated into the great World Depression of the 1930s, a brutal reduction in demand, and the paralysis of many economic activities. The phenomenon rapidly spread to all of Europe, and by 1930 Mexico saw helplessly how its export market had shrunk. The fall was aggravated by the fact that 1929 and 1930 were bad harvest years. The convergence of these factors complicated things. Relief then came, paradoxically, from weakness. Precisely because of its relative lag with respect to the great industrial nations, and because its modern and export sectors were more linked with the foreign markets than with the national economy, the economic disaster wasn't as generalized in Mexico as in Europe, the United States, or even other Latin American countries with economies that were more closely linked to the world market. Between 1929 and 1932 (the worst years of the crisis), the value of Mexican mining production fell by 50 percent, and oil production by almost 20 percent. But the gross domestic product (GDP) fell only by 10 percent, which certainly meant an economic recession, but not a catastrophe. The majority of the Mexican population wasn't directly tied to these modern activities but, rather, to the traditional agricultural activities, which didn't grow, but hardly experienced a fall.

A large part of the taxes that were imposed came from exports, and the federal government saw its income reduced; but at constant prices, the decline was only 9 percent between 1929 and 1931, and by 1932 it had increased again. The government couldn't do much to avoid the closing of mines and unemployment, but it did not stop its program of highway and dam construction, which continued at a slightly slower pace. It's true that the bureaucracy saw its wages reduced for a period, and that the external debt was farther than ever from being paid, but nothing more. The lack of resources and experience with the phenomenon prevented the federal and state governments from doing anything substantive to create employment for the fired workers and the thousands of Mexicans repatriated from the United States: the public works programs and the opening of new agricultural centers were minimal. Only the reactivation of the economy as a whole, starting in 1933, had a positive effect on unemployment.

It's impossible to know how many Mexicans were affected by the crisis, because there are no solid statistics on this. However, we can safely say that unemployment never reached the levels it did in the United States, where it affected 25 percent of the labor force. According to official data, in 1932 there were 339,000 unemployed persons in Mexico, or approximately 6 percent of the economically active population. The reason for this low unemployment rate was due in part to the fact that the traditional agrarian sector, which was not largely affected by the crisis, occupied the majority of the labor force, and it could absorb, at least temporarily, some of the workers laid off from the manufacturing industry. Whatever the case may be, by 1933 the worst of the crisis was over, and when General Cárdenas assumed the presidency in December 1934, the economic indicators were all pointing up, and Mexico was no longer in crisis.

The Great Depression left its stamp on the productive structures of the country, but not on government projects. In 1933, the PNR decided to prepare, at Calles's initiative, a government program for the 1934–1940 period. It had to define the major directions to follow in the different areas of official responsibility, and it yielded as a result a declaration of principles, strongly tinted by a spirit of populism, nationalism, and opposition to large international capital. The crisis of world capitalism, the plan said, was not over yet, and it could get worse or repeat itself. Foreseeing this, and to defend Mexican national interest, the state had to gain a greater degree of influence on the economy, not leave it in the hands of supply and demand, and to promote national control over the large export industries. It was precisely this government program that General Cárdenas adopted as his own when he was declared the official candidate of the government party. After the 1936 railroad strike, the government decided to nationalize the railroad lines and create an agency dependent on the federal government to assume control of its management. The agreement didn't last long; given the persistence of crisis in that sector, Cárdenas decided in 1938 to pass control of the railroads to a workers' administration, which continued operating until the end of his administration, although without much success. Avila Camacho placed the railroad network once again under the direct administration of the state.

The Parties of the Revolution

The 1917 constitution, as its predecessors, defined the political parties as the basic organizations to carry out the democratic struggle for power. In reality, until that moment, Mexico had been unable to channel through partisan means the feeble political participation of its citizens. For Mexicans, the electoral process had been an ephemeral experience, almost theoretical; no political group had achieved power through the vote. As of 1920, and despite the constitutional guarantees, the situation hadn't changed much. Power would still be acquired and maintained basically, although not exclusively, by force.

Besides seeking power, political parties are supposed to establish, articulate, and sum up the demands of the main groups or classes. In the Mexican reality, only the initial parties that were created with the Revolution were able to do this, albeit halfheartedly, given their limited links to the masses. In reality, the majority of those parties were created and revolved around certain revolutionary personalities: thus, they served more as a vehicle to promote the personal interests of their leaders than as representatives of more general and permanent interests. Almost all were "parties of notables," not mass political parties that circumstances would seem to indicate. The fragility of the life of the postrevolutionary parties was a consequence of this narrow and individualistic clientelism, which tied the fate of the organizations to the very risky and changing fate of their leaders. This occurred even in the case of the Labor party, the electoral vehicle of the Regional Confederation of Mexican Labor (CROM), supposedly representative of the largest organized workers' movement of Mexico. When the CROM and its leader, Luis N. Morones, fell from grace with the government at the end of 1928, the party lost importance and finally disappeared.

Until 1928, the only exception to the rule had been the Mexican Communist party (PCM), organized in 1919. Beginning in 1929, with the foundation of the official party, the National Revolutionary party (PNR), the situation changed dramatically: the parties, or at least the PNR and its descendants, gained wider recognition. Before 1929, and apart from the communists, the parties that left some mark on Mexican civic life were a few. The Catholic party, established after the fall of Díaz, supported Victoriano Huerta and vainly tried to present a presidential candidate in 1920. The Constitutionalist Liberal party (PLC) was formed in 1916, headed by Gen. Benjamín Hill, and in 1919 it named Alvaro Obregón as a presidential candidate. When Hill passed away, the leaders of the PLC began an open conflict with the president, who in 1922 dealt them a mortal blow when he favored another party that had also supported his candidacy for the legislative elections—the National Cooperativist party, established in 1917 with the support of some members of Carranza's cabinet. The Cooperativist star was in ascent until 1923, when its leaders had the misfortune of siding with De la Huerta against Calles. The defeat of the De la Huerta rebellion in 1924 did away with the party.

The National Agrarista party (PNA), established in 1920, had many leaders who had been old Zapatistas, among them Antonio Díaz Soto y Gama. In contrast with the Labor party, the PNA did not have the support of a national peasant organization, but rather the strong support of Obregón, which allowed it to have representation in the Congress and in the agrarian bureaucracy. The murder of the *caudillo* in 1928 left the PNA in a vulnerable position, and its deterioration accelerated after some of its main leaders joined forces in 1929 with the Escobar rebellion against Calles.

When the constitution was modified in 1927 to open the doors to the reelection of Obregón, Vito Alessio Robles and other politicians revived the National Anti-Reelection party to oppose the designs of the *caudillo.* They found the "man of the hour" in Gen. Arnulfo R. Gómez, but Gómez's failed rebellion and his execution ended that partisan adventure. When José Vasconcelos announced himself as an opposition candidate against Pascual Ortiz Rubio in 1929, the anti-reelectionists quickly offered him their support. The official figures gave the victory to Ortiz Rubio, the call of Vasconcelos to take up arms fell into a vacuum, and the Anti-Reelection party became part of history.

Although the parties of some importance were of a national character, there were some local parties that also left their stamp. Among them, the most prominent was the Socialist Party of the Southeast (PSS), led by Felipe Carrillo Puerto, and whose predecessor was the Socialist Party of Yucatán, founded by the Sonorense general Salvador Alvarado when he was the governor of the state. After Carrillo Puerto was murdered in 1924, the PSS lost some steam, but it was still able to participate in the creation of the PNR and to maintain some activity for a few more years. The Tamaulipas Border Socialist party, led by Emilio Portes Gil, also had its days of glory, but when Portes Gil and Calles grew apart at the beginning of the 1930s, the party lost control of Tamaulipas politics and was never able to recover.

The Party of the Government

The large number of parties of the Mexican Revolution were fundamentally modified by the creation of the National Revolutionary party (PNR)—the "party of the government"—in March 1929. With the passing of time, that official party would experience changes in name and nature, but it would conserve a fundamental characteristic throughout the decades: an almost absolute domination of the positions of popular election. The creation of the PNR put an end to the proliferation of parties. When Calles stated in his last presidential report that the Revolution should leave behind the era of personal power to enter fully into the era of institutions, he was preparing the way for the creation of a great official party that would unite all of the parties and groups of the "revolutionary family."

By November of that year, Calles had been able to reach an agreement with the multitude of existent parties to join forces in a single party. In January 1929, the first National Convention of the new party was called for Querétaro, and in March the PNR was formally constituted in the midst of a major crisis: the Escobar rebellion was exploding, the Cristero movement was still full-blown, and Vasconcelismo was challenging the legitimacy of the group in power. Calles did not formally appear as the leader of the new party, but from his position as a "simple citizen" he was able to get the majority of the delegates to the convention to stop supporting Aarón Sáenz—the favorite until then—and declare themselves unanimously in favor of the unforeseen candidate Pascual Ortiz Rubio. Another indelible characteristic of the new party was appearing for the first time: its programs and policies wouldn't be the product of a reasonably free debate among its members, but, rather, decisions prepared by the elite and transmitted and imposed by the National Executive Committee on the rank and file.

Acceptance of the necessary discipline of the revolutionary family was neither smooth nor immediate; some time would go by before the rough revolutionary politicians understood that any difference in or resistance to the official party line of the center was tantamount to suicide. But, finally, what the leaders wanted was established: the undisputed partisan discipline and the unconditional acceptance of the orders of the party chief, whatever they might be.

The 1929 program of the PNR did not differ at all from what the official Callista policy was at the time. In the first place—understandable given the Cristero conflict—it committed the party to fulfilling article 3 in educational matters, despite the opposition of the church. Second, it would promote industrialization. With reference to agrarian policy, it supported the creation of *ejidos*, the colonization of new lands, and the efforts of the new agrarian entrepreneurs. With respect to fiscal policy, it adopted a conservative attitude, by considering that it was prudent to balance the budget and reestablish external credit. The main objective was the modernization of the country through vigorous capitalist development, without losing sight of the fact that "the working and peasant classes are the most important factors of the Mexican collective."

The obvious problem of how to reconcile the contradictory interests of the different social classes was not addressed, nor was it solved, during the days of the foundation. The PNR simply declared itself open to all classes and groups identified with the Revolution and named as its first president Gen. Manuel Pérez Treviño, an individual who was clearly identified with Calles. Pérez Treviño directed the presidential campaign of Ortiz Rubio against the lone opposition of Vasconcelos, a strong alternative especially among the cohesive urban groups morally indignant at the corruption of the group in power. As has been said before, in this first encounter with the electoral opposition, it was clear that the PNR was not willing to leave in the hands of the voluble voters a decision so important as who should hold power in Mexico. The official electoral figures allotted the Vasconcelistas only 110,000 votes and granted an overwhelming 2 million votes to Ortiz Rubio. The PNR was born, then, not so much to dispute at the ballot box with its adversaries over the right of the revolutionary group to exert power, but rather to discipline the heterogeneous coalition that constituted the revolutionary group and to formally fulfill the rituals of representative democracy. The only thing lacking was the resources for such an ambitious project. At the beginning, they were obtained shamelessly through a decree signed by President Portes Gil himself, according to which state workers would have to contribute to the party a day's wages in the months that had thirty-one days. It was a crude and unpopular decree that was promptly overturned. But, from then on and for many decades to come, it was clear that the government itself would subsidize the official party directly and without any intermediaries.

When Ortiz Rubio assumed power, the command of the PNR passed to a leader close to the new president: Prof. Basilio Vadillo. Calles was soon able to remove him from that position and replace him with a notorious enemy of Ortiz Rubio, Emilio Portes Gil, whose task in the construction of the Maximato, it has been said, was to undermine the authority of Ortiz Rubio and then to cede the direction of the party to a less controversial figure, who tried to identify himself both with the president and with Calles: Gen. Lázaro Cárdenas. Cárdenas tried to maintain a delicate but difficult balance between the two powers. He did not get very far in his effort, as he soon clashed with recalcitrant Callistas who openly defied Ortiz Rubio from Congress. By then, the balance was definitely tipped in favor of Calles, and Cárdenas had to resign in favor of an unconditional ally of the Jefe Máximo, Manuel Pérez Treviño, a situation that would remain without change until the arrival of Cárdenas as president.

Introducing the basic elements of political discipline to the governing group was not an easy task. Wherever there was a local strongman—such as Saturnino Cedillo in San Luis Potosí—there were practically no problems: the local PNR was supported by the *cacique*'s strength, and vice versa. But in states with no clear dominant figure, there were fierce struggles between two or more local parties—all of them affiliated with the PNR and self-proclaimed loyalists to Calles—to try to control the governor's office, the legislature, the appointment of municipal presidents, and so on. In those cases, it was the task of the National Executive Committee (CEN) of the PNR, together with the secretary of the interior and the secretary of war, to decide who among the competing factions should obtain the position, and to enforce that decision. After Vasconcelismo, the PNR encountered certain actions of local and even national opposition parties, but their importance was secondary. To facilitate compliance with its directions, the official party modified its internal structure. From 1930, it was no longer a prerequisite to belong to a local party in order to be a member of the PNR, and three years later, in the Second Regular Convention of the party, the local parties were definitely cast aside—they quickly disappeared—and direct affiliation began. In this way, an additional step in the process of centralization and control of the political process was taken, against the hypothetical local autonomy. True political struggle would henceforth take place within the PNR, with Calles as the supreme arbiter.

The Administration of the Masses

The PNR was, without doubt, one of the greatest political innovations of the Revolution, but not the only one. It had been preceded by the organizations of workers from the countryside and the city, whose emergence the Porfiriato had attempted to prevent. The Revolution radically modified that situation; in the beginning, the struggle had taken place precisely to incorporate the working masses to full participation as citizens. The first logical step was to accept them as political actors in their own right. But the process was not so clear or simple.

When we examine the origins and nature of the Mexican Revolution, generally the 1910 insurrection is regarded as the only way out for the millions of peasants who had lost their lands, and in some regions were being forced to work for the great *haciendas* within a system of servitude that had feudal overtones.

Without the rural unrest caused by the great expansion of the *hacienda* during the second half of the nineteenth century, it is not possible to explain the downfall of Díaz, but it is necessary to recognize that the Revolution was not only and simply a peasant uprising. Otherwise, we couldn't explain the fact that, despite the political and military defeat of the landlords and the ratification of agrarian reform in the 1917 constitution, the large majority of the field workers remained without land in 1920 and the following years. The defeat of the old regime did not automatically represent the victory of peasant demands, because there were forces within the Revolution that were opposed to them. It was necessary for the representatives of the agrarian trends to fight a new and extended struggle within the revolutionary circles to ensure that their interests were taken into account. During the years of that struggle, the countryside did not remain unaltered, but, rather, the relations of production changed rapidly.

According to Frank Tannenbaum's estimations, half of the working force that lived within the *haciendas* in 1910 were no longer there in 1921, having moved on to the free wage labor market. This does not necessarily mean that their personal situation had improved. Throughout its history, Mexico had been basically a rural country, and the struggle for land was at the core of secular conflicts. From colonial times, indigenous uprisings due to land were endemic, and the situation persisted in the twentieth century. According to a chronology prepared by Jean Meyer, from the moment Díaz took power in 1876 until 1901, there was no year in which the government didn't have to put down some rural uprising. The Mexican countryside only became relatively peaceful after 1902 (with the exception of San Luis Potosí in 1905). The calm, however, lasted only a short time. The 1910 Revolution shook up the countryside once more, and calm disappeared for several decades. Just before the Revolution, 72 percent of the economically active population of Mexico worked in agricultural and cattle-raising activities, and even though a large number of persons had been able to keep all or part of their properties in the face of the onslaught of the *haciendas*, the concentration of property was greater than ever. According to the most dramatic estimates, 1 percent of the landowners held 97 percent of the disposable land. According to less extreme estimates, 54 percent of the land in 1910 was in the hands of eleven thousand *latifundios* (with an average of 19,760 acres per property); 20 percent was in the hands of small landowners; 10 percent corresponded to national lands; 10 percent was sterile land; and only 6 percent was in the hands of the communities and the towns.

During the most difficult years of the Revolution, many *haciendas*, ranches, and towns endured looting and confiscations, but once Carrancismo consolidated itself, properties were returned to their previous owners, security was increased, and the agrarian reform didn't accomplish much. Between 1915 and 1920, Carranza signed definite provisions of lands to *ejidos* for a total of 327,373 acres, compared with 217,360 million acres that were in hands of the *latifundistas* (large landowners).

Of the three great currents of the Revolution—Zapatismo, Villismo, and Carrancismo—the one most committed to the restructuring of the system of agrarian property was the Zapatista, but the faction that finally emerged triumphant was the most conservative one: the Carrancista. By 1920, agrarian reform was still in the making. Obregón and Calles didn't represent a trend favorable to the prompt destruction of the *latifundios*, although the political pressure of the *agraristas* forced them to give a relatively greater importance to the problem of land distribution.

The Agua Prieta group came to power with the support, among other sectors, of the remains of Zapatismo. Because of this and other political reasons, it was forced to demonstrate a greater concern for peasant demands. In the six months of his interim presidency, Adolfo de la Huerta handed over 207,480 acres, and in his four years of government Obregón increased the surface of the *ejidos* by almost 2.5 million acres. As expected, the state of Morelos, the heart of Zapatismo, was the region that benefited most. Starting in 1920, the political and military power was handed over to the old rebel chiefs and the *hacendados* suffered their first great defeat. By 1923, 115 of the 150 towns of the state had received *ejido* distributions. Calles continued that policy, and by 1927 there were only five *haciendas* left in the region, while 80 percent of the peasant families had provisional or definite control over their lands. According to the 1930 census, 59 percent of the cultivated land of Morelos belonged to the *ejidos*, although the area of private property still showed a high degree of concentration.

Morelos's Dream and Reality

The political value of the agrarian distribution became obvious with the 1923 crisis, when the De la Huerta rebellion had to be put down: the state of Morelos remained calm and faithful to the federal government. When Calles began his administration, he accelerated the process of *ejido* distributions, and during his administration almost 7.5 million acres were distributed. This explains the military support that the armed *agraristas* gave him during the Cristero rebellion. On numerous occasions, at the head of the government columns searching for insurgents were *agrarista* militia.

The experience of Morelos was to a certain degree similar to that of Yucatán, but it was not the case for the other states of the republic, where the *latifundio* still reigned supreme. In 1923, Obregón clearly stated that the application of the agrarian laws should be handled prudently, in order to "avoid disrupting our agricultural production"; the final objective was not to divide land, but rather to make it more productive. For Calles, the ideal situation was to "complete the agrarian distribution, indemnify the owners and form a class of modern small owners with the support of a policy of irrigation, credit [and] technical formation" (1925). The *ejido* parcel was regarded by the Mexican leaders as a transitory form of property, a useless reminder of the pre-Hispanic past.

From the perspective of the Sonorenses, the individual *ejido* parcel was preferable to communal property, because it would prepare its beneficiaries to understand the rules of the game of modern capitalist agriculture, the goal to be achieved. The *ejido* parcel, said Luis L. León in 1925, had to be simply the "family land plot" from which the "restless spirits, or those with greater ambition, would go out . . . to seek a better life." In sum, the *ejido* was far from being considered the basis of the new rural Mexican society.

In the last year of his administration, Calles distributed less land than in the previous years. From then on, as long as he retained personal influence, he threw his weight in favor of those who advocated closing the chapter on agrarian reform, a position that was not accepted by all of the ruling group. President Portes Gil considered it an erroneous policy, because he still felt it was necessary to expand the social base of support for the government by increasing the *agrarista* ranks to confront the Cristeros, Escobaristas, and other threats. Between the end of 1928 and the beginning of 1930, Portes Gil distributed 2,964,000 acres, double what Calles had distributed in 1928. According to the testimony of Portes Gil himself, when the government of Ortiz Rubio took office, the Jefe Máximo asked the new president and his cabinet to put a permanent stop to the process of land distribution. In the two years and eight months of the Ortiz Rubio administration, only 3.7 million acres were permanently distributed to the *ejidos*. The agrarian reform once again slowed its pace. Heartened by the lack of sympathy shown in high governmental circles toward the agrarian demands, the landlords in the National Chamber of Agriculture (CNA) proposed setting a time limit for the towns with rights to *ejido* lands to request them, and then proceeded to permanently close the era of expropriations. Only in this way, they said, would calm and credibility return to the countryside. By the time that proposal was made, according to the figures of the 1930 census, there still were 648 agricultural properties with more than 24,700 acres and 837 units held between 12,350 and 24,700 acres. The disappearance of the *latifundio* was far from complete.

The government did not give an official response to the petition of the CNA, but deadlines were beginning to be set by several states to put an end to agrarian reform. On May 7, 1930, Ortiz Rubio informed the National Agrarian Commission that, given the limited number of requests for *ejido* distribution that were still pending in Aguascalientes, a period of sixty days should be given to present new requests and immediately the land distribution in that state would be declared completed. A month hadn't gone by before a similar decision was adopted in the case of San Luis Potosí, and this was soon joined by Tlaxcala, Zacatecas, Coahuila, Morelos, and the Federal District. In 1931, land distribution was declared completed in Querétaro, Nuevo León, and Chihuahua. The organizations of landowners in Jalisco, Sonora, Sinaloa, and La Laguna requested similar actions for their states. By September 1931, the land distribution had "officially ended" in twelve federation entities.

Ortiz Rubio justified his policy by saying that it should not be considered an abandonment of the *agrarista* program, but rather as another proof that the Revolution had fulfilled its obligations, and there was no sense in prolonging uncertainty among private owners. To reinforce this policy, he declared at the end of 1930 that any extension of the *ejido* lands would have to be done after paying the affected properties. Given the lack of resources in the fiscal budget, it would be difficult in the future to accomplish an extension of the existing *ejidos.*

Furrows in the Gulf Region

The government's actions seemed to confirm the victory of the PNR's conservative wing, but the *agrarista* faction was not dead. The center of the struggle for land had been displaced from Morelos and the center of the country to the most populated state of the country at the time, Veracruz. In 1920, Col. Adalberto Tejeda occupied the state governor's office; he had distinguished himself sometime back by having organized several indigenous communities, until he converted them into a notable source of local power. From the governor's office, Tejeda extended his area of influence, and he promoted the resurgence of organizations of urban and rural workers. In front of this campaign of agitation, and supported by Tejeda, was a workers' leader, Ursulo Galván, who rapidly became the most important agrarian leader of the region.

As a result of the action of Tejeda and Galván, the land requests began to pile up in Veracruz, and at the beginning of 1923 the famous League of Agrarian Communities of the State of Veracruz (LCAEV) emerged, which would serve as the base of support for Tejeda and as the engine for agrarian reform in the state. During the crisis at the end of 1923, the Veracruz *agraristas* organized themselves into guerrillas and went into action against the De la Huertista general, and former military commander of the state, Guadalupe Sánchez. After the crisis was resolved, the political fidelity of the LCAEV to the federal government was rewarded when Tejeda was named secretary of the interior and the central government accepted the permanence of some armed *agrarista* corps, which would serve as the first line of defense of the *ejidatarios* against the landlords and their "white guards."

In 1926, Tejeda and Galván promoted the formation of an agrarian organization that would overflow the borders of Veracruz, the National Peasant League (LNC). In 1928, Tejeda returned to the position of state governor. Another crisis was taking place in the "revolutionary family." The Tejeda group remained loyal to Calles and repeated in that state the 1923 situation: the Veracruz guerrillas were on the side of the government in its fight against the Escobaristas in 1929. Thus, the Veracruz organization was consolidating itself precisely when the demise of the Ortiz Rubio government was only a matter of time: as the federal government's policies became more conservative, the Veracruz state government's policies became more radical.

Apart from the *agraristas*, Tejeda and his group adopted other measures that made them unpopular in the eyes of the center: they opposed a negotiated solution to the Cristero conflict, they rejected the agreements for the payment of the external debt, and they promulgated a law that allowed the expropriation in the public interest of any commercial, industrial, or agricultural firm in the state. The great national newspapers—all of them conservative—demanded Tejeda's head on a platter, which had the effect of stimulating him. While other states were putting an end to agrarian reform, Tejeda continued to expropriate, and, between 1928 and 1932, 493 provisional resolutions were adopted in Veracruz that affected 827,450 acres benefiting 46,000 peasants.

The response of the federal government to the Tejedistas was felt on several fronts. In 1930, it decided to undermine the power of the LCAEV by provoking a division resulting in one group's affiliating itself to the PNR, another to the Communist party, and a third—apparently the majority group—remained faithful to Tejeda. Ursulo Galván had just died, and the Tejedista organization adopted the name of National Peasant League "Ursulo Galván" (LNCUG). The efforts of the center at disintegrating them did not stop there, and it was soon evident that within the LNCUG a moderate tendency was starting to appear that did not follow the Tejedista line. By 1933, the conflict between the two tendencies erupted: the "red" LNCUG decided to support the independent presidential candidacy of Tejeda and the moderate faction joined the Cardenista faction within the PNR.

The federal onslaught continued until it demolished the core of their power structure, the armed organization, which in its prime had mobilized between twenty thousand and thirty thousand men. In November of 1931, the secretary of war sent Gen. Eulogio Ortiz, with little sympathy for agrarianism, to oversee those paramilitary corps, and, if possible, to disarm them. It wasn't possible, and, in August 1931, Ortiz was replaced by Gen. Lucas González, who brought with him the order of subdividing the collective *ejidos* of Veracruz, by force if necessary. In January 1933, the definite step was given when Gen. Miguel Acosta and a reinforcement of federal troops were sent to disarm once and for all the *agrarista* corps. Although they met with some resistance, the order was fulfilled in a short time.

Without arms and harassed by the government, the "red" LNCUG soon lost effectiveness, and the presidential campaign of Tejeda as a representative of radical agrarianism didn't achieve much scope.

The ex-governor of Veracruz was aware that his effort would be fruitless, but he kept his candidacy alive in order to influence the next president and Calles with respect to agrarian reform. To a certain degree, he was successful. The radical *agraristas* who proposed a profound transformation of the property system were neutralized, but the central authorities had to grant concessions to the moderate *agraristas*, who proved to be the true victors of this internal conflict in the long run.

The Triumph of Moderation

The moderate *agraristas* did not seek direct confrontations with Calles, and the "veteran" group had a very heterogeneous representation. Among its leaders, Gen. Lázaro Cárdenas stood out as someone who was always cautious not to adopt the extreme attitudes of Tejeda, to remain under the discipline of the central government, and in particular of the Jefe Máximo, but at the same time cautious not to be seen as too close to the intimate circle of Calles, corrupt and conservative.

As proof of this relative independence, while the majority of the governors eliminated or halted agrarian reform in their states, Cárdenas accelerated it in Michoacán. As Tejeda before in Veracruz, he decided to base part of his state power in a worker and peasant organization, but he did not develop a paramilitary force, such as that in Veracruz. Thus, the Michoacán Revolutionary Labor Confederation (CRMT) emerged to unite the unions and peasant leagues that were loyal to Cárdenas, and it soon became an engine for social and agrarian reform in the state. When the Michoacán division commander left the governor's office, his successor, Gen. Benigno Serratos, devoted himself to systematically dismantling the CRMT and to placing obstacles in the way of the *agraristas*. But this did not prevent Cárdenas from being clearly identified as one of the leaders of the agrarian wing.

The heterogeneity of moderate *agraristas* was evidenced in the contrast between Cárdenas and another representative of the group, the *cacique* of San Luis Potosí and also a general, Saturnino Cedillo. Cedillo did not pretend to be organizing the *agraristas* in order to eliminate the large landholdings, but only to develop a power base through the selective distribution of lands. When Carranza fell, Cedillo and the remainder of his "José María Morelos" brigade established several agricultural-military colonies in the state. The members of those colonies served as special forces against the De la Huerta rebels, the Cristeros, and the Escobar supporters. At the beginning of the 1930s, Cedillo and his group had several thousand armed *agraristas* under their control, which the central government could not easily ignore. In contrast with Tejeda or Cárdenas, Cedillo was not in favor of a total agrarian reform, but rather a very limited and selective one that would enable him to maintain an adequate recruitment of personal followers. Thus, it wasn't surprising that the federal government confronted the Veracruz *agraristas*, but seemed in no hurry to act against the Potosí agrarian corps. At the beginning of the 1930s, Cedillo accepted a decree in San Luis Potosí that put an end to the agrarian distribution, and everything seemed to indicate that in that state, under the tutelage of Cedillo, the *ejidos* and the large properties would coexist peacefully.

In May 1933, when the precandidates of the PNR were being evaluated for the presidential election of the following year, the main moderate *agrarista* leaders believed that the time had come to act on the national stage. They established the Mexican Peasant Confederation (CCM), using as a base the faction of the National Peasant League that had separated from Tejeda. The leaders of the new organization were Graciano Sánchez of San Luis Potosí, and other secondary leaders, such as Enrique Flores Magón, Emilio Portes Gil, Gonzalo N. Santos, Saturnino Cedillo, Marte R. Gómez, and León García. The CCM immediately declared itself in favor of the candidacy of Lázaro Cárdenas, and Graciano Sánchez actively intervened in the debates on the famous "Six-Year Plan" during the national convention of the PNR in December of that year. The plan had originally been an idea of Calles to impose a government project on the next president, but the final draft of the document went beyond the Callista desires. The less conservative elements of the PNR gave it its final form, casting aside the idea that it was necessary to declare the agrarian distribution over, and they insisted that there was no alternative to dividing up the large properties.

At the time, there was a political atmosphere that was appropriate for these ventures. The Abelardo Rodríguez government had been able to dismantle the machinery of the Veracruz *agraristas*, but not to continue the conservative agrarian policy of Ortiz Rubio. Rodríguez had to accept the fact that putting an end to land distribution would have been imprudent, and he reopened the channels for communities to present new requests for land distribution. Congress agreed to deny landowners the possibility of appeal, which was a clever recourse that had been diligently used by the landowners to erect obstacles to the actions that would affect them.

Rodríguez insisted on subdividing the *ejidos* into individual plots, but he also accepted the *agrarista* proposal to create an Autonomous Agrarian Department, which answered directly to the president of the republic. The concept of *ejido* itself broadened in those years and in the future would include not only the cultivable land, but also the pastures, hills, and rivers. Finally, in March 1934, the first Agrarian Code came into effect, which, among other things, allowed the *peones acasillados* to have access to the *ejido* lands for the first time.

However, the change in the agrarian policies was reflected not only in legislation. The rhythm of distribution did not increase, but rather the opposite happened: in more than two years, the Rodríguez government distributed to the peasants only 1,976,000 acres, a much smaller area than Ortiz Rubio had distributed. In opposition to that reality, Cárdenas, in his electoral campaign around the country, vowed that the Revolution would fulfill the promises made to the peasants and would distribute land to them. It is not surprising that many voters heard the official candidate's promises with skepticism, especially because they believed that Calles would remain the true power behind the throne.

The rural Mexico that Cárdenas found in his electoral tour was still a society dominated by large private properties. According to 1930 statistics, of the 324,805,000 acres registered by the census, 93 percent corresponded to private properties and 7 percent to *ejidos*. The relation between private property and *ejidos* at the regional level confirmed the politically "pacifying" character of the *ejidos*. As we have already mentioned, only in the old Zapatista center, Morelos, was the *ejido* the predominant form of property (59 percent). In the Federal District, where Zapatismo had also been an influence and agrarian agitation had been avoided, *ejido* property also had strength (25.4 percent), as well as in the nearby states of Mexico (21.8 percent) and Puebla (18.4 percent). Yucatán, with an agrarian and socialist tradition since the era of Salvador Alvarado, had a notable 30 percent of *ejido* property. In contrast, in Veracruz or Michoacán, with militant *agrarista* fronts, only 7 percent of the cultivable surface belonged to the *ejidos*. At the other extreme, were states in which the *ejidos* had not become a significant part of the property structure; in Baja California and Quintana Roo, *ejidos* were less than 1 percent of land; in Coahuila, Nuevo León, Oaxaca, and Tabasco, less than 2 percent; in Chiapas and Tamaulipas, less than 3 percent.

The Workers' Path

As one can suppose, workers had greater possibilities than peasants to create organizations to represent their class interests. Before the Revolution, and despite the Porfirian hostility toward these associations, mutual groups had proliferated. Toward the end of the nineteenth century and the beginning of the twentieth century, several significant strikes had occurred, such as those of Cananea and Río Blanco. With the Revolution, the process accelerated. The unions multiplied and, with the emergence of the House of the Workers of the World (COM), an initial attempt at unifying the workers' movement was made, with support to the working-class elements within the group of revolutionary leaders. When the COM disappeared due to Carranza's hostility, the leadership was taken over by the CROM, an organization that defined itself as socialist and opposed to a direct collaboration with the state, but whose emergence had been sponsored by the Carranza government. Shortly thereafter, there was a distancing between the president and the Cromistas, and in 1919 the CROM signed a secret pact with presidential candidate Alvaro Obregón: in exchange for the support the general would provide to the labor demands of the organization, it would support his quest for the presidency. When Carranza fell, the CROM appeared definitely on the landscape as the most important workers' organization, a privileged position that it would lose only in 1929, when unforeseen factors would modify the nature of its relationships with the government and the regime.

In its rise and fall, the CROM was directed by Luis N. Morones and his so-called action group, a small nucleus of leaders who held the main positions of the confederation. They achieved their finest moment between 1925 and 1928, when Morones was secretary of industry, commerce, and labor, and one of the most powerful politicians of the moment, so much so, that he even considered the possibility of announcing his name as a candidate for president.

In 1928, before the decline began, the CROM numbered its membership at two million workers (some observers considered that the true figure was much smaller, perhaps half as much), two thousand unions, and seventy-five federations. To the right of the CROM were the Catholic unions, which lacked an appropriate atmosphere to develop due to the crisis of the church-state relationship. The union spectrum to the left of the CROM was perhaps more interesting. By 1920, the Mexican Communist party had been formed, and it had set as one of its goals, naturally, to confront the CROM.

In 1921, the Red National Convention was held, as a result of which the General Confederation of Labor (CGT) was established—representing an anarcho-sindicalist current that had a great tradition in Mexico—which for the same reason refused to create a political party or seek some form of institutional relationship with the bourgeois government. Its independence did not ease its relationships with the new regime, and even less so after it showed sympathy for the De la Huerta movement in 1923. Just when the CROM entered into the crisis, the CGT achieved its moment of greatest influence, presenting itself as an alternative to Morones's union and proclaiming the loyalty of eighty thousand members at the beginning of the 1930s. The CGT was finally unable to capitalize on the crisis of its opponent, and by 1933 it had in its ranks only eighty thousand workers, most of them in the textile industry. The communists also tried to take advantage of the political crisis of 1929, and they reorganized, establishing the Unitary Labor Confederation of Mexico (CSUM), to replace the old Worker-Peasant Bloc, of precarious existence. Just as the CGT had, the CSUM made some inroads, but it always remained in a secondary position, confronting the government and suffering official repression.

When the crisis of the CROM grew worse at the beginning of the 1930s, none of the rival unions were able to or knew how to replace it. The situation changed only when a faction broke off from the CROM, the so-called purged CROM, at whose helm appeared a brilliant socialist intellectual, Vicente Lombardo Toledano.

By mid-1933, this CROM fraction served as the basis for the constitution of the General Confederation of Workers and Peasants of Mexico (CGOCM), whose initial membership included almost a thousand unions. Following the CROM's path, the CGOCM declared itself anticapitalist, although its immediate program was not particularly radical. It simply proposed to struggle to ensure the fulfillment of article 123 of the constitution, and other similar legal statutes. It replaced the CROM at the middle of the ideological spectrum, and it did not create obstacles to its eventual cooperation with the government. Calles did not show interest in renegotiating an alliance with the workers, but the CGOCM began to take up positions and to prepare for the appropriate moment.

It is convenient to underscore that many unions remained outside of these conflicts for hegemony between the national confederations, especially in the important industries: the oil industry, the electricians, the miners, and the railroad workers. These workers held a privileged position that allowed them to negotiate directly with the companies. They did not escape fragmentation, however, because none of the large industries had unions that covered all of the workers across the industry. The different groupings were divided, and in many cases had conflicts among themselves.

We can conclude that by 1933 the organization of the Mexican workers' movement was characterized by dispersion and by the continuing efforts to join forces. The unionized workers were constantly measuring their forces among themselves and with respect to the state.

Workers and Leaders

The workers' movement did not limit itself to the industrial workers, but also included a good number of employees of artisan shops and service firms. Of the 5 million Mexicans who made up the labor force in 1910, 1.4 million were classified as nonagricultural laborers, and of these approximately half fell in the category of industrial workers. These were concentrated in the manufacturing industry (more than 600,000) and the rest in extractive activities, power generation, railroads, and the oil industry. In 1921, the situation was still basically the same as ten years before. According to the 1930 census, the proportion remained constant, although there were 400,000 more people in the labor market. In any case, between 1910 and 1930 the workers classified as industrial workers did not exceed 15 percent of the total economically active population (see table 1). The Mexican industry virtually did not grow in that period, but the life of the workers underwent considerable transformation, not so much in the material aspect as in their ability to influence the political decision-making process that affected them.

Thanks to the alliance of the CROM and the Sonorans, after the fall of Carranza the Cromista leaders had great freedom to organize and demand the fulfillment of the new rights that the 1917 constitution had granted them. In that year (1920), 173 strikes were registered, the following year there were more than 300, and the number of striking workers exceeded 100,000. Celestino Gasca, an ex-cobbler and a prominent member of the CROM, was named governor of the Federal District, a relatively modest position, but one that would have been unthinkable a few years before.

The CROM was at the time, undoubtedly, the largest workers' organization, and its ranks were rapidly growing. By 1922, it claimed 400,000 members—50 percent of all workers—and at the end of the Obregón government it had increased its estimate threefold. Perhaps the CROM was exaggerating its strength, but it was a real force. However, together

Table 1. Structure of the Labor Force (percentage distribution)

Activities	1910	1921	1930
Agriculture*	71.9	75.2	67.7
Mining	1.7	0.6	1.0
Industry	11.3	12.4	12.9
Transport and communications	1.1	1.6	2.0
Commerce and finance	5.0	5.8	5.0
Services	5.9	3.0	4.6
Government	1.3	1.4	2.9
Other	1.8	—	3.9
Total	100.0	100.0	100.0

* Including cattle-breeding, forestry, and fishing.
Source: Nacional Financiera, *50 Years of Mexican Revolution in Figures.* Mexico City: Nacional Financiera, 1963, p. 29.

with the expansion of its influence, the leaders of the CROM had to increase their "responsibility." Beginning in 1922, the number of strikes began to decline, and they reached their lowest point precisely when the CROM occupied—through Morones—the Ministry of Industry, Commerce, and Labor, between the end of 1924 and mid-1928. Responsibility and competition: the CROM not only directly controlled its members, but on occasion prevented or sabotaged movements by opposing unions or federations. The new strength of the workers can also be measured by the outcome of court decisions. Under Carranza, the findings favorable to the workers were scarce, but beginning in 1920 the majority were favorable, together with cases in which there was an agreement between the parties that resulted in concessions to the workers.

The center of the workers' movement was located in the capital of the republic, certain regions of Veracruz, Puebla, and other mining or oil towns. Together with this geographical distribution, the most militant sectors, by industries, were the textile workers, miners, railroad workers, oil workers, tramway workers, truck drivers, and bakers.

The textile industry employed a lot of workers, to a large extent because it was lagging behind in its technology with respect to other countries. It attempted to reduce the lag in this period, but the technological innovations threatened mass layoffs, and the unions opposed this type of solution.

The frequent crisis in the world mineral market made the mining activity very unstable, and the attitude of the mining unions very defensive. The railroads, most of them in state hands, also suffered from an excess of workers, but the unions prevented a reorganization through violent strikes.

From the beginning, the oil workers were divided into multiple unions that systematically confronted the foreign companies, especially in Tampico and Minatitlán. The existence of some "white unions" was never able to neutralize the aggressiveness of the true unions, which achieved relatively high wages compared with the average wages.

The bakers represent an example of a very dispersed group, which was spread among thousands of establishments and did not hold a strategic position within the productive apparatus, but, thanks to its organization, was nevertheless able to organize some labor stoppages in the large cities. Through this pressure, the bakers were able to have their demands heard and, in some cases, accepted. The same thing occurred with the tramway workers and the truck drivers. The unions in the industries that employed a scarce but highly productive labor force, such as electricians, were better able to negotiate than the majority of the organized workers, and did not resort to strikes as often.

On the Path to Depression

Confronted with the presence of workers as a recognized social force, with their own rights, the victorious Revolution had to begin to create the specialized mechanisms to process their demands in an organized fashion. From its origins, the CROM had exerted pressure for the creation of a Ministry of Labor. In 1921, Congress rejected the proposal, and several years would go by before the project revived and became reality. Meanwhile, workers' affairs were heard by the Ministry of Industry, Commerce, and Labor. As part of the payment for worker support to the Agua Prieta movement, De la Huerta created a Department of Social Welfare in 1920, which he placed in the hands of the CROM, and later Obregón delivered the Department of Labor to the Cromistas. In 1931, a federal labor code was finally passed, extending the authority of the Department of Labor, and, under pressure from the labor organizations, the government announced that it would become independent from the Ministry of Industry. In 1933, an Autonomous Department of Labor (DAT) began to function, which immediately absorbed the Attorney General's Office for Labor Defense and the Federal Councils for Conciliation and Arbitrage.

Before 1920, most of the labor affairs were in the hands of the local authorities, but gradually the central power took control of these matters. By 1933, it was evident that the great regulator of the worker-employee relations was the federal government.

As we have said before, the fleeting millennium of the CROM collapsed after the assassination of Obregón. Calles, its great sponsor and ally, rapidly distanced himself from the Cromista leaders, so as not to irritate Obregon's followers even more. They were particularly strong among the army, which had accused Calles from the beginning and saw in Morones the intellectual author of their leader's murder. The distancing did not lead the confederation to disappear, but it did weaken it considerably and led to its fragmentation. Many of the unions no longer saw any use in following Morones's wagon, because the CROM had lost its control of the Department of Labor and the Councils for Conciliation and Arbitrage. The exodus began, and soon the CROM was an empty shell. Because of their confrontation with the government, neither the communists nor the anarcho-sindicalists of the CGT were able to replace the CROM; the PNR made weak and fruitless attempts at creating its own worker organizations. In the short term, the prevailing notes were confusion and dispersion: the *desmoronamiento* (crumbling) of Morones.

Precisely at this moment of internal crisis in the labor movement, the 1929 depression began to be felt. As we have explained, unemployment

caused by this recession in world capitalism did not have the same devastating effects in Mexico as in other regions, but it did seriously affect
certain sectors. In mining, for example, only half of the ninety thousand
miners who were working in 1927 were still employed by 1932, and
many of them had to accept pay cuts, shorter working hours, or both.

The decline in the mining sector aggravated the economic crisis of the
railroad system. The textile workers, the bureaucrats, and other workers
also suffered and accepted lower wages. Fortunately for those that kept
their jobs, the cost of living index also fell, so the decline in the quality
of life was less steep than what the simple wage decline would seem to
indicate.

The unions tried to defend their members, but they could not prevent
layoffs. Curiously, the number of strikes declined: the fear of unemployment, the lack of support from the government (on some occasions, the
workers received only repression), and the fragmentation of the unions
explain why between 1930 and 1933 only 95 strikes were registered, in
which 8,603 workers participated. The trend toward the reunification of
the workers' movement under new ground rules started to express itself
from the beginning of the crisis of the CROM. In 1930, the General
Committee for the National Worker-Peasant Unification emerged—
more a desire than a reality—which proposed the elimination of Morones
and his group as a starting point for a regenerated and vigorous workers'
movement. The economic crisis cut this impulse short, but 1934 saw
this desire reemerge with strength, fundamentally due to two reasons:
the worst part of the world crisis had ended, and the presidential
campaign was opening opportunities for a new alliance between the
workers'movement and the less conservative factions of the "revolutionary family."

The Path of Lombardo

By the end of 1933, as we have said, Lombardo Toledano established the
General Confederation of Workers and Peasants of Mexico (CGOCM).
The two large traditional noncommunist confederations, the CROM
and the CGT, had different reactions to the new organization: the
CROM fought against it, but the CGT considered for a period of time the
possibility of an alliance, which ultimately did not take place due to
tactical differences. The communists simply decided to remain outside
the conflict. By the end of 1934, the CGOCM claimed 890,000 members.
Its general and long-term position was radical—to eliminate the capitalist system—but its immediate goals sought nothing more than an
improvement in the living conditions of the proletarians, precisely the
tactic that opened the doors to a collaboration with the regime.

By 1934, once the candidacy of Cárdenas was well-established, Lombardo was promoting strikes to demonstrate the mobilization capacity of his confederation, but he was simultaneously extending a bridge toward the candidate. On July 2, 1934, Lombardo called for a general strike in solidarity with the strikers of the El Potrero sugar mill, the Landa cement factory, and the bus workers of the Federal District. In October 1934, a few days before Cárdenas was inaugurated, the CGOCM decided to participate in the National Committee in Defense of Educational Reform, which had as its main goal to support the "socialist education" that had been proposed by Calles and was part of the Six-Year Plan, that is, of the political platform of Cárdenas. They hoped that the political changes at the end of 1934 would allow them to recover part of their force. By this time, the CROM and the CGT had decided not to fall in, and they also adhered to the common front, so that their enemy wouldn't hold all of the initiative. Both groups had toyed with the idea of joining the Ortiz Rubio faction, but when the president lost power, the breach between these confederations and Calles became even wider, so that, by the time Cárdenas assumed power, the situation of the CROM and the CGT was critical, and both organizations had anxious expectations.

The unions that were independent from the large confederations were quite active, but they were very fragmented, and in several cases they had problems with the regime. Some examples: when the CROM was enjoying the peak of its power, it promoted the creation of a National Railroad Federation (FMF), which was unable to unite the majority of the railroad workers. The Confederation of Transport and Communications (CTC) remained as the main group, with an independent line with respect to the CROM, leading it on several occasions to show sympathy to the enemies of the government. In 1933, this Confederation reorganized itself as the Union of Railroad Workers of the Mexican Republic (STFRM), and it maintained its traditional antagonism toward the CROM.

The relationships between the railroad workers and the company became very conflictive dating from 1929. The workers accused the administration of the economic difficulties of the sector, and there were frequent strikes, but they were unable to prevent the layoff of eleven thousand workers as part of the reorganization plan of the system as a whole. When Cárdenas took power, the discontent among the railroad workers was considerable, and, a few days after his administration began, the workers and the police violently clashed in the streets of the Federal District.

The miners were even more divided than the railroad workers when the economic crisis affected them. After the worst was over, the CROM attempted to ensure its presence in this strategic area, and it created the Federation of Mining Industry (1934). Using as its base the Hidalgo Mining Confederation, the enemies of the CROM created the Union of Mine, Metallurgical, and Allied Workers of the Mexican Republic (STMMSRM), which the labor authorities regarded with sympathy, perhaps precisely because it neutralized the CROM.

The oil workers had become embroiled during 1933 and 1934 in a series of strikes that affected the two major companies: El Aguila and La Huasteca. At the beginning of the Cárdenas administration in 1934, they were in full swing, although they hadn't yet been able to create an industrywide union. The electricians had been able to overcome the economic crisis relatively well and had maintained good relations with the company, but toward the end of the Abelardo Rodríguez administration, they attempted to strike, without success.

The textile industry was still struggling through a serious problem, as we have said, due to an excess labor force. The conflict had subsided after a worker-employer agreement in 1927, but the tensions flared up once again with the world crisis. The industrialists threatened to close their plants, and the workers threatened to take them over. In 1933, the possibility of a general textile strike was proposed, despite the fact that there was no single industrywide union, but rather several unions controlled by the three opposing confederations. In order to prevent a catastrophe in this important industry, the government "federalized" the industry and imposed a settlement on the workers and employees, which solved the situation, at least for the moment.

From the previous paragraphs, it is easy to see that when Abelardo Rodríguez left office the Mexican workers' movement was undergoing a phase of lack of control and reorganization. At the time, it was impossible to foresee how this process would turn out, but it seemed clear that the CROM was no longer at the center of the movement. The CGOCM and Lombardo had measured their strength with respect to the other organizations and the state and had presented themselves as an alternative to the group headed by Morones, but could not speak as the voice of the majority of Mexican workers.

4.
The Cardenista Utopia:
1934–1940

When Lázaro Cárdenas was nominated presidential candidate by the ruling party, he already was, in spite of his youth, one of the most important division commanders of the army. His military career had been advanced on the battleground and not in the political arena. He knew the army well and occupied a solid position in it. By 1933, he had participated in twenty-four important armed encounters and a number of skirmishes, and had been the chief of operations of several army units.

He also was not a novice in politics, since he had been governor of Michoacán and president of the PNR, but he was not a member of the original group of revolutionary leaders, as he was younger and already considered as belonging to a new generation. He had been a loyal subordinate of Calles, without being his unconditional follower. He had not attacked Ortiz Rubio nor shared the conservative views of Calles on land reform, and this relative independence helped him to become the official candidate.

Good-bye to the Jefe Máximo

Cárdenas came to the presidency with more factors in his favor than his predecessors, but at the time few thought that he could escape the asphyxiating conservative influence of Calles. Newspapers of the period cruelly reflect that generalized opinion. Many circles underestimated the intellectual ability of the new president and many foresaw for him a fate similar to that of Ortiz Rubio. In fact, the political dice were loaded against him. In his original cabinet were Calles's followers who did not acknowledge his leadership. Tomás Garrido Canabal as secretary of agriculture, Rodolfo Elías Calles as secretary of communications and public works, Juan de Dios Bojórquez as secretary of interior, and Fernando Torreblanca as assistant secretary of foreign relations were all, directly or indirectly, a product of the powerful hand of the Jefe Máximo. Others, such as Aarón Sánchez in the Federal District Department and Emilio Portes Gil in Foreign Relations, without being fanatical followers of Calles, were far from sharing Cárdenas's political ideas. Cárdenas's followers were a minority in the cabinet, and the same thing was true in the PNR, presided over by Carlos Riva Palacio, in the Congress, and in the governorships of the states.

Tensions in the new government appeared from the beginning and finally exploded due, in great measure,to the wave of strikes that took place after Cárdenas took power and reacted mildly to them. In December 1934, Calles broke his silence and warned against "unnecessary agitation," but the atmosphere did not become calmer. By the beginning of 1935, there were problems with railroad workers, electricians, telephone workers, oil workers, and pipe fitters, among others.

Congress soon saw itself divided into two wings, as at the beginning of the Ortiz Rubio presidency: a minority identified with Cárdenas and the left, and a majority did not openly adhere to any ideology but identified itself with Calles. In June, the Jefe Máximo condemned, in the newspapers, the divisions in Congress, the "marathon of radicalism" that had erupted, and the strikes shaking the country. These statements, which Cárdenas tried to suppress, were considered an indirect criticism, and therefore a veiled warning, to the president.

Cárdenas acted speedily by exerting the military powers of the presidency, by capitalizing on the anti-Calles sentiment of many members of the ruling elite and the public, and by getting the support of the labor organizations opposed to Calles. He sent personal representatives to the Chiefs of Military Operations and the governors asking them to choose between Calles and himself. Without exception, the response was favorable and he then published a reply to Calles. Immediately afterward, he asked for the resignation of his secretaries and the president of the PNR.

These surprising actions produced the desired effect: thousands of telegrams of support started to arrive at the National Palace, the left wing of Congress immediately became stronger, and Calles left the capital and, for a time, the country. He returned in December, accompanied by Morones, the CROM leader. In April 1936, accused of hoarding arms, he had to present himself to the authorities, and had to leave the country for a political and personal exile that would last almost a decade. Before Callismo could react, the Maximato had ended, and the Cárdenas era had begun.

The Purge

With the disappearance of Calles and his group from the political scene, political life returned to normal and the presidency fully assumed the directing role that it would increasingly have in the decades to follow.

The cabinet appointed by the president on June 19 was really his, although there were people like Saturnino Cedillo, whose own strength and interests separated him from the Cardenista movement. As the PNR president, Portes Gil became the executor of the unavoidable purge of congressmen and governors disloyal to the president. Among the long list of arbitrary actions, and elimination of powers, the most spectacular was the destruction of Garrido Canabal's political machinery and his "Red Shirts" in Tabasco.

After the elimination of the unconverted Callistas from the PNR, the Congress, and the state governorships, Portes Gil left the presidency of the PNR, worn out from too much resistance and the accusation of not putting the party entirely at the service of the presidency but to himself. Cárdenas replaced Portes Gil with a man having his total confidence, Silvano Barba González, former secretary of interior, who had been succeeded in 1938 by Luis I. Rodríguez, private secretary to the president. Rodríguez shortly afterward left the party's presidency amid strong infighting to become a governor. He was replaced by the Veracruzan Gen. Heriberto Jara, an old assemblyman and a leftist, who led the party until the end of the Cárdenas government.

What is significant about these changes is that, after Portes Gil, the direction of the party was entirely subordinate to the decisions of the country's president. To the presidential control of the party, the Congress, and the governorships, we must add a key element: the army. When the cabinet was reorganized, a man who was very loyal to Cárdenas, Gen. Andrés Figueroa, was appointed secretary of war. He would die before the end of the six-year term, but not before eliminating such open Callistas as Joaquín Amaro of Military Education, Manuel Medinaveitia of the capital's garrison, Pedro J. Almada of the Operations Command in Veracruz, and others of lesser importance. Sometime later, fearing the labor policy of the president, an anti-Cárdenas faction would form in the army, personified by Division General Juan Andrew Almazán, but the armed forces would remain until the end obedient to the orders of the president. His secretary of war, Gen. Manuel Avila Camacho, would become his successor.

The New Alliance

The revolutionary regime defined itself, in contrast with the Porfiriato, as entirely open to popular participation, but when the PNR was formed, it did not fully and directly incorporate the new political actors: workers, peasants, and middle class. This was a step backward in comparison to the immediate past, in which the CROM had represented the effort to keep government and the organized masses united. During the Calles regime, the PNR left out most labor groups, and politics increasingly started to become a game played exclusively by a closed, Callista circle.

Cárdenas could have followed this orientation, at the risk of continued subordination to Calles. When he decided to get rid of the Jefe Máximo he had to strengthen the presidency by finding support in popular organizations. The narrow political circle before 1934 was destroyed, and the representatives of mass organizations joined the political world. The support given to Cárdenas by the CCM and Lombardo Toledano's Workers Confederation was accepted and appreciated.

Up to 1934, large landowners had maintained a privileged situation, not because of their own power but because of the tolerance of the government. This tolerance ended with Cárdenas. The alliance of vast peasant groups with Cárdenas had to be rewarded, and this could be done only at the expense of the *hacienda* system. Land reform was accelerated remarkably after 1935, and the new land distribution affected not only the periphery but the very core of commercial agriculture. The most notable expropriations by Cardenismo took place in La Laguna, where cotton was commercially grown; in Yucatán, center of the production of henequen (hemp); and in Lombardía and Nueva Italia, Michoacán, where grains for domestic consumption grew.

After Cardenismo, Mexican agriculture would never be the same: the large estates inherited from colonial times and strengthened in the nineteenth century were attacked. What had happened in Morelos and neighboring states was extended to the rest of the country, and by the end of the Cárdenas period the *ejido* represented almost half of the cultivated land of Mexico. In exchange for these 445 million to 495 million acres, the government counted on the support of more than 800,000 peasants who, together with those who benefited from former governments, made a total of over 1.5 million *campesinos*. It was a respectable force, and some of them were given arms to defend their recently acquired land and the government that had given it to them. By January 1936, some of the peasants had formed a rural reserve of 60,000 armed men, a number equivalent to that of the federal army. The *agraristas* and the army finished off the remnants of the Cristero rebellion and in 1938 abstained from supporting General Cedillo's insurrection. Organized in the National Peasant Confederation—created in late 1938—they became the most solid supporters of the regime.

The alliance between the workers and the government became stronger after the conflict between Calles and the president. The Jefe Máximo had directly accused Lombardo Toledano of being responsible for the tense climate in the country. The response was direct: while Morones and the CROM sided with Calles, Lombardo and the CGOCM became the core of the National Proletarian Defense Committee, which supported Cárdenas and organized large demonstrations in his favor in the cities. Once the battle was won, Cárdenas accelerated the process of labor unification until the Confederation of Mexican Workers (CTM) was created.

The reward for the renewed alliance was made at the expense of large industrial enterprises, mostly in the hands of foreign capital: mining, oil, and cable car companies, some railroad and telephone networks, electrical companies, and so forth. The domestic bourgeoisie was just starting its industrial participation and was not too affected, although it did show its resentment, as in the case of the protests by Monterrey businessmen.

The CTM, created in early 1936, became, together with the CNC, a foundation of Cardenismo, but not as unconditionally as the peasant movement. When the March 1938 crisis demanded a restriction in strikes, most unions accepted the presidential requests. When General Almazán and his conservative supporters challenged Cárdenas, labor organizations supported the candidacy of Gen. Manuel Avila Camacho, chosen by the president.

The Cardenista Utopia

Cárdenas and his predecessors were mostly concerned with the economic development of the country. Taking into account what was happening in the nation and the world, Cárdenas thought that he had to choose between two options to achieve such development: either to imitate the capitalist strategies of industrialized nations or to attempt a different approach that would combine economic growth and the creation of a more integrated and just society. The Cardenista utopia tried to go beyond Keynesianism or fascism, without falling into the Soviet model.

Between 1935 and 1940, the GNP grew 27 percent, a global figure that hides remarkable variations because, although growth was constant and uniform between 1935 and 1937, the economy became almost stagnant between 1938 and 1940. In 1939 there was a respite due to a commercial activity increase that did not affect production. The sudden economic deterioration in 1938 was a direct result of the oil crisis. The expropriation of oil fields that year affected the export not only of fuels but also, because of international reprisals, of minerals. A climate of lack of confidence in Mexico was created, and investments in a considerable part of the private sector practically stopped.

The Cárdenas regime carried out an extensive land reform, but the destruction of large estates had an immediate negative effect, and commercial agricultural production became stagnant in 1937. By 1940, it had fallen to the levels of five years before. With slight variations, the same thing happened to cattle production, and the depressing rural situation became worse with adverse weather conditions.

In this way, the traditional bases of the Mexican economy—agricultural production and oil and mineral exports—were subjected to a serious test. The beginnings of modern Mexico, nevertheless, started to show renewed vigor. Manufacturing production increased 53 percent in the six-year presidential term, more than twice that of the total economy. The country saw the beginnings of import substitution and also an intensive use of the installed (previously idle) capacity. Industrial production for internal consumption grew without being too affected by the crisis in the traditional sector. Another sector in which there was considerable growth was government expenses, which increased 4,100 percent. Between 1934 and 1940, the state assumed new functions and intensified its old ones: it became an "active state" directly involved in the production process and the creation of infrastructure.

Invisible Prosperity

During the Cárdenas administration, there was a reduction in the value of agricultural production, negatively associated with land distribution. The northern and central regions experienced the largest growth of per capita production and the lowest share of *ejidos*, whereas the Pacific North Coast where the extent of the land reform was greatest had the lowest production growth.

This was natural and foreseeable. For one thing, the *ejidatario* had less financing than the private owner. For another, there was also a change in the nature of crops. Many large estates had been totally or partially devoted to the domestic or international markets, whereas the *ejidatario* devoted the land to personal consumption, leaving the market economy. The decrease in the monetary value of production did not necessarily mean that the peasants' situation had worsened. On the contrary, the consumption of foods probably increased in rural areas.

Not all of the decrease in agricultural production was due to the change in crops or the lack of credit. Mistakes were also made and there were temporary setbacks. When 1.2 million acres of excellent wheat and cotton land were expropriated in La Laguna in the incredible timespan of forty-five days, the resulting land fragmentation prevented the advantages of large-scale production. To maintain the efficiency of the irrigation system, and access to credit, the government encouraged the creation of three hundred collective *ejidos*. After the reduction in wheat production in the 1936–1937 cycle, there was a recovery in the following cycle, and for cotton between 1941 and 1942.

Although the *ejidos*, especially the individual ones, had few inputs— capital, fertilizers, and so on—there is no doubt that they did use the available resources of land and labor more intensely, thus contributing to their more rational use, and to a decrease in rural unemployment. The increase of self-consumption, and the diminished production of certain agricultural products caused a rise in the price of foods and the resulting discontent in urban areas, but allowed for a real transfer of income from the service and industrial sectors to the agricultural sector, which fitted perfectly into the Cardenista program.

Land reform did not produce immediate economic growth, but the beneficiaries of the process saw immediate improvement in their standard of living. Peasants who had received land during the Cárdenas administration effectively improved their relative position within the complex social structure of the period.

The Financial Levers

President Cárdenas was the first to use public expenditure to encourage the economic and social development of the country. During the brief Abelardo Rodríguez administration, 63 percent of the actual expenditures of the federal government were devoted to the bureaucratic machinery. On an average, during the Cárdenas regime, expenses were divided as follows: 44 percent bureaucratic expenses, 38 percent economic development (highways, irrigation, credit, and similar expenses), and 18 percent social expenses (education, public health, etc.). At the highest point of the Cárdenas regime (i.e., between 1936 and 1937), economic development expenditures were above 40 percent, and they were devoted mainly to the development of communications, irrigation, and credit to farmers. The government's spending did not correspond exactly to its income, as can be seen in the following table:

Table 2. Income and Expenses of the Federal Government (1934–1940, in millions of pesos)

Year	Income	Expenditure	Deficit/Surplus
1934	295	265	30
1935	313	301	12
1936	385	406	-21
1937	451	479	-28
1938	438	504	-66
1939	566	571	-5
1940	577	610	-33

Source: René Villarreal, *El desequilibrio externo en la industrialización de México* (1929–1975). Mexico City: Fondo de Cultura Económica, 1976, p. 39.

This means that the government had left behind the orthodoxy that insisted on a strict balance between income and spending. Starting with Cárdenas, the government resorted to fiscal deficits, and the total monetary supply increased from 454 million pesos in 1934 to 1,060 million in 1940. Together with the benefits of accelerated spending, a dose of inflation was unavoidable, more noticeable at the end of the presidential term, due to the 1938 crisis in foreign trade and the decrease in the supply of agricultural products and cattle. On the other hand, the decision to maintain the rhythm of economic growth at any cost benefited the manufacturing industry.

The Cardenista "active state" continued widening the institutional structure. Abelardo Rodríguez had created the National Financial Institution (NAFINSA) in 1934 whose original role was to administer the properties that the previous economic crisis had left to the banking system because of borrowers' bankruptcy. With Cárdenas, this function became secondary, and NAFINSA started to act as the government's development bank. Foreign trade, thereby, was being supported by a bank devoted to its promotion. And since the *ejido* was the main unit in the agricultural economy, it was natural that a bank be created for the specific needs of this sector, whose credit with commercial banks was limited. Due to the conflicts with foreign electrical companies, whose installed capacity was not growing at the necessary rate, the Federal Electricity Commission was created, which would eventually become quite powerful.

After the railroad strike of 1936, the government decided to nationalize the railways and to create a federal government agency to manage them. The arrangement lasted only a short time. Facing a persistent crisis in the sector, Cárdenas decided in 1938 to hand over the control of the railway system to a workers' administration, which continued unsuccessfully in charge of it until the end of the presidential term. Avila Camacho put the railroad network under government supervision again.

Trade Limitations

As said earlier, the Great Depression hit Mexico's foreign trade very hard by closing markets to some of its raw materials. However, by the first year of the Cárdenas period, foreign trade had greatly recovered, and exports grew to a little more than $200 million, whereas in 1932 they had been only $96 million. The increase continued until oil was expropriated and the political effects drastically reduced exports. In 1937, Mexico exported goods for $247.6 million, but in 1938 it was able to export only $183.4 million. When Cárdenas left office, exports amounted to only $177.8 million, due largely to the decrease in oil and mineral exports.

Table 3. Oil Production between 1934 and 1940 (thousands of barrels)

Year	No. of barrels
1934	34,001
1935	40,241
1936	41,028
1937	46,907
1938	38,818
1939	43,307
1940	44,448

Source: Lorenzo Meyer and Isidro Morales, *Petróleo y nación (1900–1987). La política petrolera en México* (Mexico City: Fondo de Cultura Económica–SEMIP, 1990), pp. 54, 86.

Sales of silver to the Treasury Department of the United States were suspended in 1938, but its production and export did not suffer fluctuations. Unfortunately, prices decreased and the income in dollars from exports went down 27 percent between 1937 and 1940. In the same period, zinc exports had decreased at the same rate, and copper 22.0 percent. However, the most serious decrease was in oil revenues (see table 3).

By then, the worst of the world depression had passed and the great Anglo-Dutch company "El Aguila" had started to exploit the Poza Rica fields. In 1937, 61 percent of the production was for export (i.e., about 28.7 million barrels), but only half the following year (14.8 million barrels).

The Mexican effort to sell its oil to the Axis countries and Latin America produced sales of 19.2 million barrels in 1939 and 20.8 million in 1940. Mexico, however, would never completely recover its share of the foreign market. After that, for many years, PEMEX's (Petróleos Mexicanos) production was principally earmarked for domestic consumption. In this unforeseen way, it ceased to be a separate entity and became the main energy source for the economy. In a short time, oil had stopped being the provider of the needed hard currency.

The Cardenista Utopia, Part 2

Industrialization, as a synonym for modernization, was one of the objectives of practically all Mexican governments before and after the Porfiriato. The Cárdenas government tried to modify this scheme. According to Ramón Beteta, who at the time was assistant secretary of foreign relations and one of the principal official ideologues, Mexico found itself in an ideal position: it could benefit from the experience of industrialization in advanced capitalist countries in order to avoid their mistakes and their tremendous social cost. According to Beteta, the official project was trying to achieve a "conscientious industrialization," meaning, basically, the construction of a "Mexico of *ejidos* and small industrial communities." Industry would be at the service of the needs of an agrarian society and not, as usual, the opposite. The main objective would not be industrialization, but the development of an agricultural economy based on the *ejido*. Cardenismo viewed the future Mexico as a predominantly agricultural, rural, and cooperative country. While the largest Latin American countries, such as Brazil and Argentina, continued a clear process of industrialization based on import substitution, Mexico seemed to aim at a more balanced change, whose goal would be the integral development of the individual and society, and not solely the growth of production.

Contrary to the wishes of Cárdenas and his government, the manufacturing industry continued growing without becoming subservient to agriculture, and even started the substitution of consumer goods. The Ford assembly plant was installed in the 1920s, followed in the 1930s by General Motors and Chrysler. Such men as Gastón Azcárraga and Rómulo O'Farril, initial and lasting partners of the new automobile industry, joined the rosters of such already-established industrial entrepreneurs as Garza Sada, Benjamín Salinas, Joel Rocha, William Jenkins, and Carlos Trouyet. New industries appeared and new entrepreneurs became prominent: Harry Steele and Antonio Ruiz Galindo in the manufacture of business equipment, Emilio Azcárraga in the movies and radio, and Eloy Vallina in the processing of wood. In an atmosphere loaded with anticapitalist slogans, paying lip service to the construction of a Mexico of and for the workers, the incipient domestic bourgeoisie, both industrial and commercial, consolidated itself without great difficulties. The Cardenista utopia was overcome and negated by reality. Not much time would pass before this emerging bourgeoisie—not the *ejidos* or the cooperatives—became the core of Mexican economic development with the enthusiastic support of the government.

All Power to Organization: The Workers

Beginning with his presidential campaign, Cárdenas took a very clear position in relation to the labor movement. He took the six-year plan as a starting point and supported collective bargaining, the clause of exclusion, and the rejection of so-called white trade unions. This was the immediate political program. His dream for the long run was to create an industrial plant basically composed of cooperatives in order for the workers to be at the same time owners of the means of production.

Cárdenas's plan, his tolerance of strikes, and the confrontation between Calles and Cárdenas in relation to labor policy led Vicente Lombardo Toledano and the CGOCM in 1935 to head a bloc of labor organizations that would actively support the president: the National Committee of Proletarian Defense (CNDP), formed by nine confederations and industrial trade unions, with the conspicuous absence of the CROM, the Chamber of Labor, and the CGT. The Pact of Solidarity aimed to neutralize the pressures exerted by Callistas and to provide a basis for creating a great Workers and Peasants Congress. From this congress, a single labor central organization would emerge that would end the lack of cohesion suffered by organized labor since 1928. Its basic ideology would be different from 1928: the new organization should accept as a premise the existence of class struggle and the impossibility of cooperation with the capitalist class.

Lombardo Toledano clearly emerged as the new unifying leader, although rival organizations repeatedly attacked his group, pointing out the dangerous radicalism of its positions. In December, after a clash between members of the CGOCM and a profascist group called "The Golden Shirts," Cárdenas insisted that it was not necessary to expel Calles and his followers. In April 1936, however, he changed his mind, and the former Jefe Máximo and Morones were, without warning, taken from their homes and sent into exile. The anti-Lombardo labor front collapsed, and the field was left open for the CGOCM.

There were negative reactions to the Cárdenas policies from entrepreneurs in Mexico City, Yucatán, La Laguna, León, and Monterrey. The president responded on February 11, 1936, in Monterrey with a speech known as the "Fourteen-Point Speech." Cárdenas emphasized the need to end the conflict between labor organizations and to create a united labor front. Once the front was created, the government would discuss all labor problems with its representatives, and he would exclude from negotiations all organizations that did not join the front. He rejected fears that communists would head the new pyramid, because, according to him, the cause of workers' agitation basically was that just demands of the working masses were not being met: calm would return not by repression but by obedience to the law.

The Dialectic of the Weakest Link

The response of the labor movement was immediate. Before the end of February, Lombardo inaugurated the Congress that would start the central trade union organization. The debates were not long; the pieces had already fallen into place. Three days later, the four thousand workers who claimed to have the representation of six hundred thousand workers agreed to form the Confederation of Mexican Workers (CTM) dissolving, consequently, the CGCOM and other organizations that had participated in the Congress. Lombardo Toledano was elected secretary general of the brand-new organization.

The bylaws of the confederation reaffirmed the principle of class struggle and the eventual transformation of the capitalist society into a socialist one. At that time, however, they were not planning the overthrow of the capitalist order or the installation of the dictatorship of the proletariat, but something more compatible with the government policy: the liberation of Mexico from the imperialist yoke and the complete enforcement of article 123. The real fight would be for tangible goals: salaries, working hours, social benefits, absolute respect for the right to strike. The ideological struggle would be for the long-term goals: the attainment of a socialist society and the abolition of private property.

A short time after the creation of the CTM, in March 1936, Cárdenas received a statement from a business group questioning some of the points stated in Monterrey. He responded that in any labor dispute where the employer was not clearly right, the government would side with the workers. The revolutionary government could not be neutral and had to throw its weight in favor of the weaker party of the capital-labor relationship, and only thus could substantive justice be preserved. If this new situation led to the "fatigue" of entrepreneurs, they could leave the administration of the enterprise to its workers. The old alliance between an organized labor movement and a new government that had taken place in the 1920s returned, but with more clarity and more commitment than in the past.

The CTM and the labor movement took advantage of this favorable position to move quickly. Among his fourteen points, Cárdenas had proposed that wages should not be fixed according to the supply-demand pendulum, but in accordance with the ability of each enterprise to keep working without losses. This criterion intensified labor conflicts, and strikes became more numerous. There had been 202 strikes in 1934; there were 642 in 1935 and 674 in 1936, with a mobilization of 114,000 workers.

Among the most spectacular conflicts in 1936 was the railroad strike, which would lead to the nationalization of this sector, and the strike of the agricultural workers of La Laguna, which was also concluded with the expropriation of large estates in the region. The persistent tension in the petroleum sector threatened a strike by the recently formed STPRM (Petroleum Workers Trade Union of the Mexican Republic).

In 1937, when the strike against the whole petroleum industry became a reality, the conflict went beyond the labor problem. It became a national political problem that forced the intervention of the government to prevent the stoppage of activities, which would leave the country without fuel. First, labor courts and then the Supreme Court later decided that a raise in salaries and benefits was justifiable, but the enterprises rejected these decisions. The long and fruitless negotiation came to a deadend and the Mexican government, after studying the legal and political aspects of the conflict, punished the companies by decreeing on March 18, 1938, the nationalization of the oil industry, a decision that was to carry great weight in the future and in the shaping of Mexican history.

Beginning and End of the Party

Even at the time of its greatest splendor, and in spite of its obvious all-inclusive intentions, the CROM could not put all organized workers under its umbrella. The CTM also could not and inherited from the CROM its intentions and its failure. As soon as it was created, differences started to appear between the leadership and the strongest industrial trade unions. Soon the Mining and Metallurgic Trade Union separated, as did the Electricians Union. These were strategic organizations with enough strength to find little that was practical in the obedience to central organizations, some of them of little importance and with relatively different interests. Origin is destiny, and in the future, these and other great industrial trade unions would remain separated from the CTM, which was not able to eliminate the competition of the CGT or the CROM. Reluctantly, it had to share with them the control of certain sectors, like textiles, and this produced conflicts. On the other hand, the Communist party joined forces with Lombardo's within the popular front, but, before long, communists and Lombardistas were fighting for control of the CTM. As a result, communists were temporarily expelled from the CTM. The pressure of the international communist movement for the preservation of popular antifascist fronts made Mexican communists reconsider their position and return to the CTM, accepting the Lombardista leadership.

The regrouping of the labor movement during the Cárdenas regime and its alliance to the government improved its position vis-à-vis capital. In three of the strikes of the period—railroad workers, La Laguna, and oil workers—government support of workers' demands led to the expropriation of the companies. The strikes against the Electrical Power Company, the ASARCO mining company, the cable car company, the telephone company, the Cananea mining company, and other less spectacular strikes achieved collective contracts for their workers, with substantial gains for them. However, the actions of the labor force almost never surpassed the limits imposed by the government. To begin with, Cárdenas opposed the inclusion of peasants in their ranks, since this would have given them too much strength. Strikes against what the government declared "of national interest" were declared nonexistent by the courts, as in the case of the railroad strike of 1936. The government supported the demands of the workers against foreign oil companies, but, when they were nationalized, Cárdenas was opposed to giving PEMEX a workers' administration, although he did give the workers participation in its management. When the national crisis, partially produced by the oil expropriations, started, the CTM promised Cárdenas to reduce the number of strikes, in order not to aggra-vate the situation: there were half as many strikes in 1940 as in 1936, and the strikers involved in 1940 were only one-fifth the number in 1936.

By 1940, there were labor sectors in disagreement with official policy, and this was made clear during presidential succession. The CTM supported the candidacy of Avila Camacho, but could not avoid the creation of a workers' movement in favor of General Almazán: the pro–Andrew Almazán Railways Central party, the Almazán Mining party, and the pro–Almazán Cable Car Workers Front. It was not a very important dissident sector, but it reflected the discontent of some of the workers in the face of inflation and government control of their demands.

The Vocation for the *Ejido*

The six-year plan emphasized the need to provide land and water to all the agrarian nuclei that did not have them or had them in insufficient quantities. This included *acasillado* peons among those who had a right to the land and demanded a simplification of procedures to grant property rights. Against Calles's wishes, the plan considered that the engine of agrarian production had to be the *ejido* and reiterated the need to support it with credit and infrastructure.

In order to give peasants land by means of the *ejido*, they had to be organized. In a speech given in Guerrero in May 1934, Cárdenas stated that an important part of this organization was to arm the peasants and create self-defense units that would enable them to defend their rights against the foreseeable attacks of large landholders and their "white guards." The idea was to make the structural change in the Mexican countryside irreversible. The new rural society would revolve around the *ejido*, especially the collective one. Urban and industrial society would become secondary to the needs of agricultural economy, which would give employment to the most essential sector of the population.

During Cárdenas's regime, an average of 8.2 million acres were distributed yearly—a total of almost 50 million during the six years, to 771,640 peasant families grouped in 11,347 *ejidos*. Each beneficiary received an average of 63.7 acres. Cárdenas became the president who had distributed the most acreage and the most plots.

When Cárdenas assumed the presidency, the collective cultivation of the *ejido* was the exception, although it had been legal since 1922. Cárdenas's innovations, therefore, had two aspects: a quantitative aspect, because of the unprecedented number of grants of land and water, and a qualitative one, because of the support he gave to collective *ejidos*. These collective *ejidos* became easier to develop when at least two of the three following circumstances were present: (1) the expropriated land was fertile and irrigated, (2) its production had commercial value (e.g., cotton, hemp, wheat, or rice), and (3) there already existed important labor organizations requesting the land.

The collective *ejido* was considered the only way to prevent important agricultural regions, once expropriated, from becoming areas that grew only what they needed, especially maize, thus harming the national agricultural economy. To implement this policy the National Ejido Credit Bank was created, and its purpose was to provide the necessary capital to start and maintain these large projects of commercial exploitation.

Large Estates

The first important *ejido* was established in 1936 in La Laguna, between Coahuila and Durango, a wide plain of 3.4 million acres, of which about half were irrigated with the waters of the rivers Nazas and Aguanaval. The conflict between the peasants and the landowners was long-standing and became political with the series of strikes by the peasant unions between 1935 and 1936. Cárdenas decreed the expropriation of a third of the area (i.e., 360,620 acres). In spite of the problems resulting from the division of the large farms, production did not collapse, as had been predicted by the enemies of the decree; there were, however, serious problems, especially at the beginning. The second great expropriation took place in 1937 in Yucatán: 904,020 acres of hemp that benefited a system of collective *ejidos* of 34,000 members scattered in 384 towns. The third expropriation took place in the Yaqui valley, where a foreign enterprise—Richardson—had created at the end of the nineteenth century an irrigation system based on the waters of the Yaqui River. Cárdenas decreed the expropriation of almost 42,000 acres of permanently irrigated land and almost 89,000 acres of temporally irrigated lands—many of them in foreign hands—benefiting 2,160 members, which meant an exceptional 19.7 acres of irrigated land per capita (i.e., twice the figure for La Laguna).

The fourth great expropriation took place in Cárdenas's birthplace in 1938, where two large estates, Lombardía and Nueva Italia, in the hands of a family of Italian origin were expropriated. The almost 152,000 expropriated acres irrigated by the Tepalcatepec and Márquez rivers benefited 2,066 *ejido* members. On this occasion, taking into account the lessons of the past, the property was not divided into several cooperatives: the two *haciendas* were kept intact, and all the machinery and animals of the company became property of the new *ejidos*.

The last great expropriation was in Los Mochis, in Sinaloa, a cane-producing area irrigated by the Fuerte River, in the hands of a foreign sugar-producing company. The 1938 expropriation delivered close to 136,000 acres to 3,500 members of 28 *ejidos*, which cultivated the land as a single unit, benefiting the sugar mill, which was not expropriated. After 1938, there was no similar expropriation for the above-mentioned political and economic circumstances. But the memory of the great Cárdenista expropriations seemed unparalleled for the first time since the land distribution in Morelos during the civil war, the true agrarian heart of the Mexican Revolution.

The Peasant Wing

One of the prominent supporters of the Cárdenas candidacy had been the Mexican Peasant Confederation (CCM), the nucleus of moderate agrarianism at the end of the Maximato. Born in the electoral process, the CCM was not precisely the kind of organization that best fitted the new political stage. So, once Cárdenas had solved the Calles problem, he hurried to sign on July 10, 1935, a decree on the need to create leagues of agrarian communities in each state of the republic. The local leagues would be the bases for the creation of a great national peasant central, and the PNR—not the CCM—was entrusted with the task of implementing the decree.

Although the CTM had also wanted to incorporate the peasants, Cárdenas decided that if somebody was going to concentrate power, it should be the president and nobody else. In fact, the president himself directly supervised the initial work for the creation of the first truly national peasant organization, and attended several of the state conventions organized by the PNR. The process, however, was very slow. For instance, the first convention of the league of the Federal District took place two years after the decree was signed.

On the basis of the CCM, the National Peasant Confederation (CNC) was created, and its program stated that the only way to defend the interests of the workers in the countryside was to admit to the reality of class struggle. The land should belong to whoever tilled it, and, therefore, the organization should include *ejido* members, *acasillado* peons, sharecroppers, small landholders, and, in general, all organized rural workers.

The goal of the CNC was nothing less than the "socialization of the land." To achieve it the CNC had to make the *ejido* the basic production unit, finish off the *latifundio*, identify itself with the demands of the workers, and support the socialist education of the peasant masses.

The coordination of this organizational effort was first in the hands of Emilio Portes Gil as president of the PNR and, later, of Silvano Barba González. In 1937, the CNC was not yet organized, so the CCM was the organization that signed the pact of the electoral popular front with the PNR, the CTM, and the Mexican Communist party (PCM). The same thing happened when the PNR became the Party of the Mexican Revolution (PRM). The CCM served as the base organization for the peasant sector, together with the agrarian community leagues and the existing peasant trade unions. Paradoxically, it was only in 1938 during the Cardenista crisis when the constituting congress of the CNC could take place. The three hundred delegates claimed to represent three million rural workers. Membership in the CNC was open to *ejido* members, unionized peasants, agricultural cooperative members, members of military agricultural colonies, and small landowners. Also accepted were persons not belonging to these categories who could benefit the *campesino* cause, because of their history or skills, such as agricultural engineers.

CNC's bylaws stated that it would be the only organization to represent the *campesinos* and the CCM was dissolved, but its leader, a teacher named Graciano Sánchez, was elected secretary general of the new organization. His deputy was León García, secretary of agrarian action of the PRM. By indirect affiliation, all the CNC members were considered to belong to the PRM, and thus, from the very beginning, the CNC became the peasant wing—and, for this reason, the majority wing—of the ruling party. On the left, the "Ursulo Galván" National Peasant League did not accept the CNC and tried to achieve *campesino* unification outside political parties. It was merely a good intention and, for the time being, nobody could dispute the power of the new central peasant organization.

Splinter Groups

The main opposition to Cárdenas's agrarian policy came from the other extreme of the political spectrum. In May 1937, the National Sinarquista

Union (UNS) had been organized, a group of clear fascist sympathizers, which created a stir in the rural areas of the center of the country, where the scar of the Cristero War was still present. The UNS declared itself against the *ejido* from the beginning and asked the government to support and consolidate the small private property. The Sinarquista movement was not only an anticommunist movement of landowners but included *ejido* members and wage-earners, who had been considered obvious supporters of Cárdenas. The Sinarquistas attracted *ejido* members whose poverty had not been relieved, because of the small size of their lots and the lack of credit. When the political agitation caused by the presidential succession came to the Bajío, the UNS became the natural ally of Almazán and the people who wanted to create a wide fascist movement in Mexico. Fortunately for the government, Sinarquismo did not surpass its original bases and never became a truly national movement.

But there were some desertions. In March 1938, months before the CNC was organized, the *cacique* of San Luis Potosí, Saturnino Cedillo, one of Cárdenas's most important supporters, declared himself against his original cause and took up arms, using as a spearhead of his offensive the rural paramilitary groups that had been organized long before. He was confident that other groups would join him, but soon he was disappointed, because even most of these *agrarista* groups abandoned him.

Cedillo, almost alone, died in combat in 1939, but the defense he made of private property against the advance of *ejidos* and his denunciation of the collectivist experiments in La Laguna and Yucatán echoed a powerful and generalized opinion. In May 1938, President Cárdenas created the Bureau for Small Landholdings and announced his decision to fight the invasion of small farms, to prevent small landowners from "joining the counterrevolution." In September, barely two weeks after the creation of the CNC, a national congress of small landowners was inaugurated, claiming to represent twenty-five thousand owners, and harshly attacking both the *ejido* and the invasions. The requests of these landowners were well received by some governors, especially those of Sonora, Puebla, and Michoacán. In Michoacán, Gildardo Magaña insisted that the policies of the former regime had hit both the landless peon and the small landowner, and therefore that the revolution was forced to defend both of them equally.

Cedillo's defeat and the assurances granted to the small landowners halted or diminished the attacks of the opposition, but did not stop them completely. Almazán openly cultivated the antiagrarian tendencies and presented a platform attacking the "collectivization" of the country, which, in his opinion, revived the *encomienda* system. Almazán promised to remedy quickly what he described as the "agricultural disaster—abandoned lots, decrease in productivity" and proposed a simple solution: to purge the *ejido* censuses and grant deeds to the honest agrarians who already had lots and who would become independent owners, with average holdings of 49 acres, free from misery and political manipulation. After this, the distribution of private lands would stop.

In spite of the problems and setbacks, the Cárdenas government would see the end of the *latifundio*. Its destruction was not absolute, but the privileged status of the *hacienda* would be irreversibly ended. The second six-year plan, the platform of General Avila Camacho, was written by a group of both moderate and radical representatives. Its agricultural section made it clear that the *latifundio* was dead and the *ejido* would be the basis of the agricultural economy, but it also stated that the legal status of small properties would be clearly defined. The *ejido*, especially the collective *ejido*, would continue to receive state support, but abandoning the land or opposing production systems that benefited the majority was forbidden.

The President's Party

Given the new relationship between the ruling power and the organized masses, Cárdenas considered it necessary to transform the party system and to reorganize the official party. The PNR was replaced by the Party of the Mexican Revolution (PRM) on a semicorporative basis. It was to comprise the four sectors that supported the presidential policy: workers, peasants, popular organizations, and the military.

By then, the PNR that had put Cárdenas in office was very different from the one created by Calles in 1929. The original coalition had radically transformed itself. The October 1932 Congress decided to dissolve all the parties that had made up the PNR and to promote, instead, direct individual affiliation to the new party. This was a blow to the innumerable local leaders who until then had headed the hundreds of parties, and pseudo-parties, that proliferated in Mexico. The winners were, undoubtedly, the National Executive Committee of the party and Calles.

The head of the PNR during the Cárdenas presidential campaign was Col. Carlos Riva Palacio, who was more loyal to Calles than to the future president. The party machine worked well, and Cárdenas was declared the winner with an incredible 98 percent of the vote. At the beginning of Cárdenas's term, Riva Palacio was replaced by Gen. Matías Ramos, who was someone else Cárdenas did not trust.

Everything seemed to run normally in the party until the final fallout of the Jefe Máximo and Cárdenas in June 1935. Matías Ramos aligned himself with Calles, and Cárdenas immediately asked for his resignation. It was one of the first steps toward solving the general political crisis. At the time of the conflict, the leadership of the country was clearly divided. In Congress, which reflected the division of the party very faithfully, there were two distinct groups: a minority "left wing," which was pro-Cárdenas, and a majority openly in favor of Calles. When Congress learned that Emilio Portes Gil, former president and foreign secretary, was to replace Matías Ramos as president of the PNR, it understood that a new hour of definitions had arrived, and the "left wing" gained followers fast.

Portes Gil had accounts pending with Calles and his group, and lost no time in performing the task entrusted to him by Cárdenas: to make the PNR an instrument of loyal and efficient support of the president's policy. His immediate function was to be a political executioner: heads started rolling and the atmosphere in Congress became red-hot. The crisis came to a climax in September, when the differences between Cardenistas and Callistas resulted in a shoot-out inside the Congress—two people killed and two wounded. As a result of this scandal, seventeen Callista congressmen were deprived of immunity.

Calles returned to Mexico on December 13, 1935, starting rumors that he had come to prepare a subversive movement. As a response, on the fourteenth, five Callista senators were expelled for inciting the rebellion. On the sixteenth, the purged Senate nullified the local governments of Guanajuato, Durango, Sonora, and Sinaloa, and, later, those of other states. With the political destruction of Calles, the "power behind the throne" and, finally, the direction of the PNR were in fact in the hands of the president. From its beginning to mid-1935, no president had been able fully to take the reins of the party, and the PNR had been the basic means of maintaining the "diarchy" president/Jefe Máximo that had characterized Mexican politics since the death of Obregón. From the 1936 crisis on, the official party fast became one of the most solid bases of postrevolutionary presidential power.

The Party of the Revolution

In the opinion of many leaders, the Cárdenas-Calles confrontation and the resistance to land reform and organized labor militancy made evident the need to transform the PNR into a more active organization, where the forces that supported Cárdenas were fully represented. Until then, the party basically had been the expression of an electoral alliance of national and local political leaders, but the core of Cárdenas's policy was the organization of workers and peasants and their incorporation into the system. Popular organizations had to have direct representation in the structure of the party.

The immediate antecedent of this transformation illustrates the methods, at the same time cryptic and direct, of the Cárdenas political style, and had to do, as so many things of the period, with a Lombardo initiative: the creation of an antifascist popular front encompassing all the progressive forces supporting Cárdenas, the official party among them.

In the 1920s, Morones had succeeded in establishing a narrow liaison between the CROM and the American Federation of Labor (AFL), the great American central labor organization. They were united by a common desire to neutralize the influence of the radical left in their countries and a moderate interest in improving the standard of living of their members. The CTM broke up this relationship and looked for more radical alliances. In January 1937, Lombardo announced that the CTM would favor the formation of a popular front, as had been done in France and Spain, to counter the extreme right fascist offensive, which was the policy of the international left supported by the Soviet Union. Lombardo proposed the alliance between the CTM, the PNR, the brand-new National Peasant Confederation (CNC), and the Mexican Communist party. Cárdenas did not let the project advance too far, but took advantage of its original impulse, giving it a twist and converting the ruling party into the head of the groups interested in forming the front.

Formal reorganization of the PNR took place in 1938. The idea had been publicly stated for the first time in the presidential address of 1936, but nothing concrete was done until December 18, 1937. On this date, Cárdenas reiterated his desire that the ruling party faithfully reflect the coalition of workers, peasants, intelligentsia, and the military that supported the revolutionary government. The organizations that represented these forces were consulted, and a constitutive assembly was called. At the end of March 1938, in the middle of the general mobilization created by the oil expropriation, the PNR became the Party of the Mexican Revolution (PRM), created as a coalition of sectors: the peasant sector (represented first by the leagues of agricultural communities and the CCM and, after the CCM's dissolution, by the CNC); the labor sector, formed by the CTM, the CROM, the CGT and the two great industrial unions affiliated to the central organization, the mining and electricians' unions; the popular sector immediately identified itself with the bureaucracy; and the military sector, which in fact included all the members of the armed forces. This indirect means of affiliation permitted the brand-new PRM immediately to count four million members, a significant figure in a country with slighty fewer than nineteen million inhabitants.

History of the Oil Expropriation

The origin of the conflict between the Cárdenas government and the foreign oil companies was old. At the beginning of the twentieth century, in order to stimulate the production of the small quantities of petroleum that internal demand required, Porfirio Díaz had the Congress change the laws that had been preserved from colonial times. By a 1909 law, oil deposits—which an official study of the period did not deem rich—became the property of the owner of the land, and oil entrepreneurs (practically all of them foreigners) were granted special tax benefits—during a long period, they had to pay only a stamp fee, which amounted to less than 1 percent of production. This situation changed dramatically when the Revolution started and the government realized, for the first time, the great oil potential of the country.

By 1910, the domestic market was insufficient for the oil industry, which started to export most of its production. In 1921, 99 percent of production of a record 193 million barrels was exported. The revolutionary governments had to try to modify a situation where large foreign companies exported almost all of a nonrenewable resource, without leaving any ostensible benefits to the nation.

The nationalist attitude in regard to oil problems, which was maintained by the regimes after Díaz, was due both to the nature and the magnitude of the industry as well as to the need to obtain resources for the expenses incurred in the revolutionary struggle. The large oil exports—Mexico became the largest exporter in the world in the second decade of the twentieth century—were seen as the ideal way to cover the great deficits in the budgets. Of course, the foreign companies that dominated the industry opposed maximum resistance to the efforts to diminish their privileges and counted on the support of their governments, especially the North American and English governments. Madero, for instance, had to face a veritable international crisis when in 1912 he decreed a general tax of 20 cents per ton.

The struggle between the companies and the government became more acute from 1917 onward. Paragraph 4 of article 27 of the new constitution declared oil fields to be property of the nation. For the following twelve years, the core of the oil conflict was to decide if this constitutional rule affected fields granted in absolute ownership to foreign companies before 1917. The problem was more or less solved with the so-called Calles-Morrow Agreement in 1928, which gave origin to an oil law that explicitly recognized the principle of nonretroactivity.

After 1922, Mexican oil production began to decrease, and very soon the country lost its status as major oil producer. The great international companies started to concentrate their activity on Persia, Venezuela, and Colombia. At the beginning of the 1930s, Mexico was a marginal producer, a situation that started to change somewhat with the discovery of the Poza Rica fields in 1930.

British oilmen, anxious to exploit these new fields but afraid of the obstacles that the Cardenista government might raise—the six-year plan maintained the convenience of following a nationalist oil policy—were willing to make concessions. In November 1935, in spite of the disapproval of American companies, the English El Aguila company and the Mexican government came to an understanding in regard to the exploitation of Poza Rica. In exchange for the exploitation of one of the richest fields, the company recognized the original property right of Mexico to all oil fields, and agreed to pay the government royalties for an amount that would vary between 15 percent and 35 percent of production. It was a gigantic step in the struggle of the government to affirm its control over oil resources, since El Aguila controlled the Poza Rica area before the 1917 constitution was in effect. But the conflict had not yet started.

The negotiations between Mexico and the British consortium were not the only cause for worry for American oilmen. They were equally or more alarmed by the Expropriation Law approved by the Congress in 1936. By this law, the Mexican government could nationalize for public utility reasons any type of property and pay for it according to its fiscal value—generally lower than the market price—within ten years after the expropriation. To calm foreign investors and their governments, Cárdenas assured the American ambassador that he did not intend to use the new law against large oil or mining companies. But the companies were not pacified, knowing the little sympathy Cárdenas felt for them. At the same time, the government was late in granting the confirmation deeds that, according to the 1928 law, had to be given for properties acquired before 1917. Furthermore, the original deeds were being carefully examined because, according to the oilmen, the government was trying to find fault with them in order to annul them.

The Oil Expropriation: The Conflict

The definitive clash between the government and the oil companies, however, did not originate in a dispute about underground property, but in a confrontation between the companies and their workers. This was something completely new in the conflict between the revolutionary governments and foreign companies. Oil trade unions had distinguished themselves by their aggressiveness. Almost from the beginning of their operations, the companies had to face organized labor protests, sometimes limited to one plant, other times to all the installations of a company or to the whole industry. In part due to this attitude, oil workers were among the best paid in the country. They had not, however, achieved the creation of a single union that would negotiate working conditions for all oil workers. Encouraged and advised by the CTM and the Cárdenas policy, the main leaders of nineteen trade unions got together in the Federal District and created the Mexican Oil Workers Trade Union (STPRM), which immediately affiliated itself with the CTM and prepared to negotiate its first collective contract with the companies.

From the beginning, negotiations were difficult. The companies rejected the raise requested (65 million pesos) and proposed one-fifth of that amount. In 1937 the STPRM announced a strike. Work stopped for a short period, but the government realized that suspension in the supply of fuel disrupted the economy of the country and decided it was an "economic conflict," and the workers returned to work. Nevertheless, the Federal Conciliation and Arbitration Board had to appoint a committee to determine briefly whether the companies could increase wages and benefits on an amount higher than the 14 million pesos they had offered.

The conflict at that moment changed from a labor conflict to a political one. The government-appointed experts produced a bulky document (2,700 pages) that not only discussed the economic ability of the companies to satisfy their workers' demands, but also conducted a historical review of the role of these companies in the economic life of Mexico. Its conclusion was an open, drastic condemnation: the presence of these companies had been more harmful than beneficial to the country. As to the issue of wages, the document stated that the companies' financial status allowed them to raise wages and salaries by 26 million pesos (i.e., 12 million more than what they were willing to pay). As can be imagined, the companies considered the experts' estimates inaccurate. They insisted that if the recommendations of the document were fully carried out, the real increase would be not 26 but 41 million pesos. They admitted that they could grant a 20 million increase, and the problem went back to the labor courts.

In December 1937, labor authorities decided that the experts' conclusions were valid and that the companies could, and should, pay the assigned amount. The companies appealed to the Supreme Court and started to put pressure on the government by withdrawing bank deposits, which produced a slight panic. In this heated atmosphere and with the CTM demanding a decision that would be favorable to the workers, on March 1, 1938, the Supreme Court decided that the companies should grant a 26 million peso raise, as recommended by the experts, and with the proviso that this amount include both wages and benefits. The companies simply refused to obey the order, refusing to obey Mexican law and to recognize the sovereignty of the country itself. There was no way to hide the seriousness of the situation. If the government did nothing in response to the companies' rebellion, its prestige and leadership would be seriously questioned.

The Oil Expropriation: Lightning in a Blue Sky

The political groups, the leaders of mass organizations, and the members of foreign colonies had a sharp, and agitated, conscience about the dilemma. For many, Cárdenas's next step would be to appoint a comptroller in the companies who would make sure that the companies paid the increase decreed by court. This solution, however, would be a temporary one, because sooner or later, after negotiations, the facilities would be returned to their owners. In contrast with the ruling elite, public opinion did not seem especially interested in the problem. Actually, most radio listeners must have been quite surprised when, on the eve of March 18, 1938, all radio stations announced the suspension of all normal channels and the networking of all radio transmitters with the Autonomous Department of Publicity and Propaganda, to listen to the president address the nation. Cárdenas informed the country of his decision to settle the matter once and for all and expropriate the oil companies, since he could not allow a decision of the highest court to be annulled by one of the parties through the simple expedient of declaring itself insolvent. If this decision had not been made, he said, the sovereignty of the nation itself would have been compromised. Of course, he added, the expropriated property would be paid for, but according to the 1936 law. Mexico had taken, on that March 18, a measure without precedent in its history and with few counterparts in world history. Only the Soviet Union had dared before to take such an important step.

The large foreign investments in countries of the periphery were affected. One of the most interesting and succinct testimonies of the impact that Cárdenas's decision had produced in people in Mexico and abroad was given by the American ambassador, who said that the decision had surprised him "like a bolt of lightning in a blue sky." On the following day, March 19, the principal dailies of the country and of the world devoted their headlines to the oil company, and a popular mobilization of national scale started in Mexico. Mass organizations and media encouraged popular solidarity with the presidential decree; this campaign fell on fertile land, and support for Cárdenas became almost unanimous.

The first public demonstration in front of the National Palace took place on the March 22 and it was led by a formerly longtime critic of the government: college students. On March 23, the same place was occupied by a quarter million people, members of trade unions and the PRM, as well as independents. The president had to stay on the balcony of the palace from 11:00 A.M until 3:00 P.M. to receive demonstrations of support, and similar demonstrations were conducted in the interior of the country. The mobilization was general.

Diplomatic communications from Great Britain, criticizing the expropriation and questioning the ability of the government to pay for what it had taken, increased the nationalist exaltation. The break in diplomatic relations with the British government was well received by Mexican public opinion. In April, the president ordered the issuing of bonds for 100 million pesos for a fund to pay for the expropriations, and the Mexican Committee for Economic Liberation (CUMPLE) was created to receive popular donations. Initial response was enthusiastic. Thousands of Mexicans contributed with money, jewels, and even domestic animals to pay foreign creditors and thus maintain Mexican dignity. Enthusiasm, however, was greater than the popular ability to collect the necessary amount, and Cárdenas deemed prudent in July both the issuing of bonds and CUMPLE's activity. Its political objective had been achieved, and the American ambassador informed his superiors that there was unquestionable popular support for the expropriation decree, and, therefore, it was improbable that Cárdenas would back down, as the British were requesting and Americans and others wanted.

The Oil Expropriation: The Boycott

The official opposition of Great Britain—whose investment in 1938 was larger than the United States'—did not worry Mexico too much. With the North Americans, the problem was more delicate. To a great extent, the success of the expropriation depended on Washington's reaction. In principle, the U.S. government recognized that Mexico, as a sovereign nation, had a right to nationalize the property of foreign companies, but conditioned this right on the prompt, effective, and adequate payment of expropriated goods. And on this last point, the Mexican and U.S. positions differed irreconcilably.

Mexico, from the beginning, agreed to pay for what it had taken, not immediately, but in the ten years prescribed by law. For Washington, a deferred payment transformed the expropriation into a confiscatory act, in violation of international law. There was, furthermore, the problem of the amount of the debt. Should the value of the oil still underground be taken into account? For American oilmen, there was no doubt: property included nonextracted oil. For Mexico, the discussion touched on the meaning of the text and the spirit of article 27 of the constitution.

It was evident that the Cárdenas government was not able to pay the

$400 million or $500 million estimated extraofficially as the value of their property by the oilmen. The Mexican president, nevertheless, proposed the creation of a mixed committee, for conducting an estimate, and suggested that the payment be made in oil. The companies rejected this proposal, since from the beginning they had refused to recognize the legality of the expropriation. They declared themselves victims of a denial of justice. Washington suggested the only solution was for Mexico to return their property, a proposal rejected by Cárdenas.

The affected companies unleashed, beginning in 1938, a ferocious international propaganda campaign against Mexico, proposing, at the same time, to close down international markets to PEMEX, drowning "Mexico in its own oil" and denying it access to production machinery needed to maintain the rhythm of production. PEMEX had a very difficult time surviving, but managed partially to defy the blockade by exchanging oil for machinery and other products with fascist countries between 1938 and 1939. When World War II was declared, these European markets disappeared, and Mexico was—from 1940 to 1976—a very minor oil exporter. The American and British governments helped to block exports, prohibiting their dependencies from buying them, and putting pressure on some private companies in their own countries and on certain Latin American countries not to import Mexican oil. Internal demand, however, was increasing fast, and PEMEX basically devoted itself to meeting it. The oil industry ceased to be an enclave.

Furthermore, the Treasury Department stopped purchasing the large amounts of silver that it used to buy. Washington resorted to diplomatic and economic pressure to force Mexico to back down, but it abstained from using military force. At that time, the United States tried to get Latin America to accept and support the Good Neighbor Policy, proposed by President Franklin D. Roosevelt, to solidify a great inter-American alliance against fascism. Behind this policy loomed the menace of the Second World War, which, when it started in 1939, made the need for cooperation more evident. Given the international context, the U.S.'s national interest demanded the respect for Mexican sovereignty even if it meant sacrificing the interests of some powerful oil companies.

In 1940, Cárdenas finally reached an indemnification agreement with one of the companies, Sinclair, which, after difficult negotiations, recognized the Mexican right to expropriation in exchange for a substantial indemnity (between $13 million and $14 million) that would be paid partly in money, partly in oil. There were also informal negotiations with other companies, but Standard Oil—which was the most important and the company that spoke for the others—systematically blocked any arrangement that did not agree with its own terms. The agreement with

Sinclair allowed Mexico to maintain vis-à-vis the American government that it was possible to reach a fair, direct agreement with the companies, and, if that did not happen, it was less the fault of Mexico than of the intransigence of Standard Oil and the companies that negotiated under its wing.

At the end of the Cárdenas regime, a definitive arrangement had not been reached with most of the affected companies, but it was clear that these companies would not return to Mexico. The opinion of ruling circles in the country was that Mexican oil had to be controlled exclusively by Mexico.

The Conservative Succession

The high point of the Cárdenas regime was the expropriation of the major oil companies in March 1938. From that moment on, there were a number of factors that produced a crisis, reflected in, among other things, the decrease of land distribution and workers' organizations: the boycott decreed by oil interests, the political and economic pressures exerted by their governments, and the attacks of the right wing on the "revolutionary family."

The "veteran" politicians who had been somewhat marginalized after Cárdenas's triumph started to fight for their own interests. Within the official party itself and other government organizations there surged currents that were adverse to the presidential action. The new crisis within the "revolutionary family" became manifest inside the PRM as an explosion of "futurism" (i.e., a premature fever for presidential succession). From 1937 on, the mobilization of certain groups in favor of potential candidates had started. Political circles in 1938 bandied about the names of Gen. Francisco J. Múgica (of the most radical wing of Cardenism), Rafael Sánchez Tapia, Manuel Avila Camacho, and Juan Andrew Almazán. Outside the official party, groups were organized openly to support anti-Cárdenas candidates: Gen. Manuel Pérez Treviño tried to organize an anticommunist Mexican Revolutionary party, Gen. Ramón F. Iturbe put himself under the wing of the Mexican Democratic party, and, Gen. Francisco Coss, under the National Party of Public Salvation. From a more civilian but equally conservative perspective, the National Action party (PAN) was created, the only party of the new batch that would have a lasting and stable life. It was headed by a distinguished lawyer, Manuel Gómez Morín.

Late in 1938, two years before the end of the Cárdenas term, two secretaries resigned, Gen. Francisco Múgica and Gen. Manuel Avila Camacho, in order to work for their respective candidacies. For the same purpose, General Sánchez Tapia resigned his post as commander of the First Military Zone. Almazán's supporters also mobilized, and the PRM entered into a crisis. Luis T. Rodríguez, president of the party and unconditional supporter of Cárdenas, was openly attacked by the supporters of Sánchez Tapia and Múgica and was forced to resign at the end of 1939. His replacement was a distinguished revolutionary and assemblyman, the general from Veracruz Heriberto Jara; nevertheless, the internal crisis of the PRM could not be completely resolved. In July 1939, Almazán left the army and entered fully into the battle for presidential succession. Cárdenas had to make a definitive decision, and in November 1939 the PRM announced that its candidate for 1940–1946 would be Secretary of War Manuel Avila Camacho and not Francisco J. Múgica, who had seemed the natural successor to the Cardenista reform movement. Conditions at the time demanded a truce and a moderate consolidation of what had been achieved, and not a new radical wave. Inside the major grass-roots organizations of the party there were demonstrations of discontent. But Lombardo managed to control the CTM, Graciano Sánchez the CTM, and the president himself the army and the bureaucracy. This did not prevent numerous groups of workers, army officers, peasants, and white-collar workers from supporting Almazán. Múgica was supported by some peasant leagues and groups of workers and bureaucrats, but finally accepted the party's discipline and withdrew from the struggle. Almazán and Sánchez Tapia, however, when they saw the path closed off in their own party, decided to form new parties.

The Dispute and the Ebb Tide

Political passions were unleashed across the whole country. Of all the groups opposing Cárdenas and his candidate, the most effective and dangerous was the group headed by General Almazán. Although he was to the right of the official position, his political clientele was not reduced to the most conservative and bourgeois elements. He also counted on the support of laborers, peasants, military men, and white-collar workers, organized around the National Unification Revolutionary party (PRUN), which immediately started to create clubs throughout the country. The PRUN soon became the head of a movement with enough support to become a serious challenge to the PRM.

Almazán started his campaign in mid-1939 with a motto that was ambiguous enough to be acceptable to very varied groups: "Work, cooperation, and respect for the law." The tone was maintained throughout the campaign. Avila Camacho started his campaign in April, stating that he would advance the march of revolution. In fact, the speeches of both candidates reflected the search for a middle ground, a clear indication that the Cárdenas utopia and its radical vein were not going to be continued, either in practice or in purpose, in future years.

In spite of this shared search for moderation, the presidential campaign of 1939–1940 was far from orderly and calm. The clashes between the followers of Almazán and Avila were frequent, especially after January 1940, and the number of people killed and wounded for political reasons started to grow, climaxing on July 7, election day. On that day, there were shoot-outs, rock-throwing battles, and assaults on voting booths. Both the police and the army had to break up many clashes between rival political groups. Finally, in spite of the protests of Almazán's followers, Avila Camacho was declared the victor.

General Almazán left Mexico. His partisans insisted that he had been cheated out of his victory by fraudulent means and threatened with rebellion. There were, in fact, armed uprisings in the North, but federal forces could control them. Calm became more widespread when Almazán returned to Mexico in November and declared that he conceded and that he was withdrawing from politics. Many of his followers felt betrayed, but they could do nothing to stop the political disappearance of their leader. His withdrawal from active politics and his taking refuge in angry and nostalgic reminiscing closed a critical chapter of the history of contemporary Mexico, a chapter that is still awaiting a good historian to tell the true story of those elections, the most disputed and conflictive elections of revolutionary Mexico.

The 1938 expropriation was one of the brightest spots of the Mexican Revolution and of Cardenismo, but it had a high cost. After the expropriation, and due to economic pressures by foreign elements, there was a political and economic crisis of such magnitude that the program of reforms had to go more slowly and, in certain aspects, it stopped altogether. Cárdenas had to reach compromises with sectors of his own party that demanded an end to radicalism.

When Cárdenas handed the presidency over to Avila Camacho, the ruling party kept maintaining that class struggle was the engine of historical development, and that the ultimate goal of revolution was to build a society in which all means of production were under the direct control of the workers. The *ejido*, the cooperatives, and state property had to be the economic and social cores of the new Mexico. Opposing forces, however, were on the rise inside and outside the country, and by the end of 1940 the Cardenista plan was clearly on the defensive.

When General Avila Camacho assumed the presidency, it was clear to many people that the construction of a "Mexican socialism" had ended. The idea that with the end of the Cárdenas administration the Revolution had ended gained acceptance with the passing of years.

5.
The Mexican Miracle: 1940–1968

The Revolution as a Legacy

The Revolution ceased to be a real force after Avila Camacho's term (1940–1946), but its historical prestige and the aura of the profound transformations it produced continued to lend legitimacy to Mexican governments in the second half of the twentieth century. After Cárdenas, the mythological and real brightness of the recent past allowed the status quo, although full of failures and injustice, to be presented to the country as a passing phenomenon, since the true Mexico was the one that had not yet appeared and was to be conquered in the future. This was an ideological leap of crucial importance, and its history is the history of a revolutionary fact transformed into a continuous present and a future that was just a promise.

The belief that the Mexican Revolution was only the culmination of the great nineteenth century movements—independence and reform—is common to all Mexican leaders, starting with Venustiano Carranza. The way this belief was assumed by the revolutionary governments changed remarkably. It ended by transforming the Mexican state not only into the heir and guardian of that history, but into its patriotic vanguard.

The Mexican Revolution and the constitution of 1917 gradually lost their condition of historical facts to become, as all the history of the country had become, a "legacy," that is, an accumulation of wisdom and achievements that guaranteed the revolutionary rightness of the present.

Until Cárdenas, the history necessary to legitimize revolutionary governments started with the insurrection of 1910. After 1940, official language started to reflect the government's certainty of being the true, and uninterrupted, heir to a former history, the history that started with independence.

President Alvaro Obregón (1921–1924) paid little attention to the events of the recent revolutionary past—his desire was that this past be seen as a fait accompli—for the opposite reason that would lead future presidents (Adolfo Ruiz Cortines, 1952–1958; Adolfo López Mateos,

1958–1964; and Gustavo Díaz Ordaz, 1964–1968) to dwell on it excessively and to make it include the wars for independence. Obregón did not
doubt his legitimacy; he did not question the validity of his regime's
origin, because nobody questioned the obvious tie between his government and the Revolution. It was a clear case of a "good revolutionary
conscience." Thus, he could unblushingly speak of his "good faith" as a
source of everything that his government did, including its mistakes:
"The mistakes that are committed have no importance, because there
will always be time to correct them. They will always be committed in
good faith, and there is no problem in recognizing a mistake."

For Obregón, the "revolution" was the naked armed rebellion; his
government did not "embody" it, but simply succeeded it in a legitimate
fashion. With Calles, there is a change. The historian Guillermo Palacios
summarizes the process:

> During the Calles period, the popularity of the Revolution was not,
> as before, due to its origins or incidental components but to its
> *future* . . . Calles was not concerned, as the former president was,
> with the obvious contrast between the revolutionary movement
> and the resulting government. It is important to keep this in mind
> to understand his concept of "Revolution." Revolution, viewed like
> this, is what would permit continuity, and would grant successive
> governments the assurance of revolutionary development . . . The
> concept of Revolution as consisting of successive stages liberates it
> from its dependence on the period of armed struggle. This armed
> struggle would be considered as just one moment of the process,
> "the simplest and easiest moment" (Calles, in his last Report to the
> Nation) . . . To our days, Revolution continues to be so conceived in
> the abundant presidential and official propaganda: "The Revolution
> is generous and dignifying, and it is always on the march." . . .
> Calles wants the concept of Revolution to go into the past, and
> from it to reaffirm its advances, assure itself that it is on the right
> road, and glory in its achievements . . . The future, thus, represents
> the real stage on which the Revolution was to be fulfilled, because
> until then, in Calles' words, it would be limited to mere "essays of
> realism and socialization." The future will be the time for revolu-
> tionary consolidation, and not as fragmentary political ideas, but as
> the thought by antonomasia.

An Eternal Future

If Calles discovered the future of the Revolution, Cárdenas somehow
imposed its character of perpetuity. To the concept of continuity and

successive stages, he added that of "endless tasks," always renewed by history, which the Revolution would in each instance give an adequate solution. Looking backward, Cárdenas identified certain "stages" in the Revolution as *history*, which is connected to the present, but not simultaneous with it. A revolutionary tradition was thus established, with a progressive present and a future of continuous and ceaseless renovation. Cárdenas said: "Some had the duty of initiating the armed struggle and establishing the fundamental bases of our future. Others had to put into action the new doctrines, organizing the factors that could lead to triumph. We have to solve those problems that affect the process of our social life, and perfect our institutional regime." The Revolution completed, in this view, the integration of the nation adding economic emancipation to political independence (wars for independence) and ideological consolidation (reform, and the 1857 constitution).

The fervent concept of the nation as modern depository of an uninterrupted historical legacy, started, perhaps, with Avila Camacho. To the unsatisfied and polemical spirit of the initial Cardenismo, he contrasted the notion of a recent history full of achievement. In his inaugural speech, he stated that, for the unprejudiced mind,

the Mexican Revolution has been a social movement, guided by historical justice, which has been able to satisfy, one by one, all essential popular demands. . . . Each new era demands a renovation of ideals. The clamor of the Republic demands now the material and spiritual consolidation of our social achievements, by means of a powerful and prosperous economy.

At the end of this speech, Avila Camacho benevolently reviewed the history of the nation, regarding it no longer as a struggle but as heritage, not as a source of social friction, but as a fraternal ground of concord: "I ask with all the strength of my spirit, of all patriotic Mexicans, of all the people, to keep united, banning all intolerance, all sterile hatred, in this constructive crusade of national fraternity and grandeur." The political ideal of national unity was the wineskin in which the idea of history and spiritual values of Mexico as a treasure to be joined to the struggles of the past, would age and ripen.

The Great Change of Direction

With this ideological baggage on their backs, the "governments of the Revolution" would gravitate, starting in the 1940s, toward a central decision to industrialize the country, by means of an import-substitution policy. This seriously displaced the traditional center of gravity, which had been the countryside, to the cities. The ranks of the proletariat, the bourgeoisie, and the middle class grew, and cities, which were their natural environment, expanded. The incipient Mexican bourgeoisie—industrialists, business people, and bankers—made their primacy firmer and eventually accepted foreign partners again. So much so that by the 1960s the Mexican industrial dependence on foreign capital and technology became, as in the Porfiriato, quite evident.

When industrialization started, in part as a reaction to the popular echo of Cardenismo, which ended in the division of the "revolutionary family," governments started to doubt the role of the state and the desirable degree of direct governmental intervention in the productive process. At the beginning, this intervention was justified as being just a series of exceptional and/or temporary actions. Later on, the policy that would rule relations between the state and the private sector for several decades was developed: The duty of the state was to create and maintain the economic infrastructure; it should intervene the least in the area of direct production for the market, and engage only in those activities in which private enterprises were disinterested, fearful, or unable to maintain an adequate presence. Little by little, in spite of the protests of entrepreneurs, governmental practice and private deficiencies resulted in what was called "a mixed economy," in a persistent state of conflict, and constant negotiations between the entrepreneurial state and the domestic bourgeoisie, increasingly more consolidated. Starting in 1940, the investment ratio has averaged one-third of government investment and two-thirds of private investment.

This compromise was extremely effective, and observers and analysts started to talk unblushingly about "the Mexican miracle." Between 1940 and 1960, production increased 3.2 times, and between 1960 and 1978, 2.7 times. Those years recorded an average annual growth of 6 percent. This meant that the Mexican economy had produced a real value equivalent to 8.7 times the production of 1940, whereas population had increased only 3.4 times.

The economy not only had changed but had suffered a structural change. In 1940, agriculture represented around 10 percent of the national production; in 1977, only 5 percent. Manufacturing, on the other hand, increased from a little less than 19 percent to more than 23 percent. Other changes that were decisive, although not of a strictly economic character, were demographic: population increased from 19.6 million in 1940 to 67 million in 1977, and more than 70 million in 1980; in 1940, only 20 percent of the population lived in urban centers, and in 1977, almost 50 percent. Together with the industrialization process, the country experienced in forty years a spectacular change in its levels of urbanization and demographic growth.

The Immobile Zone

In contrast with these dramatic changes in the demography and economy of Mexico, some of the features of the political system inherited from Cardenismo were relatively unchanged. The political structures that the Revolution had created and perfected from Carranza to Cárdenas remained vigorous, with a few secondary changes.

In this system, the presidency was definitively the main piece. Neither the Congress nor the judiciary recuperated the ground they had lost up to 1940, and the autonomy of the states was as weak as before. No president promoted the disappearance of so many states' powers as Cárdenas, but all his successors acted against local governments when they fell from grace with the central government. Furthermore, with economic development, federal resources became so important that any regional or state project, in order to be carried out, depended on the decisions made in Mexico City.

The corporative official party also ratified its monolithic control, without adversaries that could challenge it. It kept in its hands all governorships and senatorial positions. The opposition was admitted only in the Chamber of Deputies, as a token minority that legitimized democratic forms without really having the ability to influence the behavior of Congress.

In December 1940, just after the administration of Avila Camacho had started, the military sector of the PRM definitively disappeared. It was a symbolic proof of the professionalism reached by the revolutionary army and of its institutional subordination to the president. This trend became a permanent political feature beginning in 1946, when Miguel Alemán (1946–1952), the first civilian postrevolutionary president, was elected. He initiated a long, uninterrupted list of nonmilitary presidents.

The PRM, as such, ended in 1946, but its transformation, like the preceding transformation, was painless and orderly. It abandoned its name and the programs that connected it to the Cardenista period, to become the present-day Institutional Revolutionary party (PRI), with interesting changes in its bylaws and platform, but very few changes in its real structure.

Economic capitalist growth based on the virtual immobility of a political system with strong authoritarian features resulted in a social structure that was very different from the one envisioned by a revolutionary government committed to social justice. Mexico joined the

Allied powers in World War II, and its remarkable economic growth produced a distributive scheme in which labor lost ground to management. The percentage of income available to the poorer half of families, in 1950, was 19 percent; in 1957, 16 percent; in 1963, 15 percent, and in 1975, only 13 percent of the total. As a contrast, the top 20 percent in 1950 received 60 percent of available income; in 1958, 61 percent; in 1963, 59 percent; and, in 1975, a little over 62 percent: a concentration of income that is very high, if we compare it to the figures for other Latin American countries, which do not distinguish themselves for fairness in the distribution of income and which have not had a revolution.

After Cárdenas, economic policy was based on the questionable idea, which came from the time of Obregón, that it was necessary to first create wealth to be able later to distribute it. Actually, there was much support for the first stage of this process and very little for the second, although in theory it was kept as a true and legitimate goal of the "revolutionary governments."

The Postwar Ally

Between 1910 and 1940, Mexico's role in the world was to clash profoundly and constantly with the great industrial powers, especially the United States and Great Britain. It was an unequal fight, and its results seemed to be the achievement of a greater independence by means of the constitution of 1917 and the destruction of the "enclave economy" through the oil expropriation of 1938.

When Mexico entered the war, however, its international situation changed drastically. Suddenly, the country found itself the ally of the country that until recently seemed to be the greatest threat to its sovereignty, and even its existence. The war created an exceptional atmosphere in which many of the problems between the two countries, such as the way to pay claims and the oil debt, could be speedily and definitively solved. The American government helped Mexico get its first international loans since the fall of Victoriano Huerta, to promote the production of raw materials required by the American war economy. To reciprocate, the Mexican government signed agreements concerning commerce, migrant farm workers, and military cooperation, although its participation in the war effort was mainly economic. Raw materials were sold to the United States at lower prices than to the free market, in exchange for which the Mexican government accumulated large reserves of dollars, which could not be easily used, since imports from the United States were rationed. Thousands of migrant workers worked on American farms, 15,000 joined the American army, and 1,492 lost their lives on the Pacific, European, and North African fronts.

When the war ended, Mexico found itself incorporated into the American area of influence. The possibility of European countries' acting as a counterweight to this influence had disappeared. The European presence in Mexico had been undermined by the nationalistic policies of the Revolution, and its international strength had seen itself weakened by the war. Furthermore, the project of industrialization that had started in Mexico during the war channeled Mexican trade even more toward the United States. Most of the raw material exports went there, and from there came most of the capital goods required by the industrial import-substitution process. Since then, between 60 percent and 70 percent of international trade by Mexico has had the United States as a source or as a destination.

To close the cycle of this decisive postwar transformation, a good part of the capital and technology demanded by the Mexican process of industrialization also came from the United States. Foreign direct investment in 1940 hardly reached $450 million; by 1960, it surpassed a billion dollars; by the mid-1970s, it reached the $4.5 billion figure, and in the 1980s it surpassed the $10 billion mark. The institutional appeasement of the Revolution facilitated this penetration by American influence in the economic, political, and cultural spheres.

In spite of the great dependence on the United States after the Second World War, Mexican foreign policy preserved a relative independence, especially with regard to hemispheric policies. Mexico did not welcome the overthrow of Jacobo Arbenz of Guatemala in 1954, did not support American aggression against Cuba starting in 1960, or the intervention in the Dominican Republic in 1965. In these and similar situations, Mexico defended the principle of nonintervention, rejected a permanent military alliance with the United States, and followed a road that was different from the other Latin American nations, but without ever reaching the direct confrontation that was typical of the revolutionary years.

From Enthusiasm to Repression

The difficult combination of economic growth and political stability that Mexico achieved after 1940 inclined many observers, in the 1960s, to present Mexico as a model to be followed by other developing countries. This enthusiasm cooled down with the political crisis of 1968, in which large groups of students challenged the legitimacy of the system and proved, by the bloody repression they suffered, that it had an authoritarian core. In a parallel fashion, from the beginning of the 1960s there were worrisome symptoms indicating that the import-substitution model of industrialization was not working well. In those years, it was necessary to admit with regret that the industrial plant that had been built with so much effort was unable to survive without strong tariff protection, was not competitive in the market abroad, and could not grow at the pace demanded by the balance-of-payments deficit and the population growth. Agriculture also showed symptoms of stagnation, its productivity decreased, it became unable to satisfy the domestic food demand and to be a dynamic factor in international trade. Products that were exported before began to be imported, and the surplus turned into a deficit. A protracted economic crisis in international economy at the beginning of the 1970s topped the already difficult economic landscape and made clearer that the favorable conditions of the until-then "stabilizing development" had eroded and that a new model was necessary.

During the presidency of Luis Echeverría (1970–1976), the highest authorities publicly expressed their doubts on the viability of the Mexican development model as it had been applied until then. Changes were demanded for an alternative way of achieving a "shared development" that would create a more just society and a more efficient economic system. President Echeverría and his secretaries finished their term without having shaped this alternative course, in the midst of a climate of economic and political distrust. Much of the immediate past had been questioned, but the new way was not clearly delineated. However, the increase in international oil prices and the important findings of new fields in Southeast Mexico in the mid-1970s prevented the propagation of the politico-economic crisis of 1976, and permitted a breathing space for searching out new strategies.

The José López Portillo presidential term (1976–1982) would prove that even the most favorable conditions in the oil market could not solve the structural problem of the disintegrated and obsolete industrial plant of the country. After four years of unprecedented increases in the income from oil exports, the country relapsed, beginning in 1981, into a deep crisis of its finances and production, caused by the drop in international oil prices and the profound imbalances in taxes, production, trade, and foreign debt.

A Final Good-bye

Few observers foresaw the great impact that WWII was to have on the Mexican economy. Cardenismo outlined its great plans under the influence of the agrarian image that had been the historical core of the country for centuries. Foreign analysts who had closely observed Mexican evolution after the Revolution, such as Frank Tannenbaum, simply thought that the necessary elements for a jump to industrialization did not exist in Mexico. According to Tannenbaum, after the euphoria of the

1940s, Mexico would return to its social roots in the countryside and to primary activities, eschewing an industry grounded on false bases. But Mexico did not return to its agricultural roots, and the change in its production patterns that had taken place in the 1940s was lasting.

The unstoppable industrializing project coincided with the Second World War, but, in great measure, investments on which it was based were already there. From 1942 on, exports of raw materials grew noticeably and Mexico obtained the necessary hard currency to import the equipment that its factories started to need. Unfortunately, the sources of machinery—the United States and Europe—were absorbed by the war effort, and could not supply what Mexico needed and could buy at that time. The industrialization impulse was unleashed only after the war, under Alemán (1946–1952). In 1939, manufacturing represented 16.9 percent of total production; in 1946, it went up to 19.4 percent, and by 1950, 20.5 percent. By then, the goal of both the official sector and the large private companies was to build the industrial society promised in the postwar period as the only way to escape underdevelopment and magnify the possibilities of independent action by the country.

For Cardenismo, the dominant preoccupation had been to establish the bases of a more just society, a society consistent with the Revolution. For the young group of civilians that came to power with President Alemán, the obsession was first to create wealth by means of industrial substitution of traditional imports, and then distribute it according to the demands of social justice. Nobody set a date for this second stage, and public and private leaders of the country seemed interested only in the first stage: to accumulate capital. Figures show their singular enthusiasm.

Between 1940 and 1945, the industrial sector grew at an annual average of 10.2 percent. After the war, the rate diminished to an annual 5.9 percent during the following five years, but, after a period of readjustment, the rate increased, and the average of the 1950s was 7.3 percent. During the war, Mexican industry, taking advantage of the vacuum left by the great powers, started to export textiles, chemicals, food, and the like. With their return to international normalcy, many foreign markets were lost because of the lack of competitiveness, and new manufactures were produced mainly for the domestic market, where tariffs limited foreign competition. Protectionism allowed these new industries to affirm themselves and even expand, but without forcing them to be efficient. In the long run, this laxness made the Mexican economy turn to itself, and prevented Mexican production from going beyond its borders, a situation that hindered the growth of a truly modern and independent industrialization.

The new Mexican industrial plant, created without benefit of any planning, required substantial imports of capital goods. However, since it did not export at the same rate, hard currency to finance them had to come from traditional agricultural and mining exports, money sent by emigrants, increase in tourism, and the inflow of foreign capital that came to share in the boom. Many foreign companies that before had to export their products to Mexico deemed it convenient to accept the government policy and establish assembly and production plants in Mexico, to avoid protectionist tariffs and not to lose their market, but almost never to export. Thus, direct foreign investment grew from $450 million in 1940 to $729 million by the end of the Alemán presidential term.

The emphasis on industrialization brought new and necessary investment in infrastructure—communications and energy—and in agriculture, the main source of exports that would finance the economic strategy. During the Alemán regime, large investments were made in irrigation and roads, which absorbed 22 percent of the federal budget. But in this instance, the developed lands were not mainly *ejidales*, but private, and this was justified in the name of efficiency.

The Stabilizing Development

By the end of Cárdenas's regime, inflation eroded the Mexican economy, worsening the unequal distribution of income and preventing the crucial expansion of exports. A consequence of this process was the 1948 devaluation in which the rate of exchange was allowed to float and went up from 5.85 pesos to the dollar to 6.80 and, the following year, 8.64. After a short boom in exports due to this devaluation and the Korean War, the problem of trade deficit reappeared, and, in 1954, a new devaluation was necessary that established the rate of 12.50 pesos to the dollar. At that time, as a reaction, the strategy of having a "stabilizing development" began, the main objective being to avoid new devaluations by putting a stop to the accelerated rise in prices and salaries. During the Ruiz Cortines regime, this strategy stopped the inflationary spiral. This spiral distorted the structure of exports and harmed wage-earners, provoking strikes, more or less violent clashes with the government, and a weakened control of official trade unionism, without which the kind of industrialization induced by the state would have been politically impossible to handle.

The immediate effect of the April 1954 devaluation was to exacerbate inflation even more, but, thanks to the political discipline imposed by their leaders and the government on the labor movement, and an improved balance of payments, the desired stability in exchange rates, salaries, and prices started to take form. In the following ten years, the wholesale price index rose by only 50 percent. The "stabilizing development" model was effective until 1973, when the convergence of a domestic and an international crisis put an end to it. The Mexican economy felt again the unpleasant effects of inflation and an increasing deficit in the trade balance. The era of devaluations returned in 1976, and the earnest search for an alternative model started. The discovery of vast oil fields in the Southeast in the mid-1970s provided a temporary solution to the country's economic problems: to become again an exporter of oil.

In spite of the differences in form between the stabilizing development model and the stage started in 1973, the basic tenets of Alemán's economics remained in force: to continue with import substitution, maintain tariff protectionist barriers, and revitalize investments in irrigation, railways, and energy. But, in fact, these measures had lost their effect. By the 1960s, the government had to revise its wage policies and admit the need to strengthen the purchasing power of majority groups. Voices were raised in alarm on the need to review industrial strategies decisively, because everything indicated that the relatively easy stage of substitution replacement was coming to an end. Those who saw clouds on the horizon thought that it was necessary to promote the substitution of capital goods, and this demanded substantial investment and larger markets. The solution would be to increase equally the domestic market and exports of manufactures (i.e., to start competing with the great industrial powers), by means of production that would make use of the most abundant Mexican resource: human labor. Mexico, then, decided to associate itself with the other Latin American countries in order to create a great regional market. This market would maintain protectionist measures vis-à-vis the rest of the world, but would be more relaxed within Latin America, in order to foster large-scale economies. The Latin American Association of Free Trade (ALALC) was created, but from the beginning it was hindered by fears of hegemony of Brazil, Argentina, and Mexico over the rest of the countries in the region. The pioneers in industrial development were not very willing to accept regional materials, because they doubted their quality and prices. Ultimately, this option was eliminated for Mexico, at least for the time being.

After the relative failure of ALALC, the Mexican government looked for markets in Europe, Asia, and Africa, but without much success. Without really planning it, the only solution seemed to be a greater participation of the state in the production process. The paragovernmental sector not only continued broadening the field of its basic activities and subsidizing private producers, but put more emphasis on the practice of assuming the control of failed companies and of creating enterprises in areas that private capital had previously neglected. For this reason, when the 1970s started, the paragovernmental sector owned some eight hundred quite disparate companies, which ranged from Mexican Petroleum (PEMEX) and the Federal Electrical Commission (CFE) to a company that made bicycles. In 1970, 35 percent of gross fixed investment corresponded to the public sector, and in 1976—a year in which the private sector limited noticeably its investments—it surpassed 40 percent. The rate of economic growth increasingly depended on the action and decisions of the public sector.

During the 1970s, the contribution of manufacturing industries to the country's production was about 23 percent. Commercial activity had a larger percentage. If we add allied activities, such as oil and electricity production, industrial participation slightly surpasses commercial activity, and it is three times larger than traditional activities (agriculture, cattle, forests, and mining). Between 1940 and 1977, the manufacturing industry proper grew 7.4 percent annually, which is higher than the total production growth, of 5.9 percent.

Fissures and Chasms

Although global growth figures seem to indicate that post-Cárdenas economic planning had been successful, some facts seem to indicate the opposite. A good part of the investment in the most modern sector of manufacturing was of foreign origin. Of the 101 most important industrial companies in 1972, 57 had foreign capital participation. Of the $2,822 million of direct foreign investment, $2,083 million were in the manufacturing industry. From 1973 on, when the Mexican economy entered a crisis, there was an effort to substitute public expenses for the decrease in private investment. But most of these resources came from foreign loans, and, therefore, although direct foreign investment lost relative importance, indirect foreign investment (i.e., foreign debt) grew. By 1971, the foreign debt of the public sector was substantial: $4,543.8 million, which would be four times larger five years later: $19,600.2 million. The government could face the increasing trade deficit and the necessary investment to maintain the rate of economic growth by means of loans from international institutions and private foreign banks. This strategy could not last indefinitely, especially if one considers that the current-account deficit of 1971 ($726.4 million) had become $3,044.3 million five years later in 1976. That year finished with a drastic devaluation (50 percent) and the floating of the peso.

By the end of the Echeverría presidency, "stabilizing development" was history, economic growth had stopped, and national and international public opinion started to question the health and viability of the Mexican economy. People quit talking about the "economic miracle," and international financing organizations acted consequently. The International Monetary Fund (IMF) imposed conditions on the handling of the Mexican economy to give its guarantee vis-à-vis international credit markets. These measures included an end to budgetary deficits and to foreign indebtedness.

The indebtedness incurred in the 1970s cannot be explained only by the lack of dynamism of the private sector and the increasing role of the public sector as the engine of the economy. What happened is that the government could not or would not carry out a thorough tax reform, and found it easier to borrow from foreign sources to administer and promote an economic growth based on an industry that was not competitive. This industry, furthermore, demanded imported materials but did not generate the hard currency necessary to import them. In a parallel fashion, the systematic decrease in agricultural growth that started in the mid-1970s not only prevented traditional exports but forced the country to spend more dollars each time to import grains and other staples for satisfying the domestic demand. Mexico started to lose the relative self-sufficiency that it had achieved in the period of the "economic miracle."

The good news about oil—the confirmation of the existence of large additional reserves—began to improve the economic picture starting in 1977. With the change of government, and the possibility of tapping an enormous hydrocarbon source in the Mexican subsoil, the confidence of investors and the general public in the economy improved. In a very short time, oil became the basis of new and ambitious plans for industrial and agricultural growth, with a projected global growth of 8 percent annually. The increase in proved oil reserves was remarkable: from 3.6 billion barrels in 1973, they jumped to 16 billion in 1977, more than 40 billion in early 1979, and 72 billion in 1981, which placed Mexico in sixth place among countries with oil potential. The lucky coincidence of an unprecedented increase in oil prices led the government of José López Portillo (1976–1982) rapidly to increase the production of PEMEX so it could export about 1.25 million barrels of crude oil in 1982, devoting approximately the same amount to internal consumption at prices below world markets.

The economic emergency of 1976 was thus solved, but the real problem still had to be dealt with: in spite of its relative industrialization, Mexico continued to be an exporter of raw materials, vulnerable to external forces, and unable to compete in the international industrial markets. It was hoped that with oil and with the passage of time, this problem would be solved in an easy, painless way, in what could become a second "economic miracle." Actually, the problem became more acute, because tariff protectionist barriers in industrial nations, far from disappearing, became stronger.

Table 4. Gross Domestic Product by Category
(in millions of pesos at 1960 prices)

Period	GDP	Agri-culture	Cattle	For-estry	Fishing	Mining	Crude Oil	Refining Indus-tries
1939	46,058	5,223	3,641	609	49	1,767	1,317	n/a
1940	46,693	4,672	3,703	626	56	1,736	1,253	n/a
1941	51,241	5,707	3,942	644	46	1,694	1,283	n/a
1942	54,116	6,433	3,968	828	62	1,939	1,189	n/a
1943	56,120	5,852	4,036	848	79	1,982	1,234	n/a
1944	60,701	6,423	4,051	836	87	1,722	1,246	n/a
1945	62,608	6,152	4,254	702	103	1,767	1,411	n/a
1946	66,722	6,220	4,566	803	110	1,363	1,581	n/a
1947	69,020	6,848	4,519	574	120	1,782	1,801	n/a
1948	71,864	7,393	4,934	579	151	1,645	1,966	n/a
1949	75,803	8,715	5,080	560	196	1,656	2,057	n/a
1950	83,304	9,673	5,194	913	188	1,739	2,467	n/a
1951	89,746	10,146	5,568	927	178	1,676	2,713	n/a
1952	93,315	9,702	5,767	726	149	1,861	2,861	n/a
1953	93,591	9,761	5,664	722	171	1,842	2,908	n/a
1954	102,924	12,202	5,935	785	191	1,734	3,128	n/a
1955	111,671	13,562	6,180	889	210	2,011	3,379	n/a
1956	119,306	12,779	6,452	886	249	2,032	3,600	n/a
1957	128,343	13,977	6,970	844	229	2,165	3,841	n/a
1958	135,169	15,189	7,297	781	264	2,154	4,287	n/a
1959	139,212	14,036	7,576	882	298	2,221	4,861	n/a
1960	150,511	14,790	7,966	882	332	2,306	5,089	39
1961	157,931	15,156	8,032	849	379	2,230	5,772	76
1962	165,310	16,187	7,913	871	368	2,429	6,080	160
1963	178,516	16,981	8,385	921	376	2,428	6,575	177
1964	199,390	18,738	8,643	921	367	2,482	7,168	251
1965	212,320	19,921	9,008	955	338	2,429	7,525	490
1966	227,037	20,214	9,202	948	376	2,498	7,898	604
1967	241,272	20,165	9,997	1,001	420	2,593	9,023	752
1968	260,901	20,489	10,671	1,024	374	2,651	9,798	1,005
1969	277,400	20,145	11,296	1,117	354	2,777	10,256	1,269
1970	296,600	21,140	11,848	1,149	398	2,859	11,295	1,380
1971	306,800	21,517	12,204	1,085	430	2,871	11,615	1,496
1972	329,100	20,955	12,832	1,173	445	2,865	12,532	1,750
1973	354,100	21,389	13,076	1,252	462	3,166	12,713	1,959
1974	375,000	22,019	13,297	1,332	467	3,626	14,524	2,319
1975	390,300	21,931	13,762	1,337	481	3,406	15,749	2,427
1976	396,800	20,352	14,202	1,395	510	3,474	17,462	2,642
1977	409,500	20,840	14,642	1,439	527	3,504	20,740	2,558

n/a: Not available.
Source: Banco de México, S.A., *Información económica. Producto interno*

Manu-facturers	Con-struction	Electri-city	Trade	Commun. & Transp.	Govern-ment	Other Serv.	Bank Serv. Adjust.
6,752	963	345	14,281	1,135	3,280	6,696	n/a
7,193	1,169	354	14,439	1,187	3,348	6,957	n/a
7,848	1,208	353	16,490	1,277	3,382	7,367	n/a
8,461	1,287	367	17,121	1,405	3,370	7,686	n/a
8,945	1,369	383	17,937	1,601	3,724	8,130	n/a
9,643	1,656	385	19,988	1,713	4,399	8,552	n/a
9,985	2,153	430	20,383	1,822	4,530	8,916	n/a
10,925	2,571	464	22,881	2,030	3,734	9,474	n/a
11,096	2,622	503	22,855	2,199	4,274	9,827	n/a
11,794	2,540	555	22,986	2,371	4,559	10,191	n/a
12,649	2,571	606	23,880	2,570	4,491	10,772	n/a
14,244	3,028	619	26,300	2,728	4,825	11,387	n/a
15,746	3,315	688	28,831	2,993	5,135	11,830	n/a
16,440	3,736	748	29,722	3,302	5,468	12,833	n/a
16,266	3,449	798	30,378	3,402	5,564	12,646	n/a
17,855	3,712	880	32,207	3,652	5,823	14,840	n/a
19,589	4,133	981	34,832	3,917	5,964	16,024	n/a
21,813	4,774	1,095	37,082	4,337	6,311	17,896	n/a
23,229	5,397	1,182	39,895	4,531	6,763	19,320	n/a
24,472	5,214	1,272	41,958	4,671	6,844	20,766	n/a
26,667	5,330	1,368	43,083	4,816	7,051	21,023	n/a
28,892	6,105	1,502	46,880	4,996	7,399	24,852	1,519
30,483	6,074	1,609	49,638	5,154	7,942	26,122	1,585
31,890	6,471	1,753	51,344	5,393	8,956	27,154	1,659
34,826	7,411	2,170	55,769	5,844	10,053	28,449	1,849
40,887	8,663	2,529	63,254	6,257	11,102	30,336	2,208
44,761	8,534	2,769	67,368	6,443	11,834	32,229	2,284
48,990	9,762	3,157	72,385	6,920	12,749	33,976	2,702
52,341	11,032	3,533	76,397	7,321	13,768	35,871	2,942
57,641	11,844	4,228	82,920	8,113	15,087	38,063	3,009
62,287	12,961	4,812	88,724	8,714	15,585	40,446	3,343
67,680	13,583	5,357	94,491	9,395	17,097	42,495	3,567
69,745	13,230	5,784	97,326	10,098	18,616	44,575	3,812
75,524	15,558	6,297	104,041	11,102	21,134	47,049	4,157
82,255	18,016	6,987	111,968	12,385	23,492	49,385	4,405
86,941	19,079	7,645	117,773	13,854	25,416	51,075	4,427
90,606	20,205	8,086	121,777	15,099	28,183	52,488	4,684
92,492	19,822	8,687	120,559	15,848	30,494	53,742	4,881
95,785	19,426	9,356	122,971	16,672	31,043	54,331	4,534

bruto y gasto, Cuaderno 1960–1977. Mexico City: Banco de México, 1978, p. 28.

By the end of the 1970s, it was clear that the average Mexican enjoyed a standard of living better than forty years before, but it was not possible to hide the fragile foundation of the economic system that permitted this new way of life: everything depended on oil's continuing to be an expensive commodity with large foreign markets. Unfortunately, until then, no oil-producing nation of the so-called underdeveloped world had succeeded in transforming oil into permanent wealth. In principle, official policy maintained that gas and oil exports should be moderate and never a substitute for the necessary reforms in the industrial, agricultural, and commercial economy. Between theory and practice, however, there was a great gap. Structural reforms were not produced—for lack of time and decision—and Mexico had to relive the cycle of imbalance, indebtedness, inflation, corruption, and depletion of resources that until then had characterized so many oil-producing countries.

Social Structure:
The More Things Change, the More They Remain the Same

Changes in social structure in the four decades after Cárdenas are unprecedented in the history of the country. In 1940, Mexico was a relatively underpopulated country with 19.6 million inhabitants. After independence (in the second decade of the nineteenth century), population had increased only threefold, but after 1940 the rate of increase became inconstant. If the country had increased threefold from 1820 to 1940 (i.e., in 120 years), it took it only 35 years to multiply by three the second time, because, by 1975, Mexico already had more than 60 million inhabitants, and, in the early 1980s, more than 70 million.

As in the past, this population was not evenly distributed. The vast spaces of the North remained as empty as before, as did the hot lands of the Pacific and the Southeast. But urban centers grew at a surprising rate. In 1940, only 7.9 percent lived in cities of over half a million inhabitants; 20 years later the percentage was 18.4 percent, in 1970 it was 23 percent, and the trend continues. In 1940, only 20 percent of the population lived in towns with more than 15,000 inhabitants. By 1970, the percentage was 45 percent, and, by 1978, 65 percent. In 1984, the metropolitan area of Mexico City became the most populated city in the world. Beginning in 1940, then, Mexico's population increased very fast—at a rate of 3 percent annually, one of the highest rates in the world—but quickly lost one of its traditional features: its peasant nature. The remarkable population growth in the last decades has been due in part to better health levels, with lower infant mortality and increased life expectancy levels. In 1940, average life expectancy was 41.5 years; in 1970, about 61 years; and, in 1980, 66 years.

The "age pyramid" inverted itself. Contemporary Mexico—in contrast with highly industrialized nations—is a country of young people. In 1940, 41.2 percent of the population was younger than 15; 30 years later, 46.2 percent. By the 1980s, the percentage decreased slowly: 42.4 in 1983. An economically active population had to support an increasing number of dependents. In 1940, 32.4 percent of the population performed some paid work; by 1970, the percentage had decreased to 26.9 percent. The need to create jobs for the waves of young people who enrolled yearly in the labor market (between 700,000 and 800,000 in the 1980s) became a problem whose solution could not wait.

Observing more closely the composition of this labor force, one can see that in 1940 six million Mexicans performed paid work compared to thirteen million in 1970. In 1940, 58.2 percent worked in farm-related jobs, and, in 1970, 41 percent. In 1980, 18 percent of the economically active population worked for industrial companies. Commerce, finances, construction, mining, and services absorbed the remaining 41 percent, but the productivity of many of these activities was very low. In reality, one of the most important economic concerns was how to offer adequate, productive work to an ever increasing and changing labor force.

According to certain estimates, in 1970, 5.8 million people were underemployed, equivalent to 3 million unemployed (i.e., 23 percent of the economically active population). This was a rate three or four times higher than that of industrialized nations. Unemployment became worse as the economy eroded prior to the 1976 crisis, but with the oil boom it improved remarkably, only to suffer a dramatic relapse in the 1982 crisis, which was structurally worse than the crisis of 1976. Unemployment was one of the most serious consequences of the economic model adopted after WWII. Along with underemployment, it proved to be a structural reality, inherent to the model that had been chosen, and not a passing phenomenon, as was claimed in the years of optimism about development. What was to be done?

For some, the solution was to promote a kind of industrialization different from that of industrialized nations: a combination of productive factors where labor would be more important than capital and thus use in an intensive way the most abundant Mexican resource, labor. But this was easier said than done since labor can substitute for capital only up to a point, and an opposite view started to win supporters: since it was not realistic to try always to find labor-intensive techniques (as shown by the examples of India and China) it was better to fully enter the stage of capital goods production, using for this purpose a large part of oil revenues. The creation of jobs along with an increase of food production were the two priorities of the federal government on the eve of the 1982 crisis. The generation of productive work had become one of the great economic and political challenges for the leaders of Mexico.

The Middle Class as a Bridge

Just before the 1910 Revolution, Andrés Molina Enríquez pointed out that one of the great national problems was the extraordinary concentration of wealth—especially wealth derived from land possession—in a few hands. For him, Mexico was a misshapen society: "Our social body is a disproportionate, malformed body: from the chest up, it is a giant's body, from the chest down it is a child's body." It was necessary, said Molina, to create a middle class to serve as a bridge between these two extremes. According to the estimate made in 1951 by José Iturriaga, 90.5 percent of the population during the Porfiriato belonged to the lower class, and the middle class represented barely 8 percent of the population.

Everything indicates that the Revolution, in fact, favored the growth of the middle class and that this was, precisely, one of its great achievements. By 1960, the middle class had doubled its 1910 numbers. According to Arturo González Cosío, 17 percent of Mexicans could be considered to be middle class in 1960. Some people believed this proved irrefutably that Mexico was slowly becoming a more just society.

Data on monthly family income reveal that, after the Revolution, income increased in absolute terms for all social groups. These data show increases in the middle class, but they also show that the income increase was not proportionally equal for all sectors, and that Mexico was not on the path to social justice, if by social justice we understand balance and equity in the distribution of national wealth. This unequal distribution was disturbing since the search for equality was one of the legitimizing goals of the political system.

According to the social philosophy of the national policy of governments from Miguel Alemán (1946–1952) on, the priority of creating wealth required first to have an initial concentration as a form of capitalization prior to the distribution of wealth. Table 5 shows us that by the end of the 1960s the process of concentration was in full vigor, and redistribution processes were nowhere to be seen. By 1975, the 5 percent of families with the largest incomes held the same ratio of national income as in 1950.

Furthermore, changes recorded in favor of the middle class were counterbalanced by a relative loss of the lower class. At the beginning of the 1980s, the social deformity described by Molina Enríquez had not disappeared, it had only transformed itself, in spite of the insistence by the government's pronouncements that it was necessary to diminish the gap between social extremes.

Bad income distribution was due in part to industrial, agricultural,

Table 5. Average Monthly Family Income, by Deciles, and Average Annual Increase Rate (1950, 1958, 1963, and 1969, at 1958 prices)

Deciles	Average Family Income				Annual Increase			
	1950	1958	1963	1969	1950–58	1958–63	1963–69	1950–69
I	258	297	315	367	1.8	1.2	2.6	1.9
II	325	375	356	367	1.8	-1.0	0.4	0.5
III	363	441	518	550	2.4	3.2	1.0	2.1
IV	421	516	598	641	2.5	3.0	1.2	2.2
V	460	608	738	825	3.6	3.9	2.6	3.1
VI	526	789	834	917	5.2	1.1	1.6	3.0
VII	669	842	056	1,283	2.9	4.6	3.3	3.5
VIII	823	1,147	1,592	1,650	4.2	6.7	0.6	3.7
IX	1,033	1,820	2,049	2,384	7.3	2.4	2.6	4.5
X	4,687	6,605	8,025	9,352	4.3	3.9	2.6	3.7
5 %	1,693	2,866	3,724	5,501	6.8	5.4	6.7	6.4
5 %	7,679	10,339	12,324	13,203	3.8	3.6	1.0	2.9
Total	975	1,339	1,608	1,834	4.2	3.8	2.2	3.5
GDP					6.3	5.1	7.6	6.3

Source: Wouter van Ginnekin, quoted in Cynthia Hewitt de Alcántara, "Ensayo sobre la satisfacción de necesidades básicas del pueblo mexicano entre 1940 y 1970," in *Cuadernos del CES*, no. 21, 1977, p. 30.

commercial, and financial concentration. According to the 1965 industrial census, 1.5 percent of the 136,000 registered concerns controlled 77.2 percent of capital and 75.2 percent of production. According to the agricultural census of 1960, 1 percent of the non-*ejido* properties controlled 74.3 percent of private landholding. The same year 0.6 percent of commercial concerns controlled 47 percent of capital and 50 percent of income from sales.

After the euphoria of the Alemán period, several analysts proposed that the government intervene in the distribution of the gross domestic product among the different classes, by means of taxes. The resulting tax reforms were insufficient. Expenses by the federal government and parastate concerns went up from 23 percent of the total in 1970 to 42 percent in 1976, but this impressive jump was financed by foreign debt and greater taxes of a general character and taxes aimed at the middle class, which affected high-income sectors very little. The determinate opposition of entrepreneurial circles and the most conservative elements of the government bureaucracy prevented the progressive taxation of capital gains. It would seem that the way to diminish social inequality in Mexico should include changes in the rules that control taxation to capital gains.

Permanence

In contrast to the great changes experienced by Mexico from 1940 on in the field of economy and class struggle, the characteristic feature of political life was one of *permanence*, although not immobility. The structures on which power was based were essentially the same as those left by Cardenismo, although with a deeper impact on society. Very few Mexicans nowadays can escape state conrol. Actively or passively, the great majority of Mexicans are affected by the actions of the government, and this is a trend that is increasingly stronger.

From 1940 on, the central elements of the political system were more distinctly defined, and on some occasions they were enlarged, but very few changed, the presidency of the republic remaining always the cohesive nucleus. Its faculties, both constitutional and beyond the constitution, were not limited or hindered by the other federal powers with which it supposedly shared power, or by informal power centers. Congress, the judiciary, secretaries, state governors, army, official party, main popular organizations, the quasi-governmental sector, and even private economic groups and organizations recognized and supported the role of the presidency and the president as the ultimate arbiter in the formation of political initiatives and the resolution of conflicts of interest in the increasingly complex Mexican society.

It is true that changes in the social and economic structure after 1940 favored the accelerated concentration of capital, and, therefore, the concentration of material resources in the hands of a few powerful groups of private entrepreneurs. But this economic power did not always become political power, although the tendency existed. Between 1940 and 1980, entrepreneurial groups increased their political power at a rate greater than other political forces. Although they have not achieved direct control over government, they *have* achieved veto power over the initiatives of the so-called political class headed by the president. However, the surprising nationalization of private banks in 1982 showed that vis-à-vis a determined action of the government, the veto of the business elite does not work. In normal situations, of course, it is common that economic initiatives of the government are modified by the concentrated pressure exerted by the highest representatives of the private sector. Some observers believe that by the end of the 1970s the state had lost ground to the other main forces of the nation, especially big capital. According to this position, business interest groups—such as the "Monterrey Group" or the "Televisa Group"—had become increasingly more powerful politically. In fact, one of the main concerns of the federal government in the second half of the 1970s was to use oil revenues to fortify the government and avoid the loss of its character as the leader of

Mexican economic development. The 1982 crisis and its sequels greatly weakened certain business sectors, which had to appeal to the protection of the state to face such basic problems as finding credit and backing for the renegotiation of public debt.

As to formal political structures, the official party changed its name in January 1946, ceasing to be the Party of the Mexican Revolution to become the contradictorily named Institutional Revolutionary party (PRI). This change did not affect its nature or its broad control over the political life of the country. The PRI, as before it the PNR and the PRM, did not lose the presidency, or a state governorship, or a seat in the Senate. The few members of the opposition who became members of the Federal Congress were members of the House of Representatives and were never in a position to question official party control over the legislative power. The few municipal governments controlled briefly by the opposition invariably returned to PRI control. In fact, partisan opposition, in spite of having its own life and strength, has been able to act only to the extent that it is permitted to do so by the group in power. It could not have had even the modest position it has in the electoral panorama if it had been openly rejected by those who exert power in contemporary Mexico. A traditional method of lessening tensions in the Mexican political system has been, precisely, not to close the doors to expressions of dissidence. This was especially true after the 1960s, when the explo-siveness of opposition, almost without institutional channels to express itself, shook the system with the railroad strikes of 1958, the student protest of 1968, and the armed urban and rural guerrillas of the 1970s.

The Silencing Machine

The analysis of the presidential campaigns and their results can give a good idea of the nature of opposition in the Mexican political system and the reaction of the government. In 1946, after the Avila Camacho regime, three opposition leaders competed with Miguel Alemán, the official candidate. Of the three, only one was somewhat important—Ezequiel Padilla—because he had recently been a prominent member of the political elite. On the strength of his performance as foreign secretary during WWII, Padilla thought that he had enough power to challenge the decision of the official party, that is, Avila Camacho's decision about the future president.

The Mexican Democratic party (PDM) that supported Padilla in 1946 did not present a real alternative to the PRI platform. It only emphasized that Padilla had forged the successful alliance with the United States during the war and that he proposed to strengthen the new pro-Western internationalism of Mexican foreign policy. This was his only distinctive contribution. Unfortunately for Padilla, his platform did not produce much enthusiasm in Mexico, and Americans did not find anything fundamentally negative in Alemán's candidacy. The official count was 77.9 percent for Alemán and only 19.33 percent for Padilla. The PDM immediately challenged the official victory as a product of fraud, but no meaningful political force supported this contention. In a short time, both the PDM and its candidate disappeared completely from the political panorama, without leaving any lasting trace.

In 1952, the phenomenon of "inside opposition" repeated itself, but this time with greater intensity. The PRI submitted the candidacy of the secretary of government, Adolfo Ruiz Cortines, and this decision by President Alemán disappointed the expectations of Gen. Miguel Henríquez Guzmán, a prominent member of the government, who thought he was entitled to the presidency because of his brilliant political and military record. The general's reaction to the presidential decision was to create his own party, the Federation of Popular Parties (FPP) to oppose the PRI monopoly.

What had happened to Padilla did not bother the followers of Henríquez, perhaps because they believed that a great part of the army and the Cardenista core supported him. Henríquez received the support of the Union of Peasant Federations, which had the slogan "Inviolability of the *ejido*, and respect to small landowners." No labor organization supported him, although his followers carried out a publicity campaign designed to appeal to the urban workers. The Henríquez opposition also counted on the always latent discontent of the middle class and the university students against the authoritarian character of the ruling party. Henríquez, as Padilla or Almazán, did not present an alternative to the official platform. On the contrary, the general insisted on the fulfillment of the political and social tenets of the Revolution, which, according to him, was impossible while the PRI was in power.

The official count gave Adolfo Ruiz Cortines 2.7 million votes (74.3 percent) and General Henríquez a little more than half a million; the PAN candidate received 285,000 votes, and Lombardo Toledano, the Popular party candidate, only 72,000. As their predecessors, the followers of Henríquez claimed that the true results of the election had been falsified, but their claims did not change the official decision or the political reality. The army remained loyal to the government, and tranquillity was disturbed only by some relatively violent demonstrations in cities of the interior and a long-forgotten massacre in Mexico City's Alameda.

For a year and a half after the elections, Henriquismo continued to be a relatively important political force, although many of its members decided from the beginning to forget their differences and rejoin the official party. Early in 1954, however, the government decided to forcibly dissolve the FPP, and the movement disappeared. In this typically authoritarian fashion, the last attempt of dissidence in the "revolutionary family" disappeared, and subsequently internal discipline in the party increased, because it became evident that there was no alternative to presidential will.

In the 1958 presidential elections, the candidacy went to the secretary of labor, Adolfo López Mateos, breaking, in a way very convenient to the president, the tradition of always choosing the secretary of government. There were no internal divisions, and the only significant opposition came from the outside, from the National Action party (PAN), which after orderly elections received only the bulk of the 10 percent opposition vote. The 1964 election had a similar character. The official candidate, Gustavo Díaz Ordaz, secretary of government, received 89 percent of the vote and the PAN candidate only 11 percent. The independent leftist opposition did not participate, and its presence in the election was practically nil (the Popular Socialist party decided to support the official candidate).

Reformed Opposition

The political crisis of 1968 did not seem to have any effect on the election returns of 1970. The PRI candidate, Luis Echeverría, secretary of interior, received 84 percent of the vote and Efraín González Morfín of PAN got 14 percent. Elections in 1976, again, did not offer any surprises, although there were some changes because the center-right opposition, the PAN, suffered an internal crisis, since a majority of its members did not want to continue playing the role of permanent minority. They thought that what they were actually doing was giving credence to the "democratic nature" of the official party. The PAN did not present a candidate. The other two registered parties, the PPS and the PARM, supported the PRI candidate, José López Portillo, who had been secretary of finance and not of interior, breaking once again the established pattern.

The only electoral opposition in 1976 was that of Valentín Campa, a candidate for the Mexican Communist party, which was not registered, and, therefore, votes for him were not taken into account. Formally, then, the official candidate was alone, and received 94 percent of the vote, an embarrassingly high percentage, which diminished even more the significance and credibility of the electoral process, since such a situation had not happened in Mexico since Obregón's election. By 1976, the supposedly pluralistic and democratic nature of the Mexican system was being questioned, even in its formal aspects. Signs were apparent everywhere of the authoritarian nature of the regime and the discouragement of participation of the citizenry. Elections in Mexico had never been a real means of selection of leaders, but rather a ritual to legitimize the previously anointed candidates. This ritual, however, demanded that there be some albeit symbolic opposition and partisan participation, and this is the reason for the December 1977 reforms to the electoral law, aimed at giving more visibility to the opposition without sharing power with it.

Even within the government, there were people who thought that it was necessary to respond quickly and efficiently to the opposition's demands for channels of expression. This response was to encourage a plurality of minority political currents, both to the left and to the right of the official party, giving them the chance of being represented in the Congress—which by itself had no capacity for substantive action—and thus revitalize the political atmosphere. Provisional recognition was also given to the Mexican Communist party, the Workers Socialist party, and the Mexican Democratic party, the first two leftist, and the last one rightist. Definitive recognition was granted after the legislative elections of 1979. In the House of Representatives, one hundred seats were created for the registered opposition parties, and it was assumed that the PRI would keep the great majority of the other three hundred seats.

The nature of the new Law of Political Organizations and Electoral Processes (LOPPE), which created three hundred mono-nominal and one hundred pluri-nominal electoral districts, was such that from the beginning it could be seen that the PRI's supremacy would not be threatened, because, among other things, the advantages given to minorities would phase out as their electoral strength increased. In this way, it was believed, the political system would not be substantially transformed, but would become more secure by the legitimization given by a minority opposition, an opposition that would be fragmented among the representatives.

Dissonance

The stability of the Mexican political system since 1929, and even more since 1941, has been remarkable. The authoritarian but flexible control exerted by the PRM-PRI on the political life of the country greatly contrasts with almost all the rest of Latin America. Unlike other authoritarian systems, the Mexican system is not interested in excluding those who want and can have political power, but rather in attracting them and incorporating them into its ranks. However, the presence of such heterogeneous interests and potential conflicts was not always resolved within the established bureaucratic channels. Once in awhile, routine and discipline were disrupted. And in those cases the central elements of the system, its mechanisms, and the forces and tendencies it represented could be seen more clearly, as through veritable X-rays of the nature of contemporary Mexican political life.

Nava's Lava: San Luis Potosí, 1959

After 1952-1954, presidential elections did not have important or violent opposition, but state and municipal elections were different. San Luis Potosí is an example. In 1938, after the fall of Gen. Saturnino Cedillo, the "strong man" of the state whose influence was based on the 1910 Revolution, another kind of boss appeared, Gonzalo N. Santos, descendant of a long line of Potosí politicians that started in the nineteenth century. When Santos left the governorship in 1949, he appointed his successors, and, in fact, continued ruling from one of his ranches in the Huasteca region. His shrewdness and violence, however, could not prevent the slow gestation of an urban opposition movement that united leftist and rightist elements in the Potosí Civic Union, which supported the candidacy of Dr. Salvador Nava—a well-known local ophthalmologist—for the post of mayor in 1959. It was a typical democratizing movement by the middle class, which eventually attracted the support of certain popular elements. The extent of this opposition and the possibility of violence were so great that central authorities thought it prudent to accept the PRI's defeat in the municipal government. This defeat demanded a reorganization of the local PRI group, and heads started rolling. One of them, of course, was that of Gov. Manuel Alvarez, appointed by Santos. After that, the domination by Santos ceased to be useful to the central government, and the brutal and picturesque politician lost his place as the center of local political life.

In this instance, the system had shown itself sufficiently flexible to accept defeat and avoid making a delicate situation explosive. This, however, was the limit of its tolerance, and when, in 1961, Nava tried to push his movement into the state government, the central government's attitude was totally negative. Without regard to the political price, it decided to confront the opposition in an open, definitive way, in order not to lose its monopoly over state governorships, which were nonnegotiable pieces in the power structure. As others before him, Nava could do nothing when the federal government declared the victory of the PRI candidate, except to accuse the PRI of fraud. After this catharsis, the Nava opposition lost vigor and for a long time ceased to be an effective political force. The civic eruption of Navismo had mortally wounded the Santos political machinery, but was not able to replace it with a state government independent from the will of the official party.

In the Peasant Underground

More dangerous for presidential power than the Potosí anti–political boss movement was, undoubtedly, the rebellious movement that took hold of key social sectors at the end of the 1950s. At the end of the Ruiz Cortines regime in 1958, the northern part of Mexico witnessed a vigorous mobilization of peasant groups that invaded lands under the direction of organizations with relatively radical ideologies, outside the official structures. It was not, of course, the first time that this happened. Cárdenas, for instance, had expropriated large landholdings in the La Laguna region, in response to the agitation of peasant organizations, which did not necessarily respond to presidential instructions.

At the end of the 1950s, the action of peasants and wage earners was directed by an independent leftist organization, the General Union of Workers and Peasants of Mexico (UGOCM), headed by Jacinto López and Félix Rubio. The eruptions of discontent culminated in land invasions in Sonora, Sinaloa, La Laguna, Nayarit, Colima, and Baja California, and a confrontation with local and federal authorities. On the one hand, the government violently stopped the wave of land invasions, expelled invaders, and imprisoned some of the leaders. On the other, the president accelerated the legal distribution of lands, a process that had a symbolic climax in the expropriation of the infamous *latifundio* of Cananea, in foreign hands since before the Revolution.

When he became president in 1958, Adolfo López Mateos (1958–1964) decided that peace in the countryside demanded a faster reactivation of the land reform process. In the first two years of his administration, 7.9 million acres were distributed, with a total of 39.5 million in his term, and his successor (Gustavo Díaz Ordaz, 1964–1970) continued this trend.

As can be seen, the stability of the political system was not based exclusively, or even principally, on the use of force, but mainly on the ability of its leaders to avoid the mobilization of social forces with independent leaders. To this end it negotiated, co-opted, and partially satisfied demands and even acted before problems became potential crises.

Children of the Railroad

After the Revolution, the control of the labor movement by central organizations and national industrial trade unions was one of the historical foundations of Mexican political stability. But it has not been an easy, guaranteed control, as labor dissidence, especially in the railway sector, showed in 1958–1959.

Since 1934–1937, Mexico had not witnessed such labor agitation as that which took place at the end of the Ruiz Cortines regime and the beginning of the López Mateos term. Agitation was produced not only by the railroad workers, but also by oil industry workers, teachers, telephone and telegraph operators, and electricians, that is, government workers and employees who formed the strategic core of the trade union movement. The discontent among teachers and workers—especially railroad workers—was in good part due to the low salaries produced by the inflationary process that took place before the "stabilizing development." The change in 1958 was led by an independent labor leadership, born from the inability of official trade union leaders, and demanded not only better salaries but also greater autonomy. The origin of the movement took place in 1954, when several sectors of the National Railroad Workers Trade Union appealed to direct action in demand of better working conditions and against the official leadership. Salaries for railroad workers were noticeably lower than in other strategic areas of the economy. The rebel leaders were accused of inefficiency and were repressed in 1955, but discontent did not disappear and grew in an underground fashion, producing by 1958 a militant, independent leadership led by Demetrio Vallejo, representative of Local 13 of the union, and Valentín Campa, veteran Communist party militant. In June, several violent trade union incidents took place and several strikes paralyzed the system, shaking the fossilized union and causing the fall of the unpopular executive committee headed by Samuel Ortega.

In August 1958, in order to avoid further agitation at the time of change of government, the regime resigned itself to the triumph of Vallejo in the trade union elections as the lesser of two evils. The presence of an independent leadership in a strategic trade union was seen by some as an invitation to open up a new era in the history of the labor movement. Certain government circles hoped for a return of the rebels. For the time being, in order not to be surpassed by them, the CTM and official trade unionism seemed to adopt a more militant attitude in the defense of the rights of workers. At the same time, the CTM did not cease in its attacks against the new railroad leaders and, in general, against all dissidents.

The new railroad leadership started to negotiate a collective contract with the new government, since López Mateos had assumed the presidency, but after long and heated discussions it was not possible to reach an agreement. The trade union called for a strike in February 1959. By then, the conflict had become a veritable national problem. The railroad workers, teachers, and oil workers were the leading edge of the movement and disrupted the normal march of economy and politics. Everything seemed to indicate that the labor movement was escaping the control of the government. The situation could lead to a fundamental change in the political system, since it surpassed the traditional limits of pluralism, either political or trade unionist, that had been the base of the pyramidlike control over strategic political sectors.

The strike started on February 25. Both the railroad company and the government declared it illegal, but agreed on a 16.6 percent salary increase. Service, but not calm, returned, and in March the trade union threatened a new strike, this time to negotiate the contracts in the Mexican Railroad and Pacific systems. Once again, the government declared the movement nonexistent, and then the surprise came. The whole railroad system struck for solidarity with the locals involved in the strike, and this was too much for presidential tolerance. The army and the police acted immediately, thousands of railroad workers were arrested, and their strike was ended with extreme violence. Once the leaders were in prison, they were tried and a new leadership was appointed. In one fell swoop, official control over the railroad union, and over all rebellious tendencies in the labor movement, was reestablished. Vallejo and Campa spent long years in prison before returning to active trade union life, and by then their courses of action were very limited.

The Night of Tlatelolco

During the subsequent ten years, Mexican political life continued without any conflict seriously threatening the leaders of the country. But in 1968 trouble reappeared. The challengers to the system, this time, were not its foundations, the worker and peasant sectors, but the middle urban groups and its more educated and less controllable elements: college students and professors. The setting was not a state, as in the case of San Luis Potosí, or the networks of a trade union, as in the railroad case, but the streets and plazas of the center of power: Mexico City.

From the beginning of the postrevolutionary government, some politicized sectors of the middle class had criticized the lack of democracy in the system. Such was the case of the Vasconcelista movement of 1929, but 1968 was a longer chapter of that story. In July of that year, a brutal escalation of repression against student demonstrations, which had little or no political content, exacerbated the deep political discontent that these sectors had traditionally had. This discontent was embodied now in the sector of college students, who were a product of the demographic change of Mexican society. By September, the conflict had degenerated into the most open, protracted, and widespread agitation in contemporary Mexican history. Large groups demonstrated in the streets, openly attacked the president and his close officials, and the system itself, accusing them of being undemocratic. Traditional student organizations, tied to the PRI and the central government, had lost all control and had been replaced by new leadership born from the confrontation.

These events were happening, furthermore, just months before the 1968 Olympic Games in a city occupied by correspondents from all over the world, whom the government wanted to impress with examples of Mexican peace and progress.

After a series of demonstrations, repression, and failed attempts at negotiation, and just before the opening of the Games, the president and his political advisers considered this challenge to the principle of authority intolerable, and on October 2, 1968, the army and the police put an end to the protest by means of an indiscriminate massacre of demonstrators at the Plaza of the Three Cultures in Tlatelolco. The leaders of the movement were arrested, and terror prevented further mobilization. But the bases of legitimacy of the regime vis-à-vis a large sector of the middle class, the beneficiary of the system and source of administration cadres, were indelibly eroded.

The administration of Luis Echeverría, who assumed power in late 1970, was especially sensitive to the university world and followed a policy of "democratic aperture" to try to incorporate at least a part of the groups alienated by the Tlatelolco massacre. Urban guerrilla and other similar movements, which were a direct or indirect result of the 1968 repression, were openly opposed, at the same time that the government showed generosity in subsidies and goodwill gestures toward universities. One can consider the 1977 political reform as the climax of this long process of "return to normalcy," a protracted, expensive, and complex process of reconciliation and co-option, explainable only by the magnitude of the original offense.

Politics and the Bowler Hat: Business and Government

The development model followed by the postrevolutionary governments greatly facilitated the accelerated accumulation of capital, but did not completely resolve the conflict represented by the privileged relation between the political elite and the foreign and domestic grande bourgeoisie. It is in the very nature of the Mexican political system that the government tries to maintain its control over all political forces, including the powerful private sector of the economy. The mechanism of capital accumulation, however, requires that the business person become increasingly stronger vis-à-vis the government and in critical moments make the state modify its decisions. A dramatic example is the attempted tax reform of the Echeverría government (1970–1976).

As we said before, from the early 1960s, Mexican and foreign observers of Mexican reality had insisted that the social stability and economic health of the country demanded some redistribution of income through a tax reform designed to give the government a higher cut of the national product and to avoid excessive concentrations of capital and foreign debt. Between 1965 and 1970, the federal government deficit had been 20 percent; in 1966, for instance, 32 percent of public investment had to be financed with foreign loans due to insufficient taxes. The Mexican government at the time received only 10 percent of the gross domestic product, a remarkably low portion, even for Latin America. Of 72 nations studied by the International Monetary Fund in 1968, only 5 had taxes lower than Mexico. When stating the need for a new Law of Federal Income in 1971, it was said, explicitly, that the moment had come to "finance public expenses principally through the tax system, emphasizing the need for its efficient administration." The ground was being prepared for a thorough tax reform. The basic proviso of this reform, according to its authors, should be to put an end to the anonymous character of shareholders. This would allow a better estimate of their real total income, and, on this base, to tax them. Never before in the history of Mexico had the government proposed to tax higher-income persons so much and so permanently.

The business sector reacted more strongly than expected. In January 1971, the Employer Confederation of the Mexican Republic (COPARMEX) handed the president a note of protest that it had not been consulted, which described the proposed reform as inconsistent and excessive. From that moment on, relations between the Echeverría government and the large private companies became tense and would end, as will be seen later, in open confrontation. But the government did not back down on its reform. In 1973, several bureaucratic negotiations were conducted between the officials responsible for economic policy and the representatives of the business sector. Without presenting a solid bloc, most business people opposed the project and pointed out that if it was carried out, private investment would diminish, there would be massive capital flight, and a devaluation would become unavoidable, putting an end to "stabilizing development" and economic growth. When the president met with his advisers, opinions were divided, and those who advised prudence and dropping the project prevailed over those in favor of paying the political and economic cost of a thorough tax reform and modernizing and cleaning up public finances in the long and medium run.

The decision resulted in the resignation of the secretary of finance. Tax changes that did take effect were relatively minor and affected mostly middle-class people with a fixed income and very few large investors. Fiscal modernization had stopped short. Companies' gains in that year (1973) were higher than in the preceding fifteen years. And, although the percentage of gross income received by the government increased to 14, so did the federal deficit, and the government had to increase its foreign debt by 29.6 percent.

The postponement of tax reform was a crucial decision of the Echeverría government. In a way, the proposal had become the touchstone of all its programs, and, when abandoned, government action lost much of its energy. The position of the state vis-à-vis private enterprise weakened, without at least improving relations between the government and large business groups, because the populist rhetoric of the government increased in inverse proportion to its withdrawal from a meaningful tax reform. In the long run, the government paid the price of a confrontation with the private sector without having achieved the structural reform it had originally planned. Public investment had to increase to compensate for the little private investment. Three years later, the situation had become impossible. With a commercial deficit of $1,749 million in 1976, an accumulated foreign debt of more than $20 billion, and massive capital drain, the government suddenly had to face the economic necessity and political shock of a 100 percent devaluation in relation to the dollar, the first devaluation in twenty-two years. The economy became stagnant and the lack of confidence became general. The wildest rumors spread about a political and economic catastrophe, and Echeverría had some of the worst moments of his administration. It was one of the most difficult periods of postrevolutionary history.

The confrontation between the government and the private sector continued with the new president and resulted in seventy-two families', some of them very powerful, losing 247,000 acres in the fertile lands of the Yaqui and Mayo river valleys. On this occasion, the loud protests of COPARMEX and the work stoppage of the private sector in Sonora and Sinaloa were to no avail. These lands were distributed among more than eight thousand *ejido* members.

From Ostracism to Cooperation

When the revolutionary process begun in 1910 climaxed with the Cárdenas government, so did Mexican nationalism. After 1940 conflicts between Mexico and foreign countries, especially the United States and Western Europe, decreased and even changed in nature. Mexico would no longer try drastically and unilaterally to change the rules of the international game. The postrevolutionary governments, however, did not ignore nationalism altogether, and the insistence on the permanent and universal value of such principles as those contained in the Carranza Doctrine helped to prove the "revolutionary" character of the government of Avila Camacho and those who followed him. Nationalism, democracy, and social justice were the ideological supports of the legitimacy of the contemporary Mexican political system. But the efforts to preserve and maintain the relative independence won during the Revolution could not prevent the character of Mexico as part of the American zone of influence from becoming more apparent after WWII.

The immediate effect was a positive one. Washington needed the close cooperation of its southern neighbor, and was willing to settle rapidly the problems pending between the two countries. In 1942 and 1943, agreements were signed on the amount and terms of payment to oil companies expropriated in 1938, with very favorable conditions for Mexico. The problem of the old foreign debt was ended, and commercial and migrant worker agreements, which would be the Mexican contribution to the Allies' war effort, were signed.

When the war ended, Mexico had moved beyond the stage of ostracism to which a large part of the international community had condemned it. Mexico participated actively from the beginning, in the creation of the United Nations and the inter-American system. Its foreign commercial exchanges increased due to its larger demands for industrialization, it was given loans again, and foreign investment returned. Cloaked in this new respectability, Mexico participated again in the international business life and flow of capital, but now as a neighbor of the undisputed first world power. Almost unavoidably its foreign relations came to mean its relations with the United States. Eventually, European investment returned and the number of countries with which it had commerce increased. Mexico opened new embassies and sent diplomatic representatives to many of the countries that had started independent life after the war. However, most political exchanges were concentrated on its northern neighbor, and the Mexican economy became as dependent as, or more than, in the past.

By 1974, the close—but forced—cooperation between the United States and the Soviet Union during the war had turned into an open confrontation that became the cold war. The international system split into two factions, and Mexico became a part, voluntarily or not, of the so-called Free World headed by the United States. However, unlike other nations of the hemisphere, it tried to maintain a relative independence in the face of the American policy of militant international anticommunism. It did not sign a military cooperation agreement with the United States, it did not participate in the Korean War, and it did not support the subversive attack against the reform government of Jacobo Arbenz in Guatemala. Mexico did not break relations with Cuba when it confronted the United States by declaring itself socialist and was expelled from the Organization of American States (OAS). On the other hand, Mexico carefully abstained from cooperating with those that had been condemned by the government in Washington. It simply stated its traditional principle of nonintervention, and avoided taking its domestic anticommunist policy to the international arena. In order for Mexican nationalism to survive, it was necessary to keep a distance, at least minimal, from the United States.

At the beginning of the 1970s, the Mexican government made an effort to take advantage of the diminishing tensions between the United States and the Soviet Union—détente—to widen its international action. It approached then, as never before, the position maintained by the countries of the so-called Third World, but its new policy had a weak basis, the weakness characteristic of the Mexican economy: its dependence. The economic crisis of 1976 put a very clear limit on the Third World action of the Echeverría government. López Portillo, who succeeded him, initially assumed a more prudent attitude, in order to face such immediate problems as the weak peso and the huge foreign debt. But as the opportunities created by the exploitation of oil increased, so did the international presence of Mexico and its international contacts as a means of breaking the close embrace that tied it to the United States.

The Benefits of the War

Let us now examine more closely the nature of this bilateral relation. Beginning in early 1941, before the United States entered the war, the American government started to explore the possibility of building naval bases on the Mexican Pacific coast, already foreseeing the strategic needs in case of a conflict with the Japanese. Mexican response was not particularly enthusiastic, implying that Mexico preferred to have help in building up its own armed forces to guard its territory on its own against possible action by the Axis. At any rate, it could not fully discuss the terms of continental security cooperation if the multiple problems pending with the United States were not resolved first.

In 1941, Mexico and the United States signed an agreement authorizing military airplanes of each country to use the airports of the other when in transit. This was done to facilitate the American effort to defend the Panama Canal. Agreements for the purchase of strategic Mexican materials were also initiated, but the oil problem blocked the way to broader cooperation. In that same year, the State Department—against the wishes of the companies expropriated in 1938—agreed to appoint a commission to estimate the value of the companies and a way to pay them. In November, an agreement was reached: a mixed committee of official experts would evaluate the expropriated enterprises, although the companies were not forced to accept their conclusions. In 1942, with the United States already at war, it was agreed that Mexico would pay

$24 million as indemnity and $5 million as interest to Standard Oil and other American companies not yet compensated by Cárdenas. The last payment would take place in 1949. It was also agreed that all claims for agricultural expropriations and damages caused to American citizens in Mexico during the Revolution would be covered by a global payment of $40 million. For its part, the United States agreed to buy Mexican silver for up to $25 million a year, grant credit for $40 million to stabilize the peso, and $30 million to improve the internal communication network, which was necessary if exchanges with the United States were going to increase. Finally, a trade agreement was reached, stating the terms under which Mexico would contribute to the Allied cause.

The Mexican army was reequipped with American credit, cooperated with the protection of the region, and even, for symbolic reasons, sent an air squadron to the Pacific theater. Mexico also agreed that its citizens living in the United States could be recruited into the army, with the totally theoretical proviso that Mexico could do the same with American citizens in Mexico. Some fifteen thousand Mexicans served in the U.S. armed forces. Finally, a treaty on *braceros* was signed, by which up to two hundred thousand Mexicans would work on American farms, railroads, and so on, replacing the labor absorbed by the army and other war-related activities.

The war also permitted Mexico to reestablish relations with two of the great Allied powers: Great Britain, with whom relations had been broken off since 1938 after the oil expropriation, and the Soviet Union, with whom relations had been suspended since 1931. Mexico could, thus, without creating any problems for anybody, become an active member of the United Nations pact.

Good and Bad Neighbors

The hemispheric policy of "goodwill" of President Roosevelt and the cooperation during the war encouraged some Mexican sectors to believe that the bilateral relationship had changed substantially and permanently. The secretary of foreign relations of Avila Camacho, Ezequiel Padilla, personified this attitude. After the war, even President Miguel Alemán—without abandoning the nationalistic theme—thought it possible to erase the basic antagonism and to emphasize the complementary economies and the common long-term political projects.

In reality, cooperation during the war was not free from friction. An agreement was reached about oil indemnization, but the State Department and, particularly, Ambassador George Messersmith, arguing that PEMEX had economic problems, tried to convince Avila Camacho to accept some type of association with the expropriated companies. After a long internal debate, the United States agreed in 1943 to grant a loan of $10 million to PEMEX to improve its refining capacity, but only because this contributed indirectly to the war effort. When, at the end of the war, Mexico asked for a second loan for PEMEX, Washington added as a condition that the new fields discovered with its aid would be kept as strategic reserves of the United States and not be exploited commercially. If Mexico wanted to exploit them commercially, it would have to ask for loans from private oil companies. Mexico did not accept these conditions, and only by the end of the Alemán regime in the 1950s did the United States finally accept that it could not intervene directly in the Mexican oil industry. Only then was the 1938 expropriation free from foreign pressures.

The Miguel Alemán term (1946–1952) marked the weakening of the Cardenista influence, the beginning of the development project, and the start of the cold war. The Mexican government reiterated its support of the Good Neighbor policy and the maintenance of close relations and friendly cooperation among the Western Hemisphere nations. In 1947, there were reciprocal visits by the presidents, characterized by official enthusiasm in both countries. The United States again supported the Mexican peso, and the EXIMBANK offered Mexico $50 million for development projects. In that year, the mixed committee for the eradication of aphthous fever (hoof-and-mouth disease) was established. This cattle disease cost the United States $20 million, and cost Mexico the loss of 160,000 cattle plus bitter disputes with the peasants and cattle owners affected.

In spite of the goodwill to maintain or at least to continue for a time the wartime cooperation, reality started to impose divergent interests in several areas.

Wetbacks

During the war, the American economy had needed unskilled labor, and it was necessary to recruit *braceros* from Mexico. But when the war was over, demobilization flooded labor market with hundreds of thousands of veterans, while at the same time the rate of production decreased in several areas. American trade unions pressured to have jobs formerly taken by the *braceros* returned to American workers. But the tide of Mexican laborers coming to the United States was far from stemmed. In 1950, American immigration officers detained and deported more than half a million undocumented Mexicans, the famous *wetbacks*.

After hard negotiations, a second *bracero* treaty was signed between the two countries. Mexico insisted that contracts were given not by the employer, as the United States wanted, but by the American government, achieving at least a minimum guarantee of working conditions. Experience had shown that farmers tended to give Mexican laborers salaries and conditions below those of the United States. Mexicans contracted under the treaty were fewer than those wishing to work in the United States, and the numbers of undocumented workers continued to increase, together with abuses against them and deportations.

In 1954, there was an attempt to renegotiate the agreement. Mexico insisted on better terms, and the American government simply let the agreement expire, thus to proceed with unilateral contracting. The official Mexican response was to try to close the borders to *braceros*, a useless effort that produced riots. Thousands of Mexican workers ignored their government's orders and entered the United States in search of jobs. Mexico could do nothing but renew the 1951 agreement. A lesson was learned: Mexico would never again try to control the flow of workers to the North.

But the pressure of American trade unions against Mexican workers did not stop, and in 1964 the United States declared the *bracero* agreement officially terminated. However, the forces that made the Mexican workers go to the United States—unemployment or need for better salaries—not only did not disappear, but in a way increased. The demand of large agricultural enterprises and certain companies in the United States continued, as did the flow of *braceros*, who were now illegal and without any official mechanism to offer them protection. By the end of the 1970s, undocumented immigration into the United States—which was largely a temporary immigration—amounted to many millions and was one of the main problems between the two countries.

The Weakening of the Special Relationship

Another central problem in bilateral relations has been that of protectionism and trade. In 1942, as was seen, trade between Mexico and the United States was regulated by a treaty, but when the war ended Mexico decided to go ahead with its incipient industrialization process based on import substitution, which required high tariffs to defend Mexican industrialists from foreign competition. For this reason, in spite of American insistence on renewing the treaty, Mexico refused, and by 1950 the United States had resigned itself to living with Mexican protectionism. In the long run, many American companies found this protectionism useful: those that decided to install plants south of the border and to produce for the Mexican market. In any case, the United States did not forget the problem and restricted a good number of Mexican exports. The second half of the 1970s and the first half of the

1980s were marked by continuous bilateral discussion on whether Mexico should join the General Agreement on Tariffs and Trade (GATT) or find other ways to open its markets to foreign goods in order to have better access to the markets of developed nations, especially the United States.

Other subjects of litigation were the return to Mexico of the border area of El Chamizal, a problem that started in the nineteenth century and was resolved only in 1963; the agreement on commercial air routes, which began to be negotiated in 1945 and was reached only at the end of 1957; and the controversy over fishing rights, which was active from 1950 to 1967 and revived at the end of the 1970s. The salinity of the Colorado River produced by the washing of brackish soil in the United States from 1961 on could be solved only in 1973. There was the problem of cotton dumping by the United States, which affected Mexican exports, and that of import quotas on lead, zinc, and sugar between 1957 and 1965; and the 10 percent surtax on all American imports, from which Mexico tried unsuccessfully to be exempt. The drug trafficking from Mexico to the United States increased in the 1970s and reached a critical point in the 1980s: on two occasions, Washington ordered a halt to the enormous flow of people crossing the border in order to put pressure on Mexico to develop more aggressive campaigns against drug dealers, thus creating serious political tensions; in 1977, the U.S. Department of Energy refused permission to American companies to import Mexican gas, at a price previously agreed on, and in spite of the fact that Mexico had started the construction of an expensive gas pipeline.

By the end of the 1970s, the idea of appealing to a "special relationship" between Mexico and the United States—born from their alliance during WWII—to solve their problems had disappeared. The nature of the bilateral relationship was seen then in a more realistic fashion: it was necessary to maintain cordial relations with the northern neighbor, but at the same time admitting the existence of structural antagonisms that made an absolute compatibility of interests impossible.

Direct dealings with the United States were not the only means of relationship, because there were also multiparty exchanges, such as Latin American organizations, the United Nations, and so on. At the end of WWII, the possibility of a permanent inter-American alliance was very attractive to Mexico. It was thought that in exchange for the political support of Latin America, the United States would grant the region sufficient aid for its economic transformation. The failure of this proposal at the Inter-American Conference in Chapultepec was a hard blow to those who advocated a closer union between Mexico and the United States. In spite of this, Mexico signed in 1947, together with the United States and the other Latin American nations, the Inter-American

Treaty of Reciprocal Assistance, which consolidated the political-military alliance with the United States and provided foundations for a joint action in case of an extracontinental attack. At that time, American aid—the Marshall Plan—was directed to Western Europe and not Latin America. Mexico lost much of its enthusiasm for the inter-American plan, and its participation in the OAS was less to fortify alliances than to object to American attempts to use the organization to legitimize its interventions, as in the case of Guatemala in the 1950s and the Dominican Republic in the following decade. In larger forums, especially the UN, Mexico maintained a prudent position: it did not contradict the American position in vital questions such as the cold war, but tried to keep a certain distance from Washington.

Doors to the Countryside

It is true that after 1940 the relationship with the United States was the core of Mexican foreign policy, but it is also true that Mexico persisted in its efforts to make the relationship less stifling. Restrictions to the importation of Mexican raw materials in the 1950s and commercial deterioration led Mexican leaders to consider diversifying markets. Between 1956 and 1961, Mexican exports were stationary, especially due to the decrease in the price of such items as coffee, cotton, lead, zinc, shrimp, and so forth. In contrast, the value of imports kept growing, and thus the weakness in foreign trade started to affect the structure of development of the country.

During the administration of Adolfo López Mateos (1958–1964), concrete steps were taken to establish political and economic relationships with newly independent nations, but without formal alignment with the group of nonaligned nations led by India, Yugoslavia, and Egypt. Efforts were also made to revitalize economic ties with Western Europe and Japan and to establish significant economic relations with the socialist bloc. Diversification within Latin America was sought through the ALALC, which was considered the initial step for the constitution of a true Common Market of the countries of the region.

The results of these efforts were meager. Neither Europe nor Japan wanted or was able to have the participation in Mexico that this country wanted. African and Asian countries with whom diplomatic relations were started were just not able to effect any substantial change, because their economies were weak and complementary. The ALALC became stagnant in the face of the impossibility that Latin American nations sacrifice their immediate particular interests in the interest of future integration.

In the context of this search for alternatives to dependence on the

United States, President Echeverría started a new, more ambitious campaign than that of López Mateos, to open new markets for Mexico and new international political forums. Two specialized institutions were created for this purpose: the Mexican Institute for Foreign Trade, to improve exports, and the National Council of Science and Technology, to decrease technological dependency by creating its own sources. Echeverría, furthermore, visited some forty nations and appointed a good number of economists as ambassadors. This diversification of international contacts was developed in a framework of anti-imperialist discourse in defense of the Third World. The major achievement of this policy was the adoption by the UN of the Charter of Economic Rights and Duties of Nations against the wishes of the major industrial countries. Once the charter was approved, the difficult or impossible task was to enforce it. There was lack of political will on the part of great industrial economies, which were more concerned with avoiding a recession by protectionist means than in helping developing nations. The Third World action of Mexico and its approach to the Chilean socialist regime of Salvador Allende irritated certain American sectors, without receiving substantial domestic support. The new foreign policy of Echeverría coincided with the general crisis of "developmentalism," which caused its weakening and ultimate failure. The commercial deficit grew spectacularly in the 1970s and, with it, foreign debt, contracted mainly with American institutions. By the end of the Echeverría regime, it was clear that a legitimate effort to diminish dependence had not produced the desired result.

The pessimistic tone that dominated political and economic circles in 1976 and 1977 turned into cautious optimism in 1978 with the important discoveries of oil and gas in Southeast Mexico. In a surprisingly short time, Mexico placed itself in sixth place in the world in oil reserves. Growth rate improved, and in that same year reached 4 percent. While other countries were in recession, a greater growth rate was predicted for the immediate future. In the face of the oil boom (more than 2 million barrels a day in the first half of 1980), the foreign debt of $30 billion did not seem so large, and the international confidence of Mexico was recovered.

The López Portillo regime did not delay in again trying to diversify economic relations, this time based on oil exports. The natural market for Mexican oil and gas was the United States, which in 1978 absorbed 88.6 percent of Mexican oil and gas exports. The percentage, however, started to diminish after a conscious effort to improve exports to Israel, Spain, France, Canada, Japan, Sweden, and so on. The idea was not only to ship oil to those countries, but to condition its sale on the establishment of a more complex exchange. Oil was even used as an element of

Mexican policy toward Central America, where Mexico showed its willingness to effectively support reform parties and governments. At the end of the 1970s, Mexico continued its perpetual search for a foreign policy that would assure a satisfactory relationship with the United States without choking its possibilities of a reasonably autonomous development. But, once again, the weakness of its economic structure was its Achilles' heel.

In 1980, in the middle of the oil euphoria, López Portillo responded to American pressure for Mexico to join the GATT by organizing a large national debate, which rejected the idea as a product of imperialist pressure contrary to national interest. The following year, when the price of oil was starting to plummet, Mexico was the seat of a summit conference between the not-too-enthusiastic heads of state of the industrialized North and some of the leaders of the many underdeveloped nations of the South. López Portillo's ambitious goal in calling the Cancún conference was nothing less than to reach an agreement of economic cooperation between rich and poor nations, that is, to succeed where the Charter of Economic Rights and Duties of States, proposed by Echeverría, had failed. By 1982, the oil market had plummeted irrevocably, and Mexico, with one of the largest foreign debts in the world— around $83 billion—was in no position to head a North-South negotiation, or anything of the sort.

In August 1982, Mexico reported that it was unable to pay its foreign debt on time. The Federal Reserve of the United States, the Treasury Department, and eleven large international banks extended Mexico an emergency loan of $1,850 million. Mexico had to repay this loan, in part, with oil sold at a low price to the Strategic Reserve of the United States. It was the beginning of a new crisis and the sad end of a policy that had been announced as the true way to economic independence.

6.
The Fading of the Miracle:
1968–1984

Two Rhythms

An overview of the past forty years of Mexican history would recognize the presence of two tempos or two rhythms. The first one, which we have called the "Mexican miracle," dates from 1940 to 1968 and was characterized by a manifest political stability and a manifest economic growth. The second period, dating from 1968 to 1984, could be called the "Mexican transition," a transition of historical importance that renewed the debate on the duration and the destiny of the political and institutional system derived from the social pact that we know as the Mexican Revolution.

As we have seen, political stability organizes itself around the consolidation of presidentialism as the center of political and social life in Mexico. The years between 1940 and 1968 witnessed, on one hand, the withdrawal of traditional sources of traditional power, such as the church and the army and, on the other hand, the disappearance of divisions within the "revolutionary family." In 1940, Juan Andrew Almazán competed against Manuel Avila Camacho for the presidency, and he was able to garner a large proportion of the vote in the cities. In 1946, the presidential candidacy of Ezequiel Padilla against Miguel Alemán had a much weaker impact.

In 1952, another independent candidate of the "family," Miguel Henríquez Guzmán, formed a party—the Federation of Parties of the People (FPP)—that continued to exist after the electoral campaign, and that was to be forcefully dissolved in February 1954, but that did not leave aftereffects. The characteristic note of the presidential succession of Adolfo López Mateos in 1958 was the unanimity of *tapadismo* (hidden candidacy), the institution par excellence of Mexican presidentialism, which from then on allowed the chief of the Executive Branch to select, by himself and without discord, his own successor. In 1957, the year his successor was elected, then President Adolfo Ruiz Cortines was successful in asking all the political forces of the country to concentrate on the debate on the government program to be implemented and to forget about the conflict surrounding who should be the candidate, an aspect of minor interest that would be taken care of in due time. As José Revueltas recalls in *México, una democracia bárbara* (Mexico, a barbarous democracy), all of the political forces of the country, both those of the opposition and those of the government, proceeded to devote themselves to a hair-splitting discussion on the government program that the national circumstances demanded, with the sole result that President Ruiz Cortines was able to decide, by himself and without any public appearance of discord, who would be his successor. Thus, a tradition of unanimity began in the most important decision of Mexican politics, which is, as in all countries, who would inherit power, who would be able to transfer power. This is the key to the political stability of the Mexican miracle: the efficient mechanism for succession.

Another decisive aspect was the state absorption of the different levels of political expression and demands. Between 1940 and 1968, Mexico experienced the dominance of a sort of institutional monologue. All of the negotiations had to take place within the state apparatus through its own channels and instruments, with its own social and pyramidal organizations, its steamroller party, and its arbitrary authorities. Whatever escaped the norms of these intramural negotiations was violently suppressed: railroad strikes and land invasions by the UGOCM in the North (1958) or student movements (1968). The main characteristic of this institutional monologue was that the conflicts were subject to a negotiation subordinated to the state and to its mechanisms of political control, or to a selective repression of extraordinary violence.

With respect to economic growth, the years from 1940 to 1968 were those of the development of the "modern" industrial base of the country, the years in which import-substitution industrialization (ISI) accelerated, in which agriculture was subordinated to industry, urbanization expanded, average growth reached 6 percent per year, exchange rate stability was achieved, and there was an equilibrium in prices and wages. They were also the years in which the central agreement of the system was in full force: the basic harmony between the political elite and the economic elite, the support for the development of the industrial, commercial, and financial sectors of Mexico.

Before 1938, foreign direct investment in Mexico was a substantial part of total investment. Between 1940 and the 1960s, foreign direct investment reduced its participation until it became between 5 and 8 percent of total investment: the economy "Mexicanized" itself, although the most dynamic sectors, those that showed the most advanced technological innovations, were still dominated by foreign capital, with the only difference that, in contrast with the past, the U.S. presence was now overwhelming. Nevertheless, nobody could deny that the Mexican bourgeoisie was definitively transformed into an industrial bourgeoisie: an industry that substituted imports, protected by a complex array of tariffs and administrative barriers, with which the government sought to allow capital to recover the time it had lost during the nineteenth century and during the Revolution.

Together with an industry that grew faster than the average of the economic activities, which by itself was almost double the demographic growth, a powerful banking system emerged, under whose protective wings important manufacturing and commercial groups took cover. Mexico became increasingly an urban society, with such a rhythm that it would end up exceeding the predictions and the capacity of the authorities to plan organized development and to meet the basic needs of the great urban settlements, in particular in the capital city.

The basic element of the economic, social, and cultural life of Mexico between 1940 and 1968 was change, the accelerated and even chaotic transformation of the physical and psychological environment of the Mexicans. This change contrasts with the permanence of the structures and forms of political life. The transformation of everything, except the political system, made clear its rigidity and inadequacy for a society that had begun to surpass its tutors.

October 2, 1968, was the starting point of a new crisis in Mexico: on that date, an interval began during which the country lost confidence in its present, ceased celebrating and consolidating its achievements and miracles, and began to confront daily, and for more than a decade, its own previously ignored insufficiencies, failures, and miseries. The crisis of 1968 was not a structural crisis that would place at risk the very survival of the nation; it was, above all, a political, moral, and psychological crisis, a crisis of values and principles, which shook up the triumphant schemes of the governing elite; it was the bloody announcement that the times had changed, without changing the means to confront them.

The 1968 rebellion was the first of the urban and modern Mexico outlined in the 1940s development model and placed above everything else. Its purveyors were the youthful elites of the cities, the students and newly graduated professionals who represented the incontrovertible proof that the agrarian, provincial, pro-PRI, and traditional Mexico was falling behind; the 1968 rebels were the sons and daughters of the middle class that had arisen in the previous three decades, the generation that would be called on to fulfill that transition and to take command of the industrial and cosmopolitan Mexico that was emerging.

In this sense, we might say that Tlatelolco killed the continuity of

Mexico's modernization, an alternative to generational transmittal. It represented the clash between an immobile and monolithic political and social sensibility—which hung onto the empty models of national unity and a provincial veneration of national symbols—and the fresh and unbending witnesses to a denationalized and dependent reality, suffering from a rapid process of neocolonial transculturation, who were extraordinarily sensitive to the causes and symbols that were their contemporaries.

In response to the official attempts of the regime to appropriate the trappings of Juárez and Morelos, the youth of 1968 offered, in their rallies of August and September of that year, the images of Che Guevara and the slogans of the French from May 1968. In response to Callista unity, which was the reaction to the political pyramid that developed in support of the "defied authority" of President Díaz Ordaz, the student strike reiterated its demand of pluralism and right to dissidence under the guise of a central organization, the National Strike Council, with which it proved impossible to negotiate without endless consultations with the grass roots. The repression of 1968 and the massacre of Tlatelolco were the numbed responses of the past to a movement that captured the heartbeat of the future, that constituted itself into the embryonic presence of another country and another society, and whose fluctuations would be increasingly difficult to manage with the old devices of manipulation and control.

Over the scars imposed by that anachronism, a new attempt of the revolutionary regime would emerge in the 1970s to update its ideological baggage, open the doors to the recognition of its accumulated inequalities and deformities, and regroup from above to create a new legitimacy, a new consensus, to revitalize the institutions and the discourse of the Mexican Revolution.

It was a six-year period of self-criticism, populist rhetoric, and the stimulation of nonconformism and criticism of the oligarchies that had grown richer with the stabilizing development pact. Toward the mid-1970s, however, the country found itself with the second rebellion of the modern sectors to which its development model had also given rise. The major beneficiaries of that model—bankers, entrepreneurs, and merchants—irate with the Echeverría populism that was more verbal than real, contrived and carried out during 1976 a financial coup d'état by reducing their investment and carrying out massive capital flight. This forced the adoption in August of a devaluation of the peso, and in the following years a long period of relative political hegemony and of favorable conditions to negotiate their interests with the state and society.

The Progress of the Crisis

The Luis Echeverría administration (1970–1976) was an intense pilgrimage from the "Mexican miracle" to the reality of those "rebellions of modernity." It was marked by agricultural downturns and industrial monopolies, land invasions, strikes, open contradictions between the forces that were growing within society and those that still demanded maintaining, through the state, the historical roles of judge and father. According to economist José Blanco, during 1975 the Mexican economy experienced its "deepest crisis" in many decades. In that year, the per capita growth of production was null, the real wage fell below the levels it had reached in 1972, private investment shrank for the first time in five years, the deficit in the current account of the balance of payments was four times greater than that of 1971, the public sector deficit was seven times greater, and underemployment affected 45 percent of the economically active population.

Thus, a climax was reached, after five bad years during which the country was affected consecutively by "atony," the collapse of agricultural products, inflation, external indebtedness, the shrinking of credit, and the lack of confidence of private capital due to the pseudo-populist style imposed by President Echeverría.

However, what was bad in the short run for the country's economy was not necessarily bad for the industrial, financial, and agricultural bourgeoisie of Mexico. The manifestations of shortages and crisis in small and medium industry also represented accumulation and monopolization in the large industry. At the beginning of the 1970s, large industry controlled at least a third of the capital stock, total production, and the employees of the sector (1,200,000 factory workers, 300,000 white-collar employees).

The agricultural shortages that led to increases in the prices of foodstuffs and basic goods forced the country to import products, such as corn, in which the country had enjoyed a surplus a few years before. It also represented the collapse of the nonirrigated lands, whose yields fell by an average of 3.9 percent per year, but not the lands of the large producers, which increased their productivity in the irrigated districts by 5.7 percent per year.

The Mexican business sector and bankers had always held sway over the state to have their demands heard. In the 1970s, they learned how to decisively demand in public whatever was not granted to them in a friendly fashion in private. The fiscal reform of 1971, which was designed to tax capital revenues, ended up being charged on the middle classes and those with high wages.

From the beginning, the private financiers had the president's promise that the banking system would not be nationalized, and in 1972 they were able to prevent the creation of unions among their employees. In 1973, the captains of radio and television liquidated the threat of state intervention in their Hertzian fields and in their accounts by forming a cohesive interest group. In 1975, the attempt to undermine some of the large landowners of the Northwest resulted in the integration of a Tripartite Commission in which those who thought they would be affected could dilute, as with the fiscal reform, the worst aspects of the initiatives that might seem negative to them.

The relative political independence achieved by people in business, bankers, and landowners, with respect to the slogans and projects of the state, reached a level of open divergence in 1973 with the assassination of the Monterrey industrialist Eugenio Garza Sada, patriarch of the Monterrey Group, the largest business group in the republic, by urban guerrilla commandos of the 23rd of September League. President Echeverría attended his funeral and listened, without uttering a word, to the very disparaging comments that a business representative devoted to him in the funeral oration, accusing him, among other things, of having created the mood of anarchy and social hatred that made possible the assassination of Eugenio Garza Sada.

Agitation and the Democratic Tendency

Part of this split in the elite was driven by the atmosphere of worker agitation that dominated a good part of the first half of the 1970s. Echeverría's administration sought initially to put an end to, or at least diminish, the power of the long reign of Fidel Velázquez and his cronies in the Confederation of Mexican Workers (CTM) and in the high reaches of the workers' bureaucracy. Sensitive to the basic needs of the union members and upheld by a vast network of national and international political interests, that workers' bureaucracy was able to resist (and even defiantly: "With the Constitution or against the Constitution," Fidel Velásquez said in Tepeji del Río, in 1972) the offensive of the executive branch of the nation. The history of what followed and its context are revealing.

The economic crisis at the beginning of the 1970s eased things for the monopolist industry, but this created the conditions for the mobilization of the workers, both with respect to the business sectors and the agencies of union control. At the apex of the industrial system, a boom was taking place, with greater concentration and creation of monopolies, but in that same sector the most significant worker struggles were taking place.

It was precisely in those highly stratified, privileged, and technical sectors of the industrial proletariat where the worker conflicts took place during the 1970s. Examples of this were the extended agitation of the electricians and railroad workers in 1971 and 1972; the strikes in the Nissan, Rivetex, Celanese, and Medalla de Oro factories in 1973; the strikes in General Electric, Cinsa-Cifunsa, and Lido in 1974; the strikes in Spicer and Manufacturas Metálicas, in Monterrey; that of Lacsa in Cuernavaca; and those of Texlamex, Harper Wayman, Cofisa, Searle, Hilaturas Aztecas, Panam, and Duramil, in Naucalpan, Mexico state, during 1975; until a climax was reached with the great electricians' march of November 15, 1975, in Mexico City.

When all of these strikes are mentioned together, they appear to be what they were not: the beginning of a workers' insurrection. They took place because, in the midst of the crisis, the traditional control of the government over the union structures could not be exerted in all the sectors of the industrial proletariat. With inflation, it seemed that the equilibrium of union control started to break down, when its main material base of support started to erode: the guarantee of stable wages and jobs, and the network of compensatory benefits. The interesting thing about the 1970s was that the upper cadres of that stagnant unionism were able to react and struggle to improve the wages of its constituents. If the inflation was seen in those years by certain elements as a "bourgeois offensive," the salary hikes negotiated in 1973–1974 by the CTM and the Labor Congress were, in some sense, a "workers' counteroffensive." Fidel Velázquez, a cautious and conservative leader, risked in those days the threat of a national strike, which clearly shows the pressure that was building up in the grass roots of the official unions, as well as the intensity of the conflict.

The reaction of the business sector to the demands of the workers' bureaucracy was no less enlightening. In 1974, confronted by Fidel Velázquez's demand of a 42 percent increase in wages, the CONCAMIN warned that such an increase "would disrupt the anti-inflation program." An employers' lockout in Monterrey in June 1974 accused the local government of not restraining the "illegal and gangsterlike" procedures of the unions that were challenging the work stoppage. The business lobbies CANACINTRA, COPARMEX, and CONCAMIN united to claim that the large unions were suffering from a "zeal for political and sectoral predominance, for the sake of an unspeakable futurism." Finally, in August, the business sector said that there would not be a raise, that they would not pay the past wages, and that in the case that a strike was called they would request that it be declared nonexistent, making the workers responsible for the factory closures that their acts would unleash.

In his presidential report of September 1974, Echeverría stated the position of the state and declared the worker demands legitimate and legal, with discussion on their "illegality" brushed aside, and the remaining debate was centered on the "percentage of raise," which was finally set at 35 percent. In the alliance with this traditional trade unionism, whose high officials he initially attempted to suppress, President Echeverría found the appropriate moment to put an end to the antagonism that he had received from the business sector since Allende's fall and the assassination of Eugenio Garza Sada in 1973. As a result of the power that Fidel Velázquez acquired and reasserted in that alliance, he was able to expel Rafael Galván from the leadership of the Union of Electricians of the Mexican Republic (SUTERM), due to the death of Francisco Pérez Ríos, leader of the union. Galván was, perhaps, the most outstanding representative of the left within the PRI and of the development of the most viable possibility of an independent working class and political vanguard in the 1970s: the Democratic Tendency of the Electricians. Toward the end of 1975, Rolando Cordera wrote: "The economic activity of the electricians, the productive and economic relations that they hold, illustrate the importance of their movement . . . the productive scenario of their struggle . . . is a strategic and unique scenario, as it is a key industry for the economy as a whole, and it also constitutes one of the main pillars of the economic and political power of the State."

The electricians' movement was a hub for the workers' mobilization against the trade union bureaucracy, the antinationalist trends within and outside the government, the isolation of other popular mobilizations, the sectarian and voluntaristic left, the party atomization, and imperialism.

In light of the circumstances of the end of the administration in which the Democratic Tendency emerged, it did not fool anyone with its name: more than the independent and organic vanguard of the struggles for democratization in the country, it was a perspective on construction, a compass that showed the way, attracted, and was beginning to give cohesion and a practical alternative to the worker and popular agitation, which, despite its accomplishments and experiences, was still the expression of what Galván himself described as a "state of mind."

Months of an intense campaign of official trade unionism against the Tendency and its leaders, a long list of provocations, and the expectant neutrality of the authorities came to a climax in July 1976, with a call for a strike of the 20,000 workers of the Tendency.

In response, the installations and workplaces were occupied by SUTERM and army personnel. The intraunion conflict had a sudden and unforeseen conclusion on July 17, when there was an armed showdown between the occupants of the electrical installations of Puebla and Tendency groups that were holding a rally in front of their workplace, a clash that left several wounded and one person from SUTERM dead. The following day, the two main branches of the Tendency—Jalisco and Puebla—accepted their readmission to the SUTERM, with which the Tendency stopped being a public, national option, to return to the original fold of its activity: the internal politics of one of the three strategic unions of the country.

The Democratic Opening

The social conflict of the first half of the 1970s had, as always, a reflection in the presidential discourse. The tradition that fed the Echeverrista style was the polemical pattern of the first years of Calles and Cárdenas, with the persistent incorporation of sections of self-criticism, dialogue and opening, the unequivocal demands of 1968, as well as Third World rhetoric. This development of the public discourse led to a surprising oxygenation of the political environment and had as its constant theme the continuous petitioning of government and society for a political opening.

The Echeverrista opening was, above all, a declaration in favor of reaffirming the ideological and institutional legitimacy of the Mexican state, eroded by the political crisis of 1968. It did not question the essential goodness of the Mexican "legacy," but rather the anachronism of a certain mentality and the ineffectiveness of some of its practices. It was a response to the demands of "updating" the legacy, in order to preserve whatever was preservable. The idea of "letting things change so that everything remains the same" went hand in hand, as an attitude and a perception, with the very anachronism of some of the major governmental policy decisions. The renewal of the instruments of ideological legitimation was an important aspect of that change of tone, because in the 1970s the public powers placed a greater emphasis on the use of publicity and the mass media. Part of its visible conflict with the private sector, in effect, had as its scenario the mass media. (The Undersecretariat of Broadcasting and the news agency Notimex were two of the administration's innovations.)

The search for mass communication was the search for a public that had deserted the traditional media for state information, motivated by the urgency to restore its credibility and to reconfigure its audience. Thus, slowly but surely, and with increasing intensity, radio and television broadcasting were infiltrated by slogans calling for planned parenthood and compelling figures on the efficiency of the parastate sector. The electoral campaign of José López Portillo, beginning in 1975, included a publicity and political strategy charged with logos, direct mailings, telephone persuasion, and commercials against corruption, the lack of union, and voter apathy. The public sector purchased and ambitiously financed its first competitive television station, Channel 13, then extended its coverage, changed its programming, and started to develop an infrastructure for television production.

The first half of the 1970s demonstrated this certainty: in order to recapture its decisive role in the formation of the national consciousness, the government would have to modify its mechanisms and sell its ideological products and educational programs through the same massive mechanisms that had surpassed it. The moment of greatest impact in the Democratic Opening was the night of June 10, 1971. On the evening of that day, a paramilitary group secretly organized by a government office put down with clubs and gunshots, machine guns, and high-caliber weapons a student demonstration in Mexico City. President Echeverría promised on television that those responsible would be punished. The words of the public authorities then seemed to coincide strongly with their actions. It was a spectacular moment because it led to the removal of high officials, including the mayor of Mexico City, Alfonso Martínez Domínguez, even though the investigations weren't conclusive and those responsible were not incarcerated.

However, the true political efficacy of the Echeverrista opening came through other channels. It had its greatest effect as a bureaucratic, budgetary, and ideological fact. It fulfilled the expectations of the protest pockets of 1968: the student leaders, the universities and centers of higher education, the progressive standard-bearers of the middle classes, and the critical intellectuals. The wide range of subsidies, recognition, exhortation, and personal treatment of those affected sectors was an unexpected avalanche of tolerance, affability, and desire for redress.

In the area of exercising freedom of expression, information, and public criticism, it wasn't a group of intellectuals, but rather a newspaper, *Excélsior*, that developed in practice the presidential proposals of opening, dialogue, and self-criticism. *Excélsior* was a vehicle that presided over the parade of news on the innovations of the 1970s, the end of the impassive Mexico of stabilizing development, and the manifestation of its defects. Every day, the front page of *Excélsior* registered the worsening political and moral crisis of the country; it searched and found the news to fulfill its program for the 1970s. *Excélsior* denounced, recorded, created controversies, and became the center of a public opinion that it created with its arbitrariness and risks, its many successes, and its solidarity with the best liberalizing causes of the nation.

On July 8, 1976, an extended manipulation of internal and external pressures determined the expulsion of seven cooperative members of

Excélsior, among them the editor-in-chief, Julio Scherer García. With them, almost the entire group of journalists and editorialists left who had made journalism a polemical, informative, and critical instrument. The governmental pressure against the newspaper and the resultant loss of confidence in certain groups were the first signs of the political crisis that was gaining ground in the country in the agitated months of the 1976 power transfer. The growing rancor of the presidential confrontation with the business sector and the conservative opinion of the country, the U.S. hostility, the excessive external indebtedness, and the instability in the balance of payments led to the first devaluation of the Mexican currency in twenty-two years in September 1976, and were condensed in the climate of political uncertainty, restlessness, and discord that marked the end of the Echeverría administration.

The "crisis of confidence" and the economic austerity were the signs of the change of government in December 1976. The financial disarray opened the doors to the stabilization and adjustment formulas of the International Monetary Fund, which imposed limits on the wage increases, limited the capacity of further external indebtedness, and established mechanisms for the international supervision of Mexican finances.

The Conquest of the Future

Then, in the midst of austerity, oil arrived. During the following five years, the country witnessed a scenario similar to the previous government, but in enormously enlarged proportions, both in its booms and its busts.

Like the Luis Echeverría administration, that of José López Portillo (1976–1982) had a first and last year of moderate economic growth, compared with the rest of the period. But, while the average growth between 1972 and 1974 was nearly 6 percent, the years of López's oil boom, 1978–1982, achieved economic growth rates that surpassed 8 percent, among the highest rates in the world. Emerging from political disarray and an economic downturn, the government of José López Portillo found in oil the Archimedes' lever to overcome the stagnation and renew the economic development process with limitless possibilities.

The discovery of new hydrocarbon resources in the midst of the 1970s allowed those expectations to emerge: the proven reserves of the country increased from approximately 10 billion barrels of oil to more than 70 billion barrels in just a few years. PEMEX, which had begun to import gasoline and other oil derivatives, was transformed in a few months into a net oil exporter of world rank, as the Mexican oil industry had already been at the beginning of the 1920s. The director of the company during the first years of the López Portillo term, Jorge Díaz Serrano—the author of the transformation of oil as the basis for the new leap of Mexico toward economic development—made clear his conviction about the historical possibilities that opened up with the newly discovered oil fields when he appeared before Congress in 1977:

> This [oil] wealth constitutes not only the instrument to solve the economic problems that we have at present times. It is also the great economic core that has been missing from the beginning of our history and whose absence has prevented the total consolidation of the nation. This wealth allows us to see in our future the creation of a new country, in which the right to work will become a reality and whose wage levels will allow in general a better lifestyle and quality of life.

The convergence of that discovery with the world's first significant energy crisis fueled the government's conviction, shared by vast segments of the population, that Mexico could buy a permanent solution to its economic problems. This was a conviction strengthened by the new oil-field discoveries and the reestimation of the potential reserves, which yielded figures of up to 200 billion barrels, at a time when the severe international crisis in the oil markets fueled a dramatic increase in the price of the product that within a decade would rise from $4 per barrel at the beginning of the 1970s to $38 per barrel in 1979.

The Limits of the Present

The value of oil exports grew very fast, but not at a rate sufficient to pay for the expanding imports, which doubled between 1977 and 1981, in order to satisfy the equally fast growth rate of the disjointed and dependent productive structure that was inherited from the stabilizing development phase. Between 1976 and 1981, the value of oil exports grew 32 times, from $560 million to $14,600 million. But even though the total imports of goods and services only grew threefold, they increased from $9,400 million to $32,000 million, a much greater absolute increase than the oil revenue.

The decisive factor of the increase of imports and its final weight on the behavior of the economy toward the end of the 1970s and the beginning of the 1980s was carefully reviewed by the observers; they determined that four factors contributed to that disproportionate growth. First was the growth in economic activity. Second was the liberalization of imports that took place between 1977 and 1981. Third were the bottlenecks in certain sectors in which demand grew faster than the productive capacity. And fourth were the effects of inflation, which was higher in Mexico than in the rest of the world, making imports more competitive. Brailowsky and Barker state:

> The estimations we have made show that nearly one-third of the difference between the observed growth rate of imports, and what had been planned, was due to the policy of import liberalization. The rest may be explained by a greater internal demand.
> Even though perhaps only one-third of the deficit in the 1981 balance of payments, of $3,700 million, may be attributed directly to liberalization, its accumulated effect during the period could have approached $8,700 million, which increased to $10,000 million in terms of additional external debt, once the interest payments are included. This is equivalent to 75 percent of the increase in the official external debt between the end of 1977 and the end of 1981, which did not correspond to the capital flight.

Expanding the economy rapidly through an aggressive liberalization of imports was the true economic policy followed until 1981, not heeding some negative indicators—inflation that was higher than what had been expected, increasing to 27 percent in 1980–1981—and celebrating some positive indicators: a higher than expected employment generation, which surpassed the natural growth rate of the work force in 1979 and 1980. In mid-1981, the world oil market suffered a severe decline, and it became evident that it would no longer be a seller's market, but rather a buyer's market. The architect of the oil boom, Jorge Díaz Serrano, resigned his position, after having suddenly cut the price of Mexican crude oil, in order to maintain the level of external sales. Together with the collapse of the oil market, the trend toward an increase in the interest rates began to accelerate in the international financial centers. Within the following two years, these increases represented an additional financial cost for Mexico that implied a disbursement of approximately $10 billion.

The specter and the reality of an acute financial crisis, with runaway speculation and capital flight, descended over the country. Despite the collapse in 1981 of the price of the main export product, petroleum, President López decided not to change the expenditure patterns or modify the international exchange rate. López Portillo even proclaimed that a "President who devalues (the currency) is a devalued President." By the beginning of 1982, the economic policies had transformed the peso into a currency that was significantly overvalued, and, in consequence, the economy quickly became "dollarized" and stimulated massive capital flight. An indicator that epitomizes these critical imbalances was the sustained and increasing presence of a serious deficit in the balance of payments. The negative factors that helped to outline this phenomenon were, according to Brailowsky and Barker: (1) the excessive internal demand, which surpassed several times the foreign exchange revenues that were obtained from oil: the third part of the deficit; (2) the increase in the foreign interest rates and growing capital flight: nearly 40 percent of the deficit; and, (3) the liberalization of imports: an additional 30 percent of the deficit. If all of these were added to the freezing of external credit due to the fear in the banks that Mexico would become insolvent, the final year of the López Portillo administration, 1982, was one of rapid deterioration of the economic and political indicators.

The Fifth Option

In February 1982, confronted with an enormous deficit in the balance of payments, amplified by speculation against the peso, the service costs of an external debt of considerable dimensions ($19 billion in 1976, $80 billion in 1982), and an oil market that did not improve, the government of Mexico was forced, belatedly, to devalue the currency by 70 percent.

A central actor and witness in those months, Carlos Tello, wrote a chronicle of the process and the manner in which the conviction that the financial system of the country was touching bottom and that it required unprecedented decisions started to develop among the upper reaches of the government:

> It was difficult to be satisfied with the four options of policy that were been discussed in those days in the government: 1) a new and considerable devaluation of the peso to discourage the demand for foreign exchange and to anticipate the expectations that were being formed that the exchange rate, which had resulted from the already disproportionate devaluation of more than 70 percent in February, could not be sustained; 2) the free flotation of the exchange rate so that "the market" would set the true parity of the exchange rate with respect to the dollar, in a situation in which there was only demand and no supply for dollars; 3) a system of exchange control that almost everybody regarded as impossible to establish in Mexico; and 4) the maintenance of the exchange rate policy that had been in practice since the February devaluation, with the purpose of giving it time to work. From the available information, and taking into account the arguments and reasons in favor of or against each of these possibilities, what later came to be known as the "fifth option" started to emerge: the nationalization of the

private banking system of Mexico . . . as the days went by in the month of August, I was under the increasing impression that we had lost the capacity to manage the financial situation of the country. Capital flight continued, and at the beginning of the month the Bank of Mexico did not have sufficient international reserves to attend the most pressing foreign exchange commitments. A few weeks earlier, the foreign commercial banks, which had benefited most from the process of rapid indebtedness of the country—and which had advocated this process decisively—decided to suspend their credit to Mexico. All of this had led the Mexican government in mid-August to make an advance sale of oil for the strategic reserve of the United States . . . and to formalize conversations with the International Monetary Fund with the purpose of requesting its help. On the other hand, the political atmosphere—which had remained favorable to president López Portillo for a longer period of time than for most previous Mexican presidents—changed radically with astonishing speed, getting worse day by day, until, in a couple of months, it became intolerably hostile.

With the development of events in the month of August, the option of nationalization of the private banks became stronger. In reality, the obvious failure of the financial policies adopted to stop the deterioration of the economic situation of Mexico . . . [That policy] had included the February devaluation, the acceleration of the daily minidevaluations of the currency, new increases in the interest rate with the purpose of keeping savings in the country, a new devaluation in August, and the establishment of a double exchange rate of the peso with respect to the dollar . . . had led the exchange rate to devaluate more than fourfold in six months, and helped to consolidate the arguments in favor of the nationalization of the banks.

The Chiaroscuro

In his sixth and last government report, on September 1, 1982, President López Portillo drew a balance of what he called the "chiaroscuro" of his government. In the luminous part of his drawing, he recalled that the public expenditure and external debt were not only part of the "liabilities" but also of the "assets," and that with those resources an enormous jump had taken place in the oil industry, with an expansion of the proven reserves from 6,338 million barrels in 1976, to 72,000 million in 1982. The oil exports in that year reached 1.5 million barrels, which yielded $14,000 million more in revenue than in 1976. Between 1977 and 1982, the electrical supply had almost doubled, in the last four years industrial production had grown at an annual rate of 9 percent, and the expansion in jobs had been 5.5 percent, a figure without precedence in the history of the country, allowing open unemployment to fall temporarily from 8.1 percent to 4.5 percent. The volume of the ten main crops, which in 1977 was 19,987,000 tons, reached 28,000,000 tons in 1981; the agricultural frontier had expanded by almost 8.3 million acres (almost 2.4 million acres were irrigated), and the agricultural sector had maintained an annual growth rate of 4.5 percent, with a jump of 8.5 percent in 1981. Primary education was being provided for 90 percent of Mexican children, medical services to 85 percent of the population, and drinking water to 70 percent, with an expansion of 87 times the resources devoted to the marginal rural sectors.

Summing up in this fashion the bright spots of his six years of government, López Portillo went on to address—albeit selectively—the shadows. First, he spoke about the negative impact on Mexico of the most severe and extended crisis that the international economy had experienced since the Great Depression of 1929, the sudden decline in the prices of all of Mexico's exports, the presence of the highest interest rates in history, the credit restrictions, and the perpetuation of protectionist barriers in the industrialized countries. López Portillo went on to say:

> The impact was suddenly felt when the price of oil collapsed . . . Afterwards, we felt the effects of that blow, in the recent increase in the external debt . . . the debt reached a total of 76 billion dollars in July of this year, of which 80 percent corresponds to the public sector and 20 percent to the private sector. . . . the increase in the interest rates explains to a large degree the economic deterioration: between 1978 and 1981, the interest rate of international loans increased from 6 percent to 20 percent and this explains, partially but fundamentally, the fact that the interest payments of the developing countries jumped from 14,200 million dollars in 1978 to 38,000 million dollars in 1981. In the case of Mexico, the interest payments on the documented public and private debt reached a total of 2,606 million dollars in 1978, while in 1981 they totaled 8,200 million dollars.

On the export side, López Portillo also recalled, Mexico had confronted, as many other developing countries, a very rapid deterioration in the prices of a good number of its basic and traditional export products. Such had been the case, between 1980 and 1981, of coffee beans (whose unit value of exports had fallen by 16 percent), raw cotton (-12 percent), mineral copper (-51 percent), refined lead (-25 percent), and, of course, silver (-75 percent). Due to this factor, the dynamism of the export revenues from primary goods, which still represented a significant percentage of the total of nonoil exports (50.5 percent in 1981), was curbed.

The Nationalization of the Banks

The president went on to analyze the negative factors of the internal political economy, focusing especially on the irresponsibility of those investors who searched for profits without risk in exchange rate speculation, capital flight, and the deep disarray of the national finances, conducted through the private banking system:

> The speculation against the peso began in the very same cashier windows of the banks in which dollarization was being recommended and supported . . . We don't know it for sure, but we have information that the newly opened bank accounts of Mexicans overseas surpass, at least, 14 billion dollars . . . Additionally, the urban and rural real estate in the United States of America that belongs to Mexicans is estimated to have a value of approximately 30 billion dollars. This has already generated an outflow of foreign exchange, through downpayments and first payments, of nearly 8.5 billion dollars . . . the accounts in Mexican banks denominated in dollars, but fed originally and in its majority by pesos, are approximately 12 billion dollars. The so-called mexdollars represent the most troubling aspect of the dollarization of the national economy.
>
> Using conservative figures, we can then assert that in the past two or three years, at least 22 billion dollars have left the Mexican economy; and a private, nonregistered debt has been generated to pay for mortgages, to pay for maintenance of properties and taxes, of more than 20 billion dollars, which must be added to the external debt of the country. These quantities, when added to the 12 billion mexdollars, would yield 54 billion dollars, which are equivalent to half of the total liabilities of the Mexican banking system as a whole, and almost two-thirds of the documented public and private debt of the country.

Unfortunately, the Presidential Report did not include the direct responsibility of the federal government for the financial disaster. After all, the action of the banks was not autonomous, but rather it followed the basic rules of the credit institutions, and these rules had been formulated with the direct intervention of the National Banking Committee.

I can assert that in a few, recent years, a group of Mexicans . . . headed, counseled and aided by the private banks, have withdrawn more money from this country, than all of the empires that have exploited us from the beginnings of our history.

We cannot continue to risk that those resources be channeled through the same conduits that have contributed in such a dynamic fashion to generate the severe situation we are going through.

We have to organize ourselves to save our productive structure, in order to provide it with sufficient financial resources to go forth; we have to stop the injustice of this perverse process: capital flight, devaluation, inflation, which affects all, especially the workers, employment, and the companies that generate it.

These are our critical priorities.

In order to respond to these, I have issued in consequence two decrees: one that nationalizes the private banks of the country; and another one that establishes the generalized foreign exchange control, not as a policy that has survived "better late than never," but rather because today the critical conditions that have developed require it and justify it. It is now or never. They have already plundered us. But Mexico has not ended. And they shall not plunder us again.

No-Man's-Land

The decisions adopted on September 10, 1982, were the unforeseen climax of a long process of structural deterioration, the end of an economic and political scheme that only needed a surge of abundance in order to demonstrate its shallowness.

During the years of the oil boom, Mexico experienced the incredible paradox that everything that enabled the country to grow rapidly would soon put it at risk of bankruptcy. The ambitious state investment during the López Portillo administration brought with it waste and inflation, which devoured its currency and its economy. The private banks transformed its yearning for secure profits into an aggressive speculation and dollarization of its operations. The disjointed national industry grew rapidly but at the cost of an unsustainable flow of imports and an increasing vulnerability with respect to the external sector. The powerful, albeit concentrated and defective, internal market spent its purchasing power on luxury consumption, smuggling, and oil tourism. Sector by sector, the Mexican society and economy found in the boom dramatic proof of its structural lack of preparation for the boom, the anachronism and vulnerability of the fundamental agreement that ruled it.

Forced by the unmanageable crisis of 1982, the most probusiness and least populist government in a long time had to scuttle the very foundation of the agreement with the private groups. It also nationalized the banks by a decision that was undertaken almost exclusively by the president, because such a momentous resolution was not part of any official project, nor were the representatives of the main political and social forces of the country consulted about it. It was, in reality, the implicit confession of a mutual failure, the recognition that the historical agreement with financial capital had ceased working, because the regime of economic concessions on which it was based did not guarantee anything but economic instability.

The Mexican society experienced the quarter after the nationalization of the banks as a pondering no-man's-land. The impending departure of the nationalizing government reduced its power as the enforcer of the expectations of society, and as the leader of the political class that sought or had already found its alignment with the new government of President Miguel de la Madrid, elected only two months before, on July 7, 1982. After attempting vainly to provide it with an orientation and to establish certain general norms for the future development of the nationalized banks, President López Portillo surrendered by the end of October to the evidence and admitted in Tlaxcala that to "reorganize" the nationalized banks in his remaining thirty-three days in office "would be irresponsible and of extreme political imprudence."

On the other side of the scale, the discretion of the incoming government and its hesitation with respect to the decree were clear indicators of its political disagreement with the decision. The months that followed the nationalization were thus a scenario of paralysis. On the one hand were the last days of a waning government, without power or a project to provide a specific orientation to its decision to nationalize. On the other hand was an elected government that was forced to redefine its objectives and commitments, due to the new and unexpected situation.

After an initial period of bewilderment, the private groups found, beginning in 1983, the way to give the opposition a single direction. They developed a coherent ideological discourse and a political action of common purpose and group cohesion, whose public face was a series of forums called "Mexico in Freedom." In these forums, it was repeated time and time again that the nationalization of the banks was the first step in a state conspiracy to impose socialism in Mexico. That certainty united the traditional voices of the right, the chambers of commerce and industry, the National Action party (PAN), the private mass media, and even the Catholic church, which spoke on this occasion through its bishops.

In its defensive movement, the business resistance touched significant civilian realms: the conservatism and the antistate belligerence of broad sectors of the emerging middle class, which had been affected by inflation, and which adhered to the defense of its consumerist liberties; the political belligerence of the reactivated church, which acted from the pulpits, preaching against the phantom of atheistic communism and socialism in Mexico; the private network of mass communications, a significant sector of the top-level public bureaucracy, and almost all of the financial public servants; and the very weight of the business sector as a productive community organized politically. Finally, the notorious corruption of the top-level political circles in the six-year period that ended in December 1982 provided a moral justification for the business sector's condemnation of almost all of the policies pursued by José López Portillo.

In the Center of the Crisis

Thus, at the end of 1982, in the advent of a change of government, after the greatest boom that it had experienced in its relationship with the world market, the country of the Mexican Revolution saw the central agreements for its stability vanish in mid-air. Its road toward the future had lost the clarity of the institutional routine that had always been present, without having put into motion the reforming mechanism that the new structure demanded. For the third consecutive time, the new government had inherited from the previous one a critical situation that had worsened considerably during the last year of administration. The Mexicans did not seem to be confronting just the typically confusing situation of transfer of power, with a simple economic crisis and disagreements in the inner circles of power. What the new government faced on the horizon was recession, financial suffocation, closing of the international monetary and commercial markets, unemployment with wage drops, reduction of public expenditure, and an economic downturn for 1983 that was already being forecast between 0 percent and -5 percent.

The nationalization of the banks was not a direct response to the main problems of the economy, because the root of the problem was not in the financial structures, but rather in the global economic development model. Nobody was able to prevent bankruptcies due to the lack of liquidity, an economic depression in the market, and the collapse of public finances due to urgent commitments that prevented importing strategic goods, leading to speculative panic. December 1982 found the country with a productive capacity that was notably larger than at the beginning of the 1970s, but extraordinarily more dependent.

The dream of "interdependence" with the trappings of a medium world power, which oil had allowed the Mexicans to dream of as a solution to the country's incorporation into the world market, had been shocked awake by the harsh realities of the international recession, the collapse in the prices of the primary products, and the oil bust of mid-1981. The increase in the interest rates in the international money market tripled the costs of the external Mexican debt that Mexico had already accumulated. The contraction of the international capital market, due to the elimination of the petrodollars from the financial circuits, narrowed the possibilities of external financing and left open only the access to short-term loans. This was the financial coup de grâce to the dream of an "interdependent" Mexican model.

Except perhaps for the years of revolutionary violence, the Mexicans of this century had not lived through such a difficult economic period as the one beginning in the final months of the oil feast. The severity of the crisis was openly recognized by the new president, Miguel de la Madrid, in his inaugural address on December 2, 1982:

> Mexico is experiencing a severe crisis. We suffer an inflation that almost reaches 100 percent this year; an unprecedented public sector deficit is fueling it acutely, and there are no savings to finance its own investment; the lag in the public fees and prices has placed the state-owned companies into a deficit situation, hiding weaknesses and subsidizing groups with high incomes; the weakening in the dynamic of the productive sectors has led us to zero growth.
>
> The foreign exchange inflow to the financial system has been paralyzed, with the exception of the revenues derived from the oil exports and some other products of the public sector and its credits. We have a public and private external debt that has reached excessive proportions, and whose service imposes a drain on the budget and on the balance of payments, and is displacing resources for productive investment and social expenditures; the fiscal revenues have weakened, becoming more inequitable. The external credit has fallen dramatically, and internal savings and investment have become unattractive. In these circumstances, the productive capacity of the nation and employment are seriously threatened. We are confronting the highest open unemployment rate of recent times. Mexicans of lower income face increasing difficulties to satisfy their basic needs for subsistence.
>
> The crisis expresses itself in the lack of confidence and pessimism in the ability of the country to solve its immediate requirements; in the surge of discord between classes and groups; in the angry search for scapegoats; in the reciprocal and growing recrimi-

nations; in the feelings of abandonment, dejection, and exacerbation of individualism and sectarianism, a trend that is corroding the
solidarity that is required for life in society and collective efforts.

The crisis is located within the international context of uncertainty and fear, a deep recession that is encroaching. There are trade
wars, even between allies, a protectionism disguised as free trade.
High interest rates, the collapse of the prices of primary products,
and an increase in the prices of industrial products are leading
many countries to insolvency. To the world economic disorder,
political instability is added, with the growing arms race, the
struggle between the world powers to extend their zones of influence. Never in recent times had we seen international concord so
distant.

We live in an emergency situation. It is not a time for hesitation
or feuds; it is the time for decisions and responsibility. We shall not
allow ourselves to succumb to inertia. The situation is intolerable.
We shall not allow our fatherland to perish in our hands. We will
act with decisiveness and firmness.

The Explosion That Never Happened

The sensation of having arrived at a dangerous limit with regard to the
stability and viability of the system that had been inherited from the
stabilizing development period was extended in the political and social
mood of the country at the end of 1982. In January 1983, high-level
government officials were estimating that if it was possible to get to the
September 10, 1983, date for the first annual Presidential Report without
a social explosion taking place, the new government could consolidate
itself and advance its own agenda. That agenda was dominated by the
conviction of having arrived at a turning point in the country, as it was
undergoing the most severe crisis in its contemporary history. And it
was bold enough to believe that facing the risk of the situation provided
an opportunity for change, because this was the appropriate moment to
introduce drastic reforms that would enable a different Mexico to
emerge. The new Mexico of which the new government was thinking
was not a centralized country, but decentralized; not populist or corporative, but liberal and democratic; not patrimonial and corrupt, but
morally renewed; not inefficient and disarticulated, but rational and
nationally planned. And it was not the large, lax, subsidizing, and
feudalized state that had administered thus far the historical pact of the
1910–1917 Revolution, but rather a small, lean state, with clear limits
on its interventionist faculties, economically realistic and not deficit-
spending, and administratively modern. The mere articulation of the

project showed its merits and also its excessive ambition. Seven themes had summed it up during Miguel de la Madrid's electoral campaign: (1) revolutionary nationalism, (2) integral democratization, (3) equitable society, (4) moral renovation, (5) decentralization of national life, (6) development, employment, and struggle against inflation, and (7) democratic planning.

In December 1984, two years after this project had been put into practice, its achievements could be summed up in the following fashion: there was not more revolutionary nationalism or simple nationalism, but less; the country, much more so than in any other previous period, had its eyes to the North and thought in terms of dollars. The integral democratization was not immediately apparent in its most obvious manifestation, the elections: the citizens had witnessed during the local elections of 1984–1986 the return of electoral manipulation and fraud.

The crisis had lowered wages, and between 1978 and 1983 they fell by 40 percent, which did not indicate progress toward a more equitable society, but rather a historical step in the direction of increasing inequality. Inflation was, by definition, a force that was leading toward a greater concentration of income in fewer hands.

Along with some highly publicized imprisonments, such as that of Jorge Díaz Serrano, oil hero of the previous administration, and the adoption of some mechanisms to prevent greater drains on the public funds, the government's campaign for moral renovation aspired to end the discredit and moral degeneration that were part of the image of Mexican society at home and abroad. The results did not correspond to the expectations generated, and the confidence of the common citizens in the honesty of their leaders was not restored.

The decentralization of national life omitted, for the sake of political realism, the proposal of municipal independence and consolidation that had been drafted by the government in its reforms to article 115 in December 1983. The decentralizing activity was basically limited to the extension of the process of administrative deconcentration that had already begun in previous administrations.

A negative growth rate of -5.4 percent during 1983 and a growth rate of slightly more than 3 percent in 1984 made evident the severe limits in the economic process and clipped the wings of the ambitious proposal for development with employment and inflation control. An inflation rate of 80 percent in 1983 grew to 100 percent by 1986 and to 150 percent by 1987, considerably exceeding official expectations and undermining the maintenance of employment and the conservation of the productive capacity.

The so-called democratic planning had been transformed, in the public's eye, into a series of roundtables with participants whose presentations merely legitimized the decisions reached beforehand by the diagnostic bodies of the government offices that convened the roundtables.

In sum, regarded through a critical eye, the panorama that unfolded was one of growing centralization and inequality, democratization in retreat, superficial moralization with self-devaluation, decentralization administered from the center, feeble growth with uncontrolled inflation, declining employment and productive capacity, rhetorical nationalism without substance, and technocratic planning. But the De la Madrid administration had gotten through not only September 10, 1983, but also December 1, 1984, without having suffered a social explosion, an irreversible or bloody split, or a substantial alteration of the peaceful and institutional coexistence among Mexicans. This achievement, given the extremely adverse situation at its start, was in itself a political victory for his administration.

The Restoration

Seen as a whole, the De la Madrid administration seemed to have two faces, which it saw as complementary. One regarded the future with a reformist aspiration; the other looked back, with a desire for restoration. A basic tenet of the project seemed to be that there would not be a stable future for Mexico if the essential agreement of the society with the state was not reinstated, and, more precisely, the agreement between private capital and the public sector.

Politically and ideologically opposed to the nationalization of the banks on September 1, 1982, the members of the new government saw in that measure the end of a social contract, and the ending point, or point of no return, of the business community's confidence in the government and of the symbiosis of private capital with the government.

By the end of 1984, the new government had devoted two years of efforts and concessions to heal at least partially the split with financial capital. In December 1983, in a process of partial privatization, they allowed private capital to repurchase 34 percent of the stock of the banks. Months later, they paid a more than generous indemnity to the ex-bankers, guaranteeing that they would have privileged access to the purchase of the nonbank companies that had fallen into the lap of nationalization. Finally, they allowed renewed access to the financial system through the very broad spectrum of "nonbank financial institutions" (stock exchange houses, insurance companies, etc.), a decision that, in the opinion of some observers, was equivalent to sanctioning the existence of a "parallel banking system." Witnessing these events, anthropologist Arturo Warman suggested that the historical experience of the nationalized railroads could be seen as a sort of "remembrance of the future" of the nationalized banks:

Between 1940 and today, the railroad system probably increased its extension by 5 percent, while all of the transportation system increased by 400 percent through the system of highways and motor vehicles. It was a parallel system that, at a certain point, became the motor force of national development, while the railroad system withered away . . . The development of the country simply sidetracked them, and the railroads languished until they arrived at their present state. And as there was no backtracking in the nationalization of the railroads, there will neither be one with the banks, as this would weaken the government. In similar fashion, the country could not simply do away with the railroad system, which still feeds it despite everything. It has not grown, it does not function appropriately, it loses money, but it still occupies a central place in the economy.

The decision to restore the agreement was also the guiding principle of the constitutional reforms of December 1983, which defined the direction of the state and of the mixed economy, as well as the offer to sell to private owners several parastate companies. It was also one of the axes of the strategy to confront the crisis and seek a recovery: once the source of external financing was closed—which had previously covered the growing shortfalls in government revenue and the deficits in the general economy, with the oil revenue tied up in the debt service and public expenditure restricted—only private investment, national and foreign, could guarantee in the midst of the crisis the possibility of a prompt and sustained recovery. Despite the concessions that had been made, foreign investment was not flowing into Mexico in the quantities that had been expected, and national investment was starting to pick up, but not of a sufficient magnitude to guarantee a sustained recovery.

The Accounts of Contadora

To the traditional problems of bilateral friction, Mexico and the United States added at the beginning of the 1980s one of strategic importance: the Central American situation. The victory of the Nicaraguan Revolution in 1979 put an end to the prolonged dictatorship of the Somoza family in that country, a dictatorship that, almost until its dramatic ending, had always counted on U.S. support. From that moment on, Central America gradually became the scenario of a geopolitical confrontation between Mexico and the United States, a scenario where the national security policies of both nations clashed. Unfortunately for Mexico, it also turned out to be the scenario where the U.S. government had decided to settle part of its global strategy of confrontation with the Soviet Union.

The arrival of Ronald Reagan to the presidency of the United States at the beginning of 1981 represented the consolidation of the most conservative visions in that country, which sought the military defeat of the Central American revolutionary forces in Latin America; the tensions in the relationship between Mexico and its great neighbor to the North became more evident. One way to prevent the deterioration of the relationship between Washington and Mexico City was to transform the Mexican policy in Central America from a bilateral to a multilateral one, coordinating it with Venezuela, Colombia, and Panama in a meeting that took place on the island of Contadora, Panama.

The configuration of the Contadora Group at the beginning of 1983, as well as its central role in the negotiation of the Central American conflict, was one of the successes of Mexican foreign policy in the midst of the 1980s crisis. From its constitution, Contadora was a diplomatic and political dam that was able to generate in the international scenario the consciousness that it was possible and urgent to find a negotiated settlement to the Central American war. To a certain extent, it put a halt on several occasions to imminent preparations for a military expansion of the conflict, and it gave continuity and Latin American support to Mexico's position, which recognized as the origin of the conflicts in the region the inequality and internal dissension of those nations, rather than the intervention of the Soviet Union and the East-West conflict.

Toward the end of 1984, after two years of excellent intermediation and under U.S. pressure and the hostility of the governments of El Salvador, Honduras, and Costa Rica, Contadora seemed to be headed toward obsolescence. The reform proposals to the Act of Pacification of the zone created by the governments of Honduras, Costa Rica, and El Salvador expressly excluded the Contadora governments in the control of the demilitarization of the zone, and effectively counterattacked by suggesting that in the guardianship of the Contadora group there was a veiled interventionism in the destiny of the Central American nations.

Contadora, since its emergence, had also been the core of an internal definition, one of the display windows of the growing U.S. influence on the networks of Mexican society. Contadora's work found opposition in broad ideological and political currents in Mexico, in the majority of the television and printed mass media, and in many segments of society that regarded with suspicion—because of self-interest or pragmatism—anything that could be equated with a confrontation with the United States.

Shaping Mexico

Observers of the U.S. press and academia detected in those years a fundamental change in U.S. policies toward Mexico in two complementary directions: on the one hand, a certain fear of the lack of governability of Mexico and distrust of the capacity of the once very trustworthy Mexican political system to confront the problems of the country; on the other hand, and as a product of the distrust in the ability of the Mexican political elite, there emerged the possibility of a new type of interventionism in the internal affairs of Mexico, to guarantee the United States "control" of its southern border. One of the most innovative aspects of this new interventionism was, for some observers, the notion of trying to shape Mexico. It was being changed bit by bit in the direction of U.S. interests, with a recognition of the real forces that modernization had created in Mexican society and that the old system of political institutions, ideas, and practices did not seem able to absorb. There was an attempt to recognize those forces and get close to them to help them develop, given that those forces would be called upon to open and erode the long-held authoritarian, corporative, and nationalist pact of post-revolutionary Mexico. They were the forces that naturally regarded the United States as a mighty friend and the path to be followed and that could be the agents of a natural process within Mexico toward a historical convergence with the United States.

In that hypothesis of trying to shape Mexico, several trends in the mid-1980s seemed to converge: the growing integration of the Mexican economy with the U.S. economy; the development of the maquiladora industry and the new automobile factories in Saltillo and Hermosillo; the incorporation of the Televisa group into the U.S. communications network as the largest Spanish-language TV network in North America (Spanish International Network); and the recognition of PAN by the Republicans as the force that was closest to embodying the U.S. ideal for its Mexican neighbor—a bipartisan system. A bipartisan system appeared attractive to the U.S. government not so much because of its possible democratic character, but rather because of its modernizing and stabilizing effect on Mexican political life. In the course of that project, the public attitudes and political loquacity of Ambassador John Gavin seemed to merge, as the most active and combative U.S. diplomatic representative in several decades.

Democracy: To Be or Not to Be

The discontent, irritation, distrust, impoverishment, and the erosion between 1982 and 1983 of previous expectations did not result in independent political movements, but rather in the search for institutional alternatives. After all, in the collective memory the traumatic experiences of 1968, 1958, and earlier were still present. As a result, the people did not take to the streets but rather to the voting booths; and not to the left, but rather to the right. There, in the elections held in the middle of the first year of government, reality quickly tested and undid the propositions of formal democracy and respect for the outcome of the elections that had been advocated by De la Madrid. There was an intragovernmental struggle between those who maintained the need to respect the electoral victories of the opposition and those who maintained the need, PRIista par excellence, of a directed democracy, which would prevent the outcome, in a crisis, from becoming a structural political change that would make the country vulnerable to foreign pressures and to the oligarchic blackmail of the capitalists and business sector, to whom concessions were already being made through other channels.

In the debate between these two positions, the latter emerged victorious, especially after PAN won in the municipal elections of Chihuahua on July 3, 1983. This was a landslide victory in the municipalities that concentrated 70 percent of the population of the largest border state with the United States. Those elections, in which the opposition PAN also won in the cities of Durango and Guanajuato, were understood by the government as an indication that the crisis had effectively arrived at the voting booths and presaged a severe decline of the PRI and the ascendance of the PAN in the North and among the urban population.

To halt that possible domino effect, the system went back to the drawing board, and the old alchemists, cajolers, and manipulators appeared. From "Operation Dragon," installed in North Baja California for the gubernatorial and municipal elections of September 4, 1983, until "Operation Tango Papas," established in Mérida for the elections held on Sunday, November 25, 1984, the recipe was "alchemy" or electoral fraud, the victory of the idea that power is not to be "given away" in the ballot boxes.

Mexican society, however, had changed, but the "alchemy" had not. The manipulation of the votes was seen and could not be hidden, among other reasons, because it was perpetrated against a population that was not nonparticipatory or unmotivated, but rather electorally mobilized against the system.

Neither the presidential decision to take charge of the PRI in its critical state nor the express decision of the federal government to reward votes in favor of the PRI with support for investment and resources was able to reverse the trend toward electoral desertion of the PRI in the urban areas of the country, particularly in the North of the republic. It already seemed impossible to convert the PRI into a convincing political product, both in those areas where it had been deserted and in the national public opinion.

The internal fissures were not a minor problem among those who prevented the PRI from acting in the critical areas, as the traditional steamroller it had been. On the one hand, the arrival to power of the Miguel de la Madrid team had displaced an important segment of the so-called political class, against whose wishes and despite whose resistance within the PRI—the trade union sector and part of the bureaucracy—the candidacy of the then secretary of planning and budget was imposed in 1981. On the other hand, part of the global project of President De la Madrid included the need for a generational change in the style and procedures of the political personnel of the country. That conviction explained the presence of numerous young politicians, of scant practical experience, in positions that until then had been reserved for experienced politicians.

Starting with the cabinet and ending with the PRI, De la Madrid seemed willing to pay the price of inexperience in order to guarantee, at least partially, the development of a new political class that would be in agreement with the objectives of economic modernization that he wanted to initiate. The assumptions and the sense of future in that initiative flatly contradicted the practices of the previous model. The basic premise of the project—summed up in the aim of achieving "structural change"—can be expressed by two profound substitutions: that of the protectionist model of growth oriented toward the internal market for a competitive model oriented toward the external market; and that of the interventionist, subsidizing, "Keynesian" state for one that simply had the function of regulating and overseeing growth, restricted to its basic task of stimulating rather than directing the energies and initiatives of society.

The Costs of Adjustment

The social costs of this change of direction can hardly be exaggerated, since they took place within the context of a recessive adjustment of the Mexican economy, which had come into the 1980s overburdened by debt and deficits as never before in its history. Also, the years of sustained development had not been sufficient to dilute the oldest and most persistent problem of Mexico: its ancestral regime of inequality.

At the beginning of the 1980s, after the oil boom and on the threshold of the economic crisis that followed it, the most severe features of inequality at the base of the Mexican society were still as dramatic and colonial as ever: only 35 out of every 100 Mexicans had an acceptable nutritional level, and 19 of every 100 showed chronic symptoms of malnutrition; 23 million Mexicans older than 15 years—or 58 percent— had not finished primary school, and 6 million lacked any instruction; 43 out of every 100 deaths that occurred in Mexico had been preventable, and 45 percent of the total population—30 million Mexicans—did not have any sort of medical coverage; only 38 of every 100 houses (31 of every 100 in 1970) had drinking water, drainage, and electricity.

A total of 22.3 million Mexicans—46 of every 100—lacked the minimum standards of welfare in nutrition, education, health, and employment. In contrast, only 14.8 million Mexicans—30 of every 100—showed low levels of marginalization. A stratum of middle class, with adequate incomes and consumption, had consolidated, but 35 of every 100 Mexican families had incomes below the minimum wage (scarcely above $100 per month) and 19 million persons were undernourished—13 million of them in rural areas. The infant mortality rate was higher than Paraguay's, and more children were born underweight (12 of every 100) than the Latin American average (10 of every 100). Forty-five percent of the population did not have access to medical services, and there were 22 million illiterates or persons who had not finished their primary education. Half of the houses in the country did not have drinking water, and 1 of every 4 did not have electricity. The distance between the richest 10 percent of the population and the poorest 10 percent, which in 1963 was 24 times, had expanded to 35 times in 1977, and everything leads us to believe that the distance has expanded in the 1980s.

The economic bankruptcy of the 1980s added the structural deficiencies of the distributive mechanisms of the country to the deepest recession of its contemporary history. During six years—1982 to 1987—Mexico had zero economic growth, the effects of which will crop up in the 1990s with an accumulated deficit in social costs of such a magnitude that it will probably represent a significant jump in Mexican inequality: not only general impoverishment, but also the concentration of resources and wealth among a smaller number of Mexicans than in the 1970s.

Research concluded in December 1987 pointed out the paradox that six years of economic crisis had made Mexican society more egalitarian, in the sense that now Mexicans were "more equal in their poverty." The number of poor (with a monthly family income below two minimum wages) had increased from 40 percent of the population to nearly 60 percent. At the same time, the 8 percent of Mexicans who at the beginning of the 1980s earned more than 14 minimum wages by 1987 had dropped to only 5 percent.

Between 1982 and 1987, the minimum wage had undergone a reduction of more than 40 percent. The participation of salary mass in the global distribution of wealth had declined from 42 percent to 30 percent, according to some authors, and from 37.4 to 28.9 percent, according to others—in any case, Mexico had returned to its wage level of a generation before, of 1966. The average wage, measured in constant 1970 pesos, had fallen from 51 pesos per day in 1985 to 35 pesos per day in 1987. The cost of the 22 products of basic consumption, which in 1982 had absorbed 33.3 percent of the minimum wage, by 1986 absorbed 42.4 percent of the same. In order to satisfy their basic needs, workers earning the minimum wage had to work 50 hours per week in 1982; to buy the same basket of goods, people had to work 85 hours in 1986.

Not only was the wage lower, but also proportionally fewer Mexicans had access to that wage. In the very decade of greatest flow of young working force into the labor market—an average of one million per year, the highest rate in the history of the country—the recession had inhibited the creation of jobs and had multiplied the exodus of new labor force to the informal economy, unemployment and underemployment, emigration abroad, and crime. According to the estimations of U.S. economist Clark Reynolds, in order to absorb the demographic avalanche of young people looking for jobs, it would have been necessary to sustain from 1980 on an annual growth rate of 7 percent. But, between 1982 and 1987, the Mexican economy fell an average of 4 percent per year. The number of permanent unemployed grew in the main cities of the country in corresponding magnitude. By the end of 1983 in Mexico City, twenty-four of every hundred persons of working age did not have a job; by 1985, the situation had grown worse: 34 percent were unemployed.

The main distributive mechanism of the Mexican model also encountered a peak and a decline. The public expenditure in social programs, which had begun a decline since the 1970s as a percentage of the GNP, began to fall in 1982 in its per capita amount. In the 1980s, each Mexican received less money per capita of social expenditure from the state: a quarter less in health investment, a third less in educational investment. Consequently, by 1986 some troubling phenomena began to crop up that presaged long-term retrogressions and deviations in two central aspects of Mexican welfare: on one hand, in the conservation of the human resources of the country; on the other, in their qualification and training, the only lasting guarantee of economic improvement and social mobility.

In 1986, public expenditure on health was the lowest it had been in twenty years: 35 million Mexicans remained outside the health system of the country, public or private. The number of persons attended by public health institutions and social security increased proportionally between 1982 and 1985, but the total number of inhabitants without any health services also grew significantly, from 37.2 million in 1982 to 41.4 million in 1985. There were indicators of a fall in the quality of services, such as the multiplication of patients with respect to hospital beds and available doctors, and a parallel fall in wages, salaries, and funds devoted to social benefits—credits, child care services, retirement pensions—of the institutes of social security. Above all, there was a negative trend in the rates of infant mortality, which increased from 40 deaths per thousand in 1980 to 51 deaths per thousand in 1984. There was also an increase in work accidents, as a product of the decline in the funds for training, maintenance of the installations, and the system of work security, which made the number of permanent disablements paid by the Mexican Institute of Social Security (IMSS) jump from 16,000 in 1981 to 24,000 in 1986.

The decline in education was even more severe. Stable, with a tendency to decline, were the physical installations—the number of students per teacher increased from 43 in 1982 to 45 in 1985—with the resulting fall in the quality of education aggravated, as in the case of medical doctors, by the parallel fall in teachers' wages.

The revealing process that truly expressed the crisis was perhaps the severe change in the high schools. It is the segment of greatest challenge for the nation, the millions of young teenagers en route to unemployment, frustration, and the closing off of their futures and their opportunities. By the mid-1980s, the crisis was pulling students from the classrooms—due to family poverty, millions of youngsters were put to work by their families to improve the fallen income. In 1982, 42 out of every 100 students were able to finish their high school studies; by 1986, the figure had fallen dramatically to only 21 of every 100.

An even greater hardship, although perhaps its long-term effects might be as hidden as the others, is the decline in nutrition. The decline in family income, the reduction of compensatory public expenditure, the elimination of subsidies for basic foods, and the prices of goods and services, in the midst of an accelerated inflation, explain the fact that between 1982 and 1986 the annual consumption of beef by Mexicans fell by half (from 35.3 to 17.4 pounds per capita), the consumption of milk by a third (from 114 to 78 quarts per capita), and that of chicken by a similar proportion (from 11.9 to 7.7 pounds per capita). Once the figures are estimated for the purchasing power of wages with respect to the eight basic food items—corn tortillas, beans, beef, sugar, coffee, eggs, milk, and lard—the purchasing power of the minimum wage in 1986 was the same as in 1940—a return to the origins of the "Mexican miracle" and preindustrial society.

As a consequence of such adverse conditions, the level of crime and the lack of safety also increased very rapidly. The burglaries reported in Mexico City increased from 44,000 in 1982 to 74,000 in 1984. What is truly significant, however, is the incredible jump in the number of cases of juvenile delinquency: the estimated growth in criminality in young people under the age of 18 till the end of the century is 50 percent in property crimes—burglaries, and the like—and 23 percent in such misdemeanors as intoxication, violent conduct, and vagrancy.

At the other extreme of the struggle for survival and diminishing compensations is the vertex of the income pyramid. For these people, the crisis of the 1980s represented an unprecedented boom. The share of capital income in the distribution of national income, which had been declining during the 1970s, increased from 43.1 percent in 1982 to 54 percent in 1985, an increase of 10.9 percent at the expense of labor's share and the public sector. Mexico experienced in those years a concentration of wealth in the hands of those who already controlled it through several mechanisms: inflation, financial income, speculation, and exchange policies. In effect, the acute Mexican inflationary process of the 1980s— which by itself made the wealthy richer and those who weren't, poorer— added to the Mexican inequality of the end of the century created extraordinary advantages: (1) high interest rates that rewarded bondholders with secure earnings of two or three times the rate of inflation and made the value of the financial rents increase from 4.2 percent of the GNP in 1970 to 13.5 percent in 1985; (2) a stock market that, before its collapse in November 1987, yielded an average return of 600 percent per year, and that was the center for the swift and legendary creation of speculative fortunes; and (3) a policy of sustained overvaluation of the peso until 1982, which rewarded with the devaluations of that year those who had extracted their money from the country to convert it to dollars. Estimated in a conservative fashion by specialists, those profits were equivalent in December of 1982 to 12.2 percent of the GNP of that year. The reverse policy, of aggressive undervaluation of the peso since 1983, rewarded, on the other hand, another type of sectoral concentration— exporters, maquiladoras, and the tourism industry. To give an idea of the volume of the transfers to those sectors, between 1986 and 1987 the Mexican exporters obtained, according to estimations by the French economist Maxime Durand, an additional profit of approximately $4 billion, almost half of what was needed to service the Mexican foreign debt.

Thus, at the end of the 1980s, income distribution and inequality in Mexico had taken a regressive jump, or, if preferred, a qualitative jump forward in the process of concentration of wealth. In a population of 85 million inhabitants, almost half, some 40 million, survived with an income below two minimum wages (some $200), and only one-twentieth, some 4.5 million persons, lived with incomes that exceeded twenty minimum wages (over $2,000 per month).

It had been a "lost decade" not only for development, but also for the distribution of income, even in its most gradual mode, which had previously taken place in Mexico: the large-scale creation of middle-class strata, sectors, and mobility. Even more so: the adjustment of the Mexican development model, with the shrinking of the state, the end of the subsidized economy, and the expansion of the external market, at the expense of a strong decline in the internal demand and consumption, had a concentrating effect in the upper class, and an effect of absolute and relative impoverishment even on the successful middle classes. At the end of the 1980s, inequality had increased poverty at the base of the pyramid, ratified and extended the economic hegemony of the top, and paralyzed the middle strata by limiting the expectations of growth.

Foreign Policy

In the 1980s, Mexico's foreign policy was centered, directly and indirectly, on its relationship with the United States, as it hadn't been for several decades. As was already expressed in the previous pages, at the beginning of this decade, the political relationship of Mexico with its northern neighbor was marked by an increase in the tension level. However, regarding the economic field, the dominant trend was the reverse: that of collaboration. There was, in consequence, an element of schizophrenia in the dialogue held in those years between the governments of Mexico City and Washington.

The main reason for the deterioration of the political relationship between Mexico and the United States may be found in the attempt by the López Portillo government to take the activism of Mexican foreign policy—which had begun in the previous administration—to new heights. In effect, since 1979 an attempt had been made to use the resources that oil was providing, directly and indirectly, to transform Mexico into a mid-level international power. Central America was the place chosen to inaugurate this policy, which aspired to leave behind the traditional defense of the national interest through isolationism and passivity with respect to the external world. By attempting to support to the south of its border those moderate forces that were committed to change, the Mexican Foreign Office sought to attain several goals at the same time. In first place was a historical goal: to reduce the enormous U.S. presence in the region. Mexico attempted to gain influence over moderate and nationalist Central American sectors by offering, together with Venezuela, oil to all those countries in the region under more favorable conditions than existed in the world market, besides credit, technical assistance, and markets. Even though the Mexican offer was modest, it was hoped that it would be of interest to some Central American governments and political groups that sought to diversify their ties abroad as a way to reaffirm their relative independence. That seemed to be especially the case of the Nicaraguan government after the victory of the Sandinista Revolution against the Somoza family dictatorship.

The Mexican policy not only attempted to open a space in what had been till then a region of exclusive U.S. influence. It also attempted to contribute to pacifying a neighboring zone in the throes of civil war, supporting those forces that sought stability in the long-term through the destruction of the oligarchic structures that were already obsolete. For Mexico, the Central American peace was a form of preventing a greater influx of refugees into its territory and a way to stop the growing polarization of the political atmosphere, because such a situation opened the doors to a greater presence of Cuba and the Soviet Union and, consequently, to a U.S. reaction of similar or greater magnitude, all of which would reduce the possibilities for Latin American autonomy.

In the end, the Mexican strategy didn't produce the expected outcome. To begin with, the fall in the international prices of oil in 1981 and the beginning of the great Mexican economic depression in the following year considerably weakened the material base for the Mexican international activism. Second, the Nicaraguan revolutionary leadership lost its original pluralism and radicalized its internal and external policies to such an extent that a U.S.-Nicaragua negotiation became impossible. Given the increasing U.S. hostility, the government of Managua decided to carry forth its national revolutionary project by resorting increasingly to Soviet and Cuban aid, openly confronting Washington's government and putting aside moderate proposals such as the Mexicans'. Third, and related to the previous point, the U.S. government, headed by Ronald Reagan, defined the Nicaraguan radicalization, as well as the increase in offensive actions by the revolutionary forces in El Salvador, as a situation that was not compatible and reconcilable with U.S. national security in the Western Hemisphere. Under these conditions, the Mexican policy toward the Central American region was seen in Washington as contrary to U.S. vital interests. As a consequence, in a short time, political relations between the governments of Ronald Reagan and Miguel de la Madrid became tense, and that tension would not disappear until the end of both administrations in 1988-1989.

This situation had some paradoxical aspects. In their economic projects, for example, the two administrations shared many common points of view and interests. Thus, and despite the political differences between Mexico City and Washington, cooperation between both countries in the economic field remained the same. In effect, beginning with the Mexican economic crisis of 1982, the two governments tried to give the market forces greater action in the distribution of the social resources and, consequently, reduce the growing role that the state had played in that field since the 1930s. The United States had tried fruitlessly for some time to get Mexico to open its economy, and it was De la Madrid who began to dismantle the old protectionist structure of the Mexican industry, as part of a general reformulation of the Mexican economic project. In sum, the new policies adopted by Miguel de la Madrid drew together the dominant economic visions in Mexico and the United States as they had not been since the Second World War. It was precisely for this reason that Washington decided that its political differences with Mexico should not prevent it from encouraging this part of the evolution of its neighboring country.

It was the basic compatibility of the schemes that De la Madrid and Reagan proposed for the economy that prevented the tensions generated in the political-diplomatic field to translate into a greater conflict. Despite the enormous social cost, the Mexican government made a great effort to maintain its payments of interest and capital on the huge external debt, the accumulated sum of which did not fall with time, but rather grew larger. The Reagan administration, for its part, supported the Mexican requests for new loans from the international financial institutions—the International Monetary Fund and the World Bank—in which the voice of the U.S. representatives was decisive. In the same fashion, the U.S. authorities in charge of the financial policies of the country did not oppose requests made by Mexico to the international banking community to consider reducing the burden of the debt payments. If the De la Madrid government was ultimately unable to modify in its favor the original terms of the external debt, this was due not to the opposition of the Washington authorities, but rather to the stubbornness of the creditor banks.

To reduce the U.S. pressure on Mexican diplomacy in Central America, but without admitting to a change in position, the Mexican Foreign Office decided to transform its political actions in Central America from bilateral to multilateral. Mexico was the engine behind the creation of the Contadora Group, at the beginning of the De la Madrid administration. This group, originally formed by Venezuela, Colombia, Panama, and Mexico, allowed this last country to distance itself from the Sandinistas, but at the same time to continue to insist that the solution of the Central American problem should take place within the framework of respect for the principle of nonintervention, and, above all, for the peaceful solution of controversies. The final outcome of Contadora was ambiguous. On the one hand, there is no doubt that it helped to limit the possibilities of a direct action by the United States against Nicaragua. But, on the other hand, it did not achieve an effective respect for the principle of nonintervention, as the United States openly created and financed a counterrevolutionary Nicaraguan army that operated from sanctuaries in Honduran territory. Finally, the Contadora Peace Plan to end the conflicts within and between the states of the region did not receive support from all of the interested parties, but it did help as a framework and a stimulus for the Central American governments, headed by Costa Rica, to propose their own scheme for pacification (the Esquipulas Agreements). Although this plan also did not achieve the definitive solution to the regional problem, both plans prevented what at some moments seemed unavoidable: an armed conflict between Nicaragua and its neighbors, and between Nicaragua and the United States.

The political differences between the governments of Mexico and the United States did not express themselves only or basically as an incompatibility of projects for Central America. They also reflected a disagreement with respect to an internal problem that was shared by both countries and that acquired particular importance for the United States: drug trafficking.

The "war" against the consumption of drugs by a significant part of the U.S. population became in the 1980s one of the most important points of the internal agenda of the U.S. administration. In this context, Washington's pressure on the governments of the drug-producing or drug-exporting countries transformed itself into a policy with broad support in U.S. public opinion. And Mexico became a target of that pressure due to its production of marijuana and heroin, as well as for being an important point of entry into the United States for South American cocaine.

The 1985 assassination in Guadalajara of an agent of the U.S. Drug Enforcement Administration (DEA), by drug traffickers protected by the local and federal police, set into motion an intense international campaign of discredit of the Mexican police apparatus, in particular, and of the Mexican political system, in general. The authorities in charge of the "drug war" in the U.S. federal government, as well as a good number of the U.S. Congress, presented to U.S. and world public opinion the image of a Mexican police apparatus and a justice administration system that were thoroughly corrupt. The figures on thousands of tons of marijuana and thousands of pounds of heroin and cocaine that had been confiscated by the Mexican army and police—as well as the millions of dollars and numerous personnel that the Mexican government was devoting to the fight against the drug producers and distributors, and the capture in Costa Rica of the Mexican drug trafficker accused of the murder of the DEA agent—did not satisfy U.S. demands. Washington continued to insist that Mexico restructure its own antidrug apparatus in order to eradicate the persistent ties between its officials and the drug traffickers.

The other aspect that helped those groups in the United States—and to a lesser extent in Western Europe and Latin America—interested in reinforcing the image of a deficient Mexican government was the electoral process. The emergence of a true electoral opposition to the government during the Miguel de la Madrid administration allowed the foreign mass media, especially from the United States, to become an important factor in the Mexican political process, by giving international credibility to the accusations by the center-right opposition—the PAN—about electoral fraud by the PRI in the northern part of the country. Some U.S. political circles let it be known indirectly that they would consider a positive development the possibility that the democratic conservative opposition in Mexico, with sympathy for the dominant policies in the United States, put an end to the long monopoly of political power by the PRI. The doubts expressed by foreign mass media about the legality of the electoral processes reached a climax in the 1988 presidential election, when the front page of the *New York Times* included direct testimonies of concrete examples of fraud by the government party, which gave credibility to the doubts about the general validity of the official figures. However, the original enthusiasm in the United States in favor of the Mexican opposition became more subdued once the political direction of the main challenging force suddenly changed from the right to the left.

With the almost simultaneous presidential change in Mexico and in the United States at the end of 1988 and beginning of 1989, the attitude of the U.S. government toward the Mexican government changed noticeably. After the first encounter between George Bush and Carlos Salinas in Houston, Texas—where both leaders offered to collaborate in achieving the other's goals—a new relationship developed that was dubbed "the spirit of Houston," representing an end to the mutual recriminations of the immediate past. The motives for the change in U.S.-Mexican relations in 1989 were diverse. Among them, as was stated before, an important element was the emergence of an important center-left opposition force—neo-Cardenismo—and the relative weakness of the new Mexican government. Confronted with this situation, those in Washington in charge of developing the U.S. policy toward Mexico easily arrived at the conclusion that the best way to protect the U.S. national interest south of the Rio Grande was to provide open support to the political system that existed in Mexico and, above all, to the government of Carlos Salinas. Both were the guarantee that the structural change of the Mexican economy would proceed without risking the loss of social or political stability in Mexico, which constituted the main interest of the United States south of the border.

Immediately after taking power, the Salinas administration began to act in a dramatic and decisive fashion against certain conspicuous representatives of official corruption, which were opposed to the modernization of the Mexican economic and political system: the arrest of the leaders of the powerful oil union and of the former chief of the Federal Security Division, who, due to his position as head of the political police, had become linked to drug trafficking. The new government also achieved the capture and conviction of the person who for years had headed the DEA list of Mexican drug traffickers: Félix Gallardo. These events reinforced the arguments of those in Washington who advocated decisive support of the new Mexican government. In official and private circles in the United States, as well as in the mass media, there were numerous positive opinions with respect to the new Mexican president and his political agenda. Finally, the disappearance of the last traces of Mexican activism in Central America, and a concordance in the Mexican and U.S. positions in the case of Panama—both condemned the authoritarian policies of Gen. Manuel Noriega—reinforced this atmosphere of optimism in the United States with respect to the Mexican government in 1989.

Shortly after his inauguration, President Bush, and his secretaries of state and of the treasury, openly sided with the Mexican authorities in their demand that the international banks accept a substantial modification of the amount and conditions for the payment of the Mexican external debt. Otherwise, the main political project of Carlos Salinas would not stand a fair chance of success: putting an end to the extended Mexican economic depression in order to reactivate an important trade partner and prevent the emergence of political instability south of the border.

In mid-1989, U.S.-Mexico relations at the government level were notable for the lack of friction or substantial disagreements. A similar atmosphere had not prevailed since the end of the 1960s. This, of course, did not mean that the contradictions between the two countries had disappeared. These remained, for example, with respect to the undocumented migration of Mexicans to the United States, the prices of primary products, technological transfer, the integration of the maquiladora industry—basically of U.S. ownership—into the national economy, and the interpretation of the principle of nonintervention.

At the end of the period under study, the main issue in Mexican foreign policy was the form and the extent of the integration of the Mexican economy into the world economy, and in particular into that of the United States. The questions in this area were numerous and the risks and opportunities enormous.

The Elections: From Irrelevance to Center Stage

The main goal, almost the only goal, of the government headed by Miguel de la Madrid from December 1982 was to achieve the structural transformation of an economic system that had just shown its historical lack of feasibility. This process had to take place in the midst of, and due to, the great depression into which the economy fell after the dramatic fall in world oil prices in 1981. As the De la Madrid administration proceeded, the main goal of the president and his circle became clearer; the need to subordinate the complex political problems to the achievement of the primary goal: to transform the economic model through the opening and readjustment with respect to external economic forces.

Even in the best of circumstances, the change from a productive structure that for forty years had grown based on the internal market and tariff protection, to another whose principal engine was the demand in the world market and free trade, implied a great cost for the society as a whole. The logic of the new national project required, among other things, that the role of the state as a producer should be cut back drastically, that private investment—internal and external—grow in the same proportion as the reduction in the state investment, and that the share of oil in the export total be increasingly smaller, while the share of the manufactured products and services should expand. The cost of this enormous readjustment in the factors of production became more acute given the great weight of the external debt, which by the beginning of 1989 had reached $105 billion, and whose service absorbed 6 percent of the GNP.

The initiation of this ambitious and urgent economic project took place within a process of price increase that in 1987 dangerously approached hyperinflation, with an average growth rate of 160 percent. Of all costs, one grew at a much slower rate than the rest: the price of labor. The level of social irritation increased parallel to the inflation rate. In order to reverse or at least slow down this dangerous situation, the government, with the support of the corporative organizations, put the Pact of Economic Solidarity (PESE) into effect in 1988, which consisted of a relative freezing in prices and wages, together with a fiscal adjustment and the establishment of a fixed exchange rate.

Understandably, the catastrophic ending of the "Mexican miracle" and the effort toward economic modernization had to have political repercussions. Despite the severe blow that the 1982 depression represented for the quality of life and the expectations of the majority of Mexicans, the extended political stability of the country—the most long-term in Latin America—was not disrupted, nor did the party in power lose its traditional monopoly over the exercise of power in

Mexico. Both were kept intact thanks to the enormous power of the institutions, in particular those concentrated around the president, as well as the burden of an authoritarian and nonparticipatory civic culture, and, above all, the absence of a strong opposition capable of providing a political orientation for the dissatisfaction that had been generated by the end of economic growth and the social cost of the structural adjustment of the productive apparatus.

Even though the economic failure of the 1980s was not accompanied by an upheaval in the political or social order (as some foreign observers had feared), the essence of the authoritarian and repressive political system, worn out to the same extent as the decline in the welfare of the majority of Mexicans, was seen by an important part of society not only as a result of the blind forces of the economy, but also as a product of the errors in the political direction of the immediate past: of the lack of control in public spending, including corruption, and of bad administration of the external debt.

The social tensions generated by the great economic depression were channeled laboriously and even awkwardly, and, despite the obstacles placed by the powers that be, through a constructive mechanism: the electoral one. Until the beginning of the 1980s, Mexican elections historically had been almost entirely formal and devoid of content. This was particularly true after 1958 when the presidency controlled from beginning to end, and practically without opposition, the process of internal selection of the candidates in the state party, and the subsequent development of the electoral process that confronted that party with a group of mostly ineffective competitors. In 1982, Mexico had a party system on paper, but not in reality. The iron-clad presidential control of the party in power—the PRI—and its extreme dependence on governmental resources were such that it was not really a political party but rather part of the structure of the federal government. In the opposition, the left experienced a permanent marginality, and only a center-right party, the PAN, had some of the organizational characteristics and social penetration required to be a true political party in the modern concept of the term. But the government's action and the general environment provided it with scarce opportunity to develop its political potential.

Despite what has just been said, the economic crisis led the traditional political landscape to change in a dramatic fashion in a relatively short period of time, six years. By 1988, something entirely new began to emerge in Mexico: an authentic party system, and together with it the possibility of making the elections in the future, and for the first time, the central source of governmental legitimacy. As we were writing this book, the transition from postrevolutionary authoritarianism toward a modern political democracy had just begun, in the midst of great contradictions. In 1989, democracy was still a promise, and certainly not inevitable. Let's review some of the events that have opened up this possibility.

As a presidential candidate in 1982, Miguel de la Madrid did not confront any significant opposition. He did, however, have to accept a less lopsided electoral victory than most of his predecessors, because it was no longer possible to ignore the political and social tensions that had begun to sprout, given an economic crisis that was still being presented to the public as a serious but short-term downturn. That was why the victory of the presidential candidate of the official party was obtained with only 71.7 percent of the votes cast. This figure, although quite acceptable as a basis for victory, placed the new president in the lower extreme of electoral support in the history of the PRI.

During his campaign, and even after, De la Madrid underscored his commitment to the renewal of the political processes through elections. In this area, his agenda seemed to be the search to recover the legitimacy that the political system as a whole had lost due to the economic crisis. Thus, at the beginning of 1983, everything seemed to indicate that the government could support the economic transformation with a gradual political transformation. However, the speed and magnitude of the victory of PAN in the local elections after 1982 seemed to go beyond what the government had predicted and was willing to tolerate. In effect, in the 1983 elections in Chihuahua, the PRI lost eleven municipal presidencies to the PAN, including the capital and Ciudad Juárez, which altogether represented half of the electorate. Not only that, but the PRI also lost to the PAN opposition five of the eleven local deputies. After recovering from their shock, the president and the PRI corporative elites agreed on the convenience of backpedaling and postponing for the time being the opening up of the political system. Otherwise, the PRI could soon lose control of the northern region of the country. However, the economic recovery did not take place according to the original plans of the government; instead, the dissatisfaction increased.

The local elections in several northern states with a strong opposition, especially in Chihuahua in 1986, were characterized by the open and massive use of federal government resources to support the official candidates by widespread suspicion of electoral fraud, and by the use of the government's control of the Federal Electoral Commission and the local commissions to sustain PRI victories that national and international public opinion did not consider legitimate. The atmosphere created by the government's tenacity in confronting the resistance of the power mechanisms to the economic changes and social transformations was characterized by an informed observer of the process, Juan Molinar, as an atmosphere of "electoral suffocation."

From 1984 on, the government was able to obstruct the progress of the external opposition, but at the cost of considerable credibility. However, the pressure finally resulted in a fissure in the governing party. In effect, the exacerbation of the social contradictions and the uncharacteristic narrowness of the presidential circle led a group of PRI leaders who had been marginalized by De la Madrid to defy traditional party discipline in 1987. In that year, a handful of PRI activists—headed by the ex-governor of Michoacán, Cuauhtémoc Cárdenas, and the ex-president of the National Executive Committee (CEN) of the PRI in the Luis Echeverría administration, Porfirio Muñoz Ledo—created a political offshoot within the governing party, the Democratic Current, that publicly questioned the merits of the president's economic policies and demanded that an internal debate be established on this issue.

The very existence of an organized political offshoot within the PRI, which publicly acknowledged its existence as such, represented a tremendous challenge to one of the central rules of the prevailing political system: the subordination of the entire state party apparatus to the discipline imposed by the president. And, as if this were not enough, the rebel group also demanded the establishment of mechanisms of true internal democracy within the party, which, if accepted, would have represented a fundamental change not only within the PRI but in the entire political system. This was because any expansion of the effective independence of the party cadres would have to take place at the expense of the weakening of the central political institution: the presidency.

The Democratic Current was finally marginalized and then abandoned the PRI to begin the constitution of an independent center-left political force, which participated in the presidential elections of June 1988. Using the prevailing electoral laws and some of the marginal parties—PPS, PARM, PST—the Democratic Current established a coalition known as the National Democratic Front (FDN), which presented Cuauhtémoc Cárdenas as a presidential candidate. After a series of difficult negotiations, the former Mexican Communist party abandoned its initial idea of fielding its own candidate and joined the FDN, which became a true center-left alternative to the PRI. The Cardenista agenda focused on the need to reverse the process of impoverishment of the majority, to reduce the speed of the dismantling of the parastate apparatus and the opening of the economy to the external sector, and to give priority to the need for renewing economic growth over payment of the external debt.

The PRI, for its part, in an internal process designed by the president of the republic, presented six possible precandidates, after which, and without great internal debate, a single precandidate emerged: the young Ph.D. in economics and secretary of planning and budget, Carlos Salinas de Gortari. Salinas de Gortari presented a program that consisted, basically, of continuing the economic project initiated by Miguel de la Madrid—the reduction of the role of the state as an economic producer, the opening of trade, the modernization of the industrial capacity, and insistence on the renegotiation of the external debt—of which Salinas de Gortari had been one of the main architects.

The center-right opposition—represented by the PAN—after an open selection process with the participation of the grass roots, elected as candidate a recent arrival to the party: the extroverted northern businessman Manuel J. Clouthier. The PAN proposal did not differ much from the official one, especially with respect to the reduction in the economic role assigned to the state and the increase in the role of market forces on the allocation of resources. However, the fundamental theme of the PAN was not economic, but rather political: the demand for effective suffrage, for democracy.

The July Election and the First Months of Government

The PRI candidacy of Carlos Salinas de Gortari for president in 1987 was a clear indicator that the governing team persisted on the path to modernization for which it had been elected, and had unforeseen political consequences. Cuauhtémoc Cárdenas—at the time, an ex-governor of Michoacán, ex-senator of the republic, and ex-undersecretary of forestry—was able to congregate around him a broad array of political leanings and the support of four parties that formed the National Democratic Front, as well as a political group without legal registration: the Authentic Party of the Mexican Revolution (PARM), the Popular Socialist party (PPS), the Cardenista Front of National Reconstruction party, the Mexican Socialist party (PSM), as well as the Democratic Current.

The Cardenista candidacy grew steadily in the months of the electoral campaign and came to the July 1988 elections with sufficient strength to become the second electoral force of the country, displacing the National Action party (PAN) and defeating the PRI in the capital of the republic and other central regions of the country, as well as in some northern cities.

The slowness in the tallying of electoral results, the surge of the opposition, the ostensible manipulation of the process by the authorities, and the skepticism of public opinion cast a dark pall over the July 1988 elections, amid accusations of fraud. The official results that declared Carlos Salinas de Gortari the victor by slightly more than 50 percent of the vote (30 percent for Cardenismo and 20 percent for the

PAN) were disputed by diverse national sectors and by the international mass media, and paved the way for a climate of confrontation and strife.

Ultimately, no one was satisfied: not the opposition, the government, or a high percentage of voters. The contradiction between the expectations of the public and the slowness of the process, the lack of legal channels of redress, and the governmental manipulation of the spectacle made evident a delicate and critical aspect of the political life of the country: the lack of adequate institutions to accommodate the new civic presence in the ballot boxes and the need for political reform in order to adjust those institutions to the new reality.

The July elections made evident, even for the most cold-blooded and traditional observers, that Mexico should begin to travel the road to the configuration of a solid party system with competitive elections. But the electoral laws still privileged the structure of a state-party, virtually a one-party, system. Its political practices led to increasing confrontation with the expectations of an emerging citizenship, as a product of the social and economic modernization that the country had undergone in the last quarter of a century.

The July elections had direct political effects in other spheres. First, they reformed de facto Mexican presidentialism, cutting back on its powers and creating new checks and balances. They eliminated, for example, the possibility of introducing constitutional reforms without the approval of the opposition, by creating a Chamber of Deputies in which the PRI held only 260 of 500 seats. Given that any constitutional reform requires the approval of two-thirds of the Congress—approximately 332 deputies—the president would need to maintain all of his votes firmly and convince more than 70 members of the opposition in order to pass a reform.

Second, the elections balanced the power between the executive branch and the Congress, transforming the latter into an institution capable of opposing and even defeating some presidential initiatives. The slim PRI majority in the Congress in the future could garner victories, but not landslides; it could impose itself, but not crush the opposition.

Third, the July elections territorially fragmented the regime's power. They took away its majority in the Federal District, thus avenging a major citizen complaint: the lack of elections to name the local government for the most important city of the country. The regime also lost the second city of the republic—Guadalajara, won by the PAN—and there were opposition electoral victories in states that had traditionally been controlled by the PRI—Morelos, Michoacán, and Guerrero. The republic as a whole soon emerged as a map of intense electoral competition and equilibrium. According to the official results of the 1988 elections, a slight increase in the negative sentiments against the government—equivalent to 10 percent of the electorate: 1.9 million votes—would be required in the following years in order to balance the national vote of the PRI with that of the second electoral force of the country.

Thus, the July elections opened the doors to the possibility of a credible and competitive party system in Mexico, a regime capable of guiding the nation toward a democratic experience that Mexicans have not enjoyed in this century or in the previous one: a peaceful transfer of power.

The New Government

When Carlos Salinas de Gortari was inaugurated as president of the republic on December 1, 1988, the political novelty seemed to capture the attention of the nation. But it was not the only challenge. The territory of the Mexican transition was starting to show its rough edges, on all fronts.

Even for the most optimistic observers, it was clear that the years of economic rebuilding, after the collapse of the 1980s, would demand immense efforts on behalf of the nation in order to obtain modest results. One million new jobs had to be created each year simply to prevent the unemployment rate from increasing. If the payment of the external debt was conditioned on the growth of the economy, and enough resources were liberated in order to guarantee until the year 2000 an annual growth rate of 2.5 percent—the average between 1982 and 1988 was -0.4 percent—by the end of the century, Mexicans would have recovered simply the per capita income already reached in 1980. If, in the course of the following six years, the real wage of Mexicans doubled—something that has never occurred in the history of wages in Mexico during all previous administrations—by the end of the Salinas de Gortari administration in 1994, the real wage of Mexicans would barely recover the level it had reached in 1982.

The productive infrastructure and the communication networks of the country demanded drastic measures in many areas. Thus, for example, the disinvestment during the 1980s in the oil industry foreshadowed a period of progressive decline in oil production, unless exploration and exploitation activities were reactivated immediately. There were half a million unattended applications for telephone lines, and a similar number of unstable, precarious, and low-quality lines. And for a long time there had been warnings in the electrical industry anticipating the effects of disinvestment: if the country kept growing, there would not be enough energy production to satisfy demand.

Finally, Mexican society was undergoing deep political doubts, apart from electoral qualms, at the beginning of the Salinas de Gortari administration. First, there were doubts regarding the ability of the government to control the armed populations that traversed its territory: police, drug dealers, criminals, Mafia, gangs, and small private or corporative armies that seemed to have mushroomed until they made the need for public safety one of the strongest public demands.

Second, there were doubts regarding the ability of the regime and the government to overcome the pressure and the autonomy of the corporative enclaves that its own clientelistic action had created: unions taken over by strong leading cliques, capital that demanded endless support for speculation without regulation or risk, and a government trapped between its agenda for a necessary but unpopular change and the abusive inertia of an unjust and predatory, albeit powerful and threatening, corporative establishment. The first six months of the Salinas government made progress on these two last fronts by displacing in a series of quick and dramatic actions this entrenched corporative impunity.

At the beginning of January 1989, Joaquín Hernández Galicia, until then an untouchable leader of the powerful oil-workers union, was thrown in jail. One month later, in the midst of a campaign to penalize tax evaders, the prominent private businessman Eduardo Legorreta was also incarcerated for violation of banking laws and stock market fraud. The independent teacher-union's mobilization of March and April 1989 also led to the downfall of another symbol of the corporative union corruption in the nation: Carlos Jonguitud Barrios, leader of the National Union of Education Workers.

Almost at the same time, the government announced the incarceration of the greatest druglord of the drug-trafficking Mafia in Mexico, Félix Gallardo, whose capture brought a series of successful operations against drug traffickers, mass imprisonments, confiscations of tons of pure cocaine in a single operation, and the like—all of which led to a positive reaction in U.S. official circles and press. Revelations by the captured drug traffickers themselves led to additional unexpected events, among them, the discovery of archaeological artifacts that had been stolen in December 1985 from the National Museum of Anthropology.

Finally, at the end of June 1989, as a result of the sustained pressure of public opinion and the national press, the murder of journalist Manuel Buendía was solved. He had been shot in the back in May 1984 under orders of the then commanding officer of the Federal Security Division (DFS, the political security police of the country), José Antonio Zorrilla Pérez. Through his death, according to the official version, the DFS had attempted to prevent publication of his article documenting the relationship between the DFS and drug traffickers.

The investigation of the murder of Buendía also unleashed the biggest scandal in the police ranks in the history of Mexico: it revealed the extent to which the Mafia and the police had become intertwined and to which citizen demand for security was justified, as well as the continuous protests against the impunity of police officers. Thus, as a consequence of solving the Buendía murder, the recently created Division of Intelligence of the Federal District was dismantled. This entity had been formed in large part by ex-agents of the DFS, several of whose commanders were criminally prosecuted as partners in drug trafficking or as responsible for the conspiracy that ended in Buendía's death. The public demand for a responsible and efficient police force was, however, still not satisfied.

Short and Long Term

On the economic recovery front, the new government set as its priority the renewal of growth. With this purpose, it chose as the centerpiece of its strategy what had already become a public outcry in the country in the final years of the government of Miguel de la Madrid: a renegotiation of the debt to reduce substantially its payments, to free up fresh resources for development, and to compensate for its dramatic aftermath in all aspects.

The new proposal Mexico presented its foreign creditors was a 50 percent reduction in the debt owed to the commercial banks—which amounted to some $55 billion—a reduction in the interest rates, and the guarantee of new and substantial financing during the next five years. The introduction of the so-called Brady Plan by the Bush administration at the beginning of March 1989 covered the Mexican initiative by establishing the need for bank acceptance of voluntary agreements to reduce the debts of the developing countries. At the end of the first half of 1989, the international private banks and the Mexican government were still continuing their difficult negotiations in order to achieve a mutually beneficial agreement; as a backdrop was the possibility that Mexico might join the group of countries that had already suspended their payments to the unyielding international creditors.

The maintenance of the Pact of Economic Stability and Growth—an agreement that virtually froze the prices that had been introduced in January 1988—reduced inflation from an annual rate of 150 percent in December of 1987 to 18 percent in June 1989. But, keeping the price of the dollar frozen until December 1988, and beginning in January 1989, a slight lowering of its value, equivalent to an annual devaluation of 10 percent, had a negative impact on Mexican international reserves. The aggressive trade liberalization that accompanied the implementation of the pact as a mechanism to reduce and contain the internal prices had allowed imports to grow and also had a negative impact on the foreign reserves. The trade surplus in Mexico's trade with the United States, for example, fell by 50 percent between 1987 and 1988—from $5,023 million to $2,409 million.

Under these conditions, and in order to prevent speculative attacks against the peso and capital flight due to possible devaluations, the government was forced to support extraordinarily high internal interest rates—50 and 60 percent, compared with an inflation of 19 percent—thus increasing the internal debt and slowing the flow of capital to productive activities. Only the positive signs in the negotiations with the creditor banks could guarantee the future stability of the peso and allow a gradual transition to lower interest rates and the gradual transfer of capital from the speculative circuits to productive investment.

At the beginning of June 1989, the government could postpone for another nine months—until March 1990—the basic conditions of the pact and give itself an additional waiting period to conclude its negotiations with the international banks. However, the internal conditions that have been described, and in particular the nervousness and the pressure of capital, created a situation that was basically unstable and that still required an urgent favorable solution in the external sector.

With the situation as described in the short term, the government presented its proposal for the medium and long term on the last day of May: the National Development Plan (PND) for 1989-1994. It was, in effect, the conceptualization of a new type of development that the government of Miguel de la Madrid had begun to establish in the previous years, a different type of development, opposed in many respects to what Mexico had followed in the last forty years.

The conceptual changes proposed by the PND began by stating a notion of the state different from the prevailing one in Mexico since the 1930s: the corporative and authoritarian political stability, the protected industrialization process to substitute imports, the expansion of public expenditure and the state in order to address the social and productive failures of society. In other words, it was the whole model of inward-oriented growth that had given such good results until it had started to falter.

The PND proposed a different kind of state from the omnipresent, absorbing, and subsidizing state of the postrevolutionary tradition. It proposed a state that would "guide society in a modern sense," not as an interventionist and nationalizing state, but rather one that would provide "incentives." The Salinas document proposed new rules with respect to Mexico's ties abroad. It began by recognizing the process of global integration and the conditions necessary for outward-oriented growth, capable of inserting itself in a competitive fashion into the currents of the world economy. According to these new rules, an open national market that would compete with the world market, and not a protected market as in previous development, would be the new judge of the industries and services that were desirable for Mexico and the Mexicans.

In order to guarantee successful development in the future, the new government proposed doing exactly the opposite of what had been done in the past. It was necessary to deregulate the economy and the market: to attract foreign investment; to place private investment at center stage; to cross the borders in search of markets, partners, investments, and technology; and to exchange the labyrinth of solitude for the supermarket of world integration.

Inequality and Democracy

Two programs of internal equilibrium and reform completed the design of the Salinas National Development Plan (PND). The first was the state compromise of addressing the accumulated social debt, which the plan called the "Agreement for the Productive Improvement of the Quality of Life." The compromise was derived from the certainty, implicit in the 1989–1994 PND, that the misery inherited and aggravated by the crisis would not be eradicated by the logic of the modernizing process itself, but rather required an explicit political will and programs of state investment oriented toward breaking the vicious circles that reproduced poverty. The articulation of this investment with the proposal of giving absolute priority to the market forces in the allocation of resources was not very clear.

The second program that referred to the democratic political reform placed on the agenda by the July 1988 elections was called in the PND the "Agreement to Extend Our Democratic Life." The plan seemed to understand and accept that the authoritarian crutches inherited from the previous model were now anachronistic for the Mexican society that had voted on July 6, 1988, and would prove intolerable for the society that would emerge from a successful economic modernization—open to the world and to the free circulation of goods, ideas, capital, technologies, and opportunities, as the PND proposed. In effect, the limits of Mexican democracy—electoral results delayed for weeks, the substantial transfer of public funds to the official party, the lack of a reliable voter registration list, the metaphysical impossibility of simply counting the votes—were already absurd in 1988, but would prove explosive for the society that could emerge from the modernization foreseen in the Salinas PND.

Six months after the Salinas government had been inaugurated, the likelihood of fulfilling the commitment to improve the welfare of an impoverished society seemed very low. The logic of the dominant economic processes was acting against this possibility.

In first place, inequality and poverty were the oldest and least solved problems of Mexico: a centuries-old social debt that did not have and could not have a quick solution. Second, even if the PND fulfilled its goals and timetables, its offer was limited to renewing gradual growth. A truly solid path toward improvement in living conditions—the demands for new formal employment, the improvement in purchasing power, the consolidation of internal consumption—would become clear in many months, perhaps many years. And, third, the instruments at the disposition of the state to implement its programs against absolute poverty had so far provided very poor distribution effects.

More feasible, despite the difficulties and inertia, seemed the path toward a democratic consolidation of the system. For many months, beginning in March 1989, the parties and citizens within the Federal Electoral Commission debated several options and a possible consensus in order to introduce the political reforms that the country was demanding. An agreement had been reached to call a special session of Congress to begin on August 28, 1989, and to proceed to the debate of appropriate legislation.

But even more revealing of the true political trends in the matter were the elections held in the first week of July 1989 in five states of the republic: Campeche, Zacatecas, Chihuahua, Michoacán, and North Baja California.

In these five local elections, the vices that still burden the Mexican political system were clearly portrayed, but also evident were the possibilities of transforming the vote and the party system into an effective mechanism to channel the political energies of the new Mexican society. In the cases of Campeche, Zacatecas, and even Chihuahua, voter absenteeism and the traditional forms of politics still dominated: the PRI won without major problems.

In Michoacán, the official figures that handed the victory to the PRI candidates over those of the PRD were not credible and unleashed a legal conflict and challenge similar—on a regional scale—to that of the national elections the year before. In mid-1989, it was clear that the political modernization of Mexico through democratic reforms still had to overcome many barriers, and that society still had not found the path to impose its preferences over the will of the government. But it had been able partially to fulfill the democratic promises of July 1988.

But in North Baja California the absolute victory of the center-right opposition—the PAN—opened up the possibility of an alternation of the party in power and showed that a well-organized opposition that had been able to penetrate the weave of the society in which it acted was capable of attaining victory. With a governor and a local Congress in the hands of the PAN in North Baja California in July 1989, the first case of an entity ruled by the opposition developed since the establishment of the state party in 1929. It was the most significant event announcing the arrival of a new era of anticipated Mexican democracy.

7.
The Beginning of a
Painful Transition

The Last Decades

Mexican society of the mid-1980s had the general feeling of a change of era, and it was showing the signs of a great historical transition. The accumulated symptoms of change the country and the institutional system had undergone during the last four decades made the transition increasingly evident.

Beginning in 1968, the constitutive elements of the pact of stability had eroded, one by one. The student rebellion of that year was the most well known, but by no means the only, rejection of the institutional monologue of the decades of the Mexican miracle. In the course of the 1970s, an organized dissident movement also emerged within the workers' movement, the Democratic Tendency, which merged broad coalitions and offered momentarily an alternative to the traditional workers' leadership. Beginning in 1975, the system witnessed an increasing entrepreneurial rebellion, and the gradual independent organization of groups and capital that until then had been satisfied with the symbiosis of the years of the miracle and stabilizing development. The institutional monologue was also broken by the antiguerrilla campaign that was conducted in the first years of the 1970s, a war that faced off insurrectional elements in the countryside and in the cities, especially in Guerrero, with the movements led by Genaro Vázquez and Lucio Cabañas, and by the sequel to the 1968 repression: the urban armed groups whose action is associated with the "23rd of September League."

As a consequence, and in parallel fashion to all this turmoil, the Mexican political system was oriented toward an opening and dialogue (1971–1976), and later to an institutional political reform (1978–1982), thus recognizing explicitly that the institutional concert no longer included all the notes, or even some of the most important ones.

Stabilizing development also met its end as an economic reality and as a political pact. In the 1970s and 1980s, Mexico not only ceased to maintain a sustained growth, but suffered extremely severe decreases in its GNP, with some years of zero economic growth, and others, such as 1983 with -5.4 percent, of economic downturn. The process of modernization of the country, which seemed to be one of the major advantages of the industrializing model of the 1940s, emerged in the 1970s as a severe national problem. It was precisely with the productive and investment boom of the oil years (1978–1981) that the industrializing scheme revealed itself to be unfeasible, and marched off to bankruptcy just at the time when there were the largest number of resources to feed it. Why was this so? It was because of the productive disarticulation, its vulnerability, its external dependence and its traditional inefficiency; because it was unable to grow without massively expanding imports, and because it was incapable of exporting to prevent the ensuing crisis in the balance of payments. On the other hand, the deterioration of the agrarian economy led the country to lose its food self-sufficiency, and to be forced to use the scarce foreign exchange to import food instead of industrial inputs. The nationalization of the private banks on September 1, 1982, finally led to the collapse of all that remained of that political symbiosis in the higher echelons of the financial, industrial, and commercial bourgeoisie with the state and the political bureaucracy. Already nervous, and avid for greater independence and guarantees during the Luis Echeverría administration (1970–1976), those groups saw the bank nationalization of September 1982 as a socializing offensive that broke the basic agreement on a mixed economy and demonstrated the uncontrollable authoritarianism of Mexican presidentialism, its "socializing" trends, the faculty to expropriate without compensation, and the "totalitarianism" of the government. In the mid-1980s, the attempts to reestablish advantages, benefits, and broad political concessions for these business sectors, with the purpose of restoring the broken agreement and symbiosis, had been unsuccessful in reestablishing the political agreement of the 1940s and 1950s. These attempts were also unable to make the business sector feel represented once more by the state institutions and reasonably secure that its historical destiny as a class was in some way guaranteed by the decisions of the national state.

The general characterization of the political, productive, and social conditions of the disappearance of the miracle and the rending of the transition must include the examination of at least thirteen central actors and/or situations within the system: four from the political elite (the presidency, the bureaucracy, the state party, and the so-called political class); four associated with the representation of the social classes and their action within the system (peasants, workers, business sector, and middle classes); three related to movements in society (political parties, public opinion, and church); and, finally, two other vital actors: the army and U.S. influence. In the following pages, some ideas are outlined regarding this, which do not include everything that these short histories should have but do include the elements that they should not lack.

The Presidency

The presidency of the republic is the first and fundamental part of the Mexican political system. Between 1934 and 1982, it underwent the consolidation of Mexican presidentialism under Lázaro Cárdenas and Avila Camacho (1934–1946), the imposing rule of the Alemán, Ruiz Cortines, and López Mateos administrations (1946–1964), and a new phase during the 1970s. In this period, without losing his role as the undisputed center of political life in the country, the president started to act and function as a great coordinator of special interests and bureaucratic agencies ("The role of the President of Mexico is to pick up the banners of society," President Luis Echeverría once commented). The Mexican presidents of the 1980s held an absolute power that was much greater than that of their forerunners. We have already mentioned at the beginning of this chapter some of the factors for the consolidation of this essential actor: the political withdrawal of the army and the church. Some other factors can also be mentioned. First, there is a problem at the roots. The 1917 constitution placed emphasis on the construction of a strong executive branch. In the minds of the drafters of the constitution, the idea was present that the Porfirian dictatorship was partially caused by the fact that the 1857 constitution had designed a weak executive branch, which, in order to rule effectively, was forced to accumulate power by appropriating the faculties that had been given to the legislative and judicial powers of the states of the federation. The decision by the Constitutional Assembly of 1916–1917 was to grant to the executive branch broad faculties, much greater than the other constitutional branches. As a consequence of that strong executive, the legislative and judicial branches suffered a loss of power.

To that constitutional reason, a historical one may be added: the paternalistic and authoritarian tradition of the indigenous and colonial past of Mexico and the political attitudes of the viceroys established a type of ruler similar to those we later know as presidents, a clever politician who must engage and negotiate with various powers, seeking to conciliate the different forces, who must act simultaneously with a great discretionary power and with a great need for conciliation and negotiation. The nineteenth century added its own *caudillo* heritage to the colonial tradition, the deep-rooted culture of a man sent providentially, whether his name was Iturbide or Santa Anna, Benito Juárez or Porfirio Díaz.

Still immersed in that tradition, Obregón and Calles in the twentieth century appeared to the nation as irreplaceable rulers. One of the important political aspects of the twentieth century in Mexico is that, beginning in the 1940s, charisma and authority no longer rested with a *caudillo* or a *cacique* (as a person), but rather started to be associated with the position itself. The presidential institutionalization has been definitive, in the sense that it grants power to the president only while he occupies the presidential chair. A president ending his tenure is almost a nobody; an incoming president is nearly everything. As an effect of that institutionalization, the holders of those positions pass from the "nothingness" to power, and from power once again to "nothingness." This is one of the reasons for the stability of the country and one of the characteristics of the presidential institution. It is a position, furthermore, that has immense power in a bureaucratic and patrimonial culture such as Mexico's. In 1970, a president of the republic could distribute among his followers six thousand positions, among the best paid and best regarded of the country; in 1982, the distribution reached ten thousand positions. We are talking of an enormous power to reward, punish, and distribute income, concentrated in a single institution, the most important in the Mexican political system.

Without ignoring the central character of the presidency, its short history would be incomplete if it did not question the platitudes that populate this aspect of our political life, with the intention of eliminating it: the idea of an almighty president, of a "six-year monarchy," the idea that presidents make a whimsical selection of their successors, that everything is decided by the president and is his direct responsibility, the idea that all of the secretaries are merely blind executors of his policies, and that the government as a whole is only a ridiculous court of worshipful attendants. Carlos Monsiváis wrote:

What are the powers of a President? They are extraordinary in a certain sense: he appoints and protects, grants, obstructs or facilitates corruption, he is the measure of all of his political career, provides the tone to the style of his administration. In another sense, however, they do not seem so immense: in the realm of the fundamental transformations. If this power should not be underestimated, neither should it be magnified. But Presidentialism is the theory of the lack of restraint, and the myth of Presidentialism that pervades the bureaucratic institutions, simply disregards the international financial order, North American imperialism, the bans and the interests of the Catholic Church, of national capitalists, the growing autonomy of the bureaucracy, the police force "independence," in sum, the very structures of the country.

The Bureaucracy

The bureaucracy is perhaps the only segment of the political system that has grown systematically in the last decades, accumulating an increasing power and decision-making capacity over a society that is also ever-expanding. The political displacement in the character and the power of this bureaucracy also expresses some of the central characteristics in the transformations of the system. One indicator of this displacement is that the presidents of the republic were designated from the Ministry of Defense until Manuel Avila Camacho (1946), and from the Ministry of the Interior until Luis Echeverría (1970–1976)—with the sole exception of Adolfo López Mateos (1958–1964), who came from the Ministry of Labor. But beginning with the government of López Portillo (1976–1982), they have come from the Ministry of Finance, showing how the political weight of the bureaucracy seems to have been displaced from the traditional political-military sector to the financial and planning sector: from the Ministry of the Interior to that of Finance, and later to that of Planning and Budget, from which President Miguel de la Madrid (1982–1988) emerged.

This considerable bureaucracy has some characteristics that no history should ignore. The first is that it is primarily constituted of persons who have emerged from the middle classes, who have scarce relationship with the dominant economic groups in society, but who are also not of popular extraction. These members of the middle classes made their fortune within the state, and see it as the source of their own social mobility, the scenario that they are interested in advancing and developing.

Second, the Mexican bureaucracy works as a mechanism for the circulation of the ruling elites. Every six-year period brings forth a substantial change of public officials. The lack of a civil service allows substantial changes every six years in the upper reaches of government and in the middle strata as well, which leads to a great deal of inefficiency, voluntarism, wastefulness, and squandering of human resources, but also to fresh air and political mobility.

Third, the bureaucracy is a scenario for discretionary income, an occasion for personal enrichment and for the net transfer of public resources to private hands, a transfer that usually transforms politicians into business leaders, or simply into rich people, who abandon their public activities in order to concentrate on their private activities.

Last is a fourth aspect that has been little studied but is fundamental: the bureaucracy is a basic scenario for the political struggle between different interest groups in society; it thus represents a possibility for political negotiation between the diverse, and occasionally contradictory, tendencies within the state apparatus. The bureaucratic infighting is, despite the lack of attention it has received, one of the most important elements in the development of political conflicts. A short history of this much-desired and despised caste of the Mexican bureaucracy should be able to quantify and describe these different tendencies and attempt a political sociology of this sector, so that we could study the true face of the Mexican public administration. This is a face that would probably be equidistant from its commonplace image as nonexistent or archaic and its dark legacy as uniformly corrupt and irresponsible.

The National Revolutionary Party

A third fundamental actor is the state party, the old National Revolutionary party, transformed under Cárdenas into the Party of the Mexican Revolution and under Alemán into the Institutional Revolutionary party. In its most recent incarnation, the party has moved toward a state that we could call revolutionary inanition. The pervasiveness of its presence in Mexican political life, however, is as notable as is the absence of a history to reveal this presence. A history of the PRI era would be incomplete if it did not include the mention of at least four of the main functions that the state party has had in the decades of the Mexican miracle and transition. It has been, first, a recruitment instrument for a large part of the primary political cadres (although not of the high-level cadres); second, the instrument for controlling the mass organizations; third, the great apparatus for the administration of the social demands and welfare; and, last, the machinery for electoral legitimation.

The state party has worked because it is mainly a pragmatic coalition of interests, the timely incarnation of what some authors call the "interclassism" of the Mexican Revolution, the possibility to reunite in the same political task the interests of all classes: conservatives and revolutionaries, poor peasants and large landowners, workers and business people, in such a way that in pragmatic negotiation, behind closed doors, everyone may get something, and those who do not at least receive hope. The problem of the PRI in the transition is that it seems to be a political party designed for a Mexico that arose before the last decades of modernization. The PRI has begun to be surpassed in the enclaves and regions that are under the sway of modernity: cities, middle sectors, universities and intellectual spheres, and the mass media of communication. It keeps its capacity for cohesion—in fact, a form of national organization—in the marginal, traditional, and recently modernized zones. Since these zones are still the majority of the country, it could be said that the PRI, despite its decline, is still the instrument of majority organization in Mexico. But clearly the road to the future for the economy and society will probably not allow the PRI to maintain its cohesion. It will lead, rather, to modernization in the urban, industrial, and service sectors, in response to which the corporative resources of the party will not be the most effective.

Sergio Zermeño has suggested the existence of two political arguments, or logics, that coexist and struggle in the confusing heart of present-day Mexico: the popular, national-corporative logic, which arose from the fundamental pact of the Mexican Revolution, and the democratic-liberal practice, born from urban and industrial Mexico, which tends to question and repudiate the authoritarian and top-down responses of the other logic. The society and the economy generate sectors, social strata, life-styles, and cultural and material desires that fall beyond the traditional boundary administered thus far by the popular national logic. They are by no means different worlds, because they are intertwined, but they are worlds in conflict, and in an era of unresolved conflict between opposites lies one of the historical knots of the Mexican transition. The state party exists thanks mainly to the surviving political reserves of the first logic; but it is losing importance and presence as the second one nurtures and seduces the spirits of Mexican society.

The Political and Bureaucratic Elite

A fourth fundamental actor is what we have taken to calling the political class, despite the legitimate protests of the sociologists. It is the political and bureaucratic elite of the country, the equivalent of the Soviet *nomenclatura*, which effectively rules and occupies the key positions in the execution of governmental decisions. In the last forty years, the Mexican political class has undergone essential transformations, most of which are related to its own origin: it no longer derives from the PRI militants in the public schools, but rather from students with graduate studies abroad or in the private schools. From the point of view of the dominant professions, there is a transition from lawyers to economists and, in the crisis of the 1980s, a great presence of accountants, who in effect are in charge of recording the accounts of the excesses (after the party come the bills). In this evolution of the political class, a central conflict that in itself defines a change of era is what the press has called the conflict between the politicians and the technocrats, a conflict that is clearly present since López Mateos. Why? Because the bureaucratic apparatus has become sophisticated, complex, and enormous, with its own self-interests, and has become impossible to rule in a direct fashion, without the intermediation of complex levels of a technical nature.

Ever since the López Mateos administration, the so-called political-politicians count the hours they have left before they disappear, while more of the so-called technocratic-politicians emerge, people who originate from the universities and technological institutes, who over time have assimilated the mechanics of the operation of political-politicians (clientelistic relationships, qualms, virtues, and manipulations), and are trustworthy in the planning of investments, public works, education, health, and other central aspects of public administration. The last decades of stabilizing development have witnessed the displacement of this old political class in favor of a new type of technocratic politician that burst forth onto the national scene with an uncontainable force in the 1970s.

Together with that displacement, there is also a basic transformation of other essential mechanisms of political control and aggregation. The *caciques*, in particular, have been the main instrument for local and regional manipulation. The *cacique* mechanisms, which offer effective guarantees for political control, are no longer only the old *caciques* in the style of Gonzalo N. Santos in San Luis Potosí, Leobardo Reynoso in Zacatecas, or Rubén Figueroa in Guerrero. The reformulation and the territorial implantation of the federal bureaucracy throughout the country helped configure *caciques* of a new type, positioned around occupants of management offices of the large parastate companies, managers of the agricultural banks, and federal delegations. These are now the intermediaries between the federal or bureaucratic powers and the social reality of the different regions of the country. And they have accumulated a vast capacity for administering local power and clienteles.

The Peasantry

The drama of the political representation of the peasants has to do, among other aspects, with this displacement of the traditional axis of regional organization. Between the years of the Mexican miracle and the crisis of the 1980s, peasant control was gradually transferred from the previously active and powerful National Peasant Confederation to the new *cacique* examples of modernization, a new type of *cacique* whose headquarters are in the cities, not even in the countryside or the local arena. The last forty years have witnessed an effective bureaucratization in the social and productive relations in the countryside, to the extent that there are those who consider the presence of state and parastate agencies as the main structural obstacle to agricultural development in Mexico. In a parallel fashion, there is a terrible political invisibility of the true peasant movements. Their organizations have been relegated backstage as groups capable of pressing and negotiating their demands.

This drama of political representation takes place within a scenario of structural transformation and a strategic weakness of the nation. First, as a consequence of the process of industrializing modernization, Mexico experienced in recent decades a decapitalization of the countryside in favor of the city, a growing internal migration, day laborers, and what some have called the *depeasantization* of the countryside, a countryside that is increasingly eroded and more difficult to transform in the direction of the desired self-sufficiency and modernization. Second, there is the offensive of agribusiness, capitalist agriculture, and the expansion of cattle breeding in lieu of cultivated lands.

Thus, a strategic weakness of food dependency is building up, as a consequence of years of inefficiency and sleight of hand in the productive organization of the Mexican countryside. The political consequence of these factors is that the old organizational forms for control and mobilization are increasingly ineffectual, lack vitality, and are demanding a new historical form.

Workers and Business People

With respect to workers and their organizations, it could be said that Mexico has experienced, both under the miracle and under transition, the era of Fidel Velázquez, the era of responsible trade unionism. Beginning with the crisis of the 1980s, that unionism has confronted a collapse of the real wage that might extend until the next decade. It is a fundamental negative fact in the historical perspective of a responsible trade unionism, because the maintenance of the real wage during many years, and its occasional increase, had been the only decisive and true conquest of that trade-union movement; their leaders had guaranteed this to the union members ever since the era of Morones in the 1920s. With their real wage in decline, what do they have to offer? It is not a modern workers' organization: the attempts at union organization by industry have not achieved much, to a large extent due to the opposition of old-style trade unionism. The Confederation of Mexican Workers (CTM), Velásquez's enclave, is far from being a form of union organization adequate for organizing the workers in the most dynamic industries.

It is not only a problem of the CTM. Even a union such as the Mexican Union of Electricians (SME), which was able in 1936 to negotiate basic questions characteristic of modern trade unions, such as work rules, found in 1984 that its successes were "obstructing" the productivity of the Light and Energy Company and was forced to negotiate on a more modern basis its collective contract. Here resides the central problem that has decisively altered the relations (and consequently the organization) of the popular classes: what has been the technological impact on the working conditions, worker organization, and mobilization? What has happened within the factories and with the lines of union negotiation that technological innovation rendered obsolete? To what extent is this form of responsible trade unionism genuinely derived from the Mexican Revolution, based on an unsustainable productive prehistory?

These same questions should be answered in a history of the entrepreneurial class over the last four decades. It is an entrepreneurial class that has also undergone a long transition: from the profitable symbiosis of the elites during the Mexican miracle to the anti-Echeverría rebellion of the 1970s, and to the historical closing of what remained of the old agreement in 1982 and the beginning of a new agreement that has yet to bear fruit. It has also gone from a relatively easy import substitution, with which it replaced foreign capital under the protection of the state, to a new dependency that clearly begins in the 1960s with the technological innovation and the process of trasnationalization. In 1965, almost 17 percent of the 980 largest companies in Mexico were controlled partially or totally by foreign capital (if we consider only the 50 largest companies, then 48 percent were controlled by foreign capital, and if we consider only the capital-goods sector, then the percentage becomes 53 percent). In other words, after a honeymoon period of easy import substitution and the displacement of foreign investment that took place during the Mexican miracle, the national bourgeoisie was or began to be displaced once more by the high-tech sectors of industry, and retained its predominance only in the traditional sectors, and this thanks only to protectionism. None of this prevents the business class from becoming one of the most active, visible, and belligerent political groups during the years of transition. The intensification of its antigovernment discourse corresponded to the appearance of new organizations of entrepreneurial political representation, such as the Enterprise Coordinating Council in 1975. Another substantial change was that of the successive vanguards of the Mexican entrepreneurs: in the 1940s and 1950s, the leaders of the business sector were the industrialists and capitalists who flourished under the shadow of the state; in the 1960s and 1970s, the center stage was occupied by bankers and financiers; Televisa and the private mass media establishment became the effective entrepreneurial vanguard beginning with the bank nationalization in 1982.

The Middle Classes

If one were to summarize what has happened to the middle classes in the last forty years in Mexico, one would have to say that the administration of their conduct and ideology is no longer exclusively confined to the Catholic traditions and the miter, and has become the domain of universities, consumerism, mass media, and the state bureaucracy. It is perhaps one of the decisively profound movements of society; beginning with the industrialization of the 1940s and 1950s, it has gradually become a new social majority. It is no longer the traditional majority of the old Mexico—rural, provincial, Catholic, or indigenous; neither is it a new proletarian majority. It is a new urban majority, related both to the students of 1968 and the opposition voters of the 1980s; it is related to the new society of Mexican masses, the peasants who emigrate to the cities and lose their peasant origins or already have one generation in the cities; it is the expression of the base of the demographic pyramid of young people, fully incorporated into urban life, for whom there seem to be no prospects, and who have begun to find their own forms of barbarous organization in the juvenile violence organized in gangs, in the popular *barrios* (neighborhoods) of the great cities.

For several years, Mexico has experienced a new era of younger customs and social expressions. The manifestation of this fact is quite visible on the walls of the cities painted by gangs, in the demographic statistics, in the entertainment industry that has successfully created child and adolescent musical groups on the television screens, the theaters, the radio, and the bedroom walls of millions of Mexican youth. The face of this new majority that Mexico has generated in the last decades does not seem to respond either to proud Mexican traditions or to the folkloric clichés with which we attempt to comprehend them. It is a new majority, for whom the PRI and the political corporatism of the old system will become less attractive with the passing of time; a new majority integrated with the perspective of modernization and approximation to the "American Way of Life," a new majority without tradition, lay, urban, and massive, without whose social and mental history it will be impossible to comprehend the Mexico that we live in, or imagine, even approximately, the Mexico that will come.

The Political Parties

Another actor is the political parties. They have advanced in these last forty-four years from a loyal opposition to a bipartisan perspective. There is not much that we can add to this. The Mexican pluri-party system was always a sort of unavoidable masquerade, a form of concealing the quasi-dictatorial reality of the dominant party, the state party. However, it was always the form that the state found to channel and legitimate the participation of forces that, at times, seemed uncontrollable. The political reform of the mid-1970s was, to a large extent, a reform made in order to allow the participation of the left, because the years before had witnessed an anti-institutional rebellion from the left: the student movement, the union insurgency, the guerrilla movements. The accommodation of scruples and the failure of the system have led to a new political reform that clearly favors the right.

The July 1988 elections brought to the political scene the greatest novelty of the last decades: a true political competition between parties and the transformation of the elections into a new paradigm of legitimacy for the country. The citizen demands for clean elections and the conflictive position of the PRI before increasingly demanding voters seemed to open Mexico up to a credible and competitive party system by the end of the 1980s. So much so that in 1989, for the first time since the creation of the PNR sixty years before, a candidate of the opposition won a state governor's position: Evaristo Ruffo Appel, of the PAN, in North Baja California.

Public Opinion

A key scenario in which the struggle for the consolidation of the party system and democratization has been won is public opinion. The press and the movies were no longer its formative media; starting in the 1970s, radio and television assumed greater influence. It is the Mexican version of the global village, a fundamental transformation of the political and social life of Mexico. Since 1982, for the first time in the history of the country, a communications system is in place that is able to transmit a uniform message to the whole country or at least to broadcast it uniformly. Television and radio have become the preferred mode of communication of the government and the state, at the expense of the press. This is a fundamental process in the field of ideological struggle and the formation of national consciousness, which no political history of recent years could avoid describing and analyzing.

The Church

Also in the tide of conservative consolidation have been the changes in the Catholic church, which in the last forty years has been transformed from the church of silence to the church of the microphone. The church in the 1940s and 1950s had a sort of institutional agreement with the state. In exchange for its submission and silence, it was no longer attacked and was able to prosper on several civic fronts, especially in education, where it accomplished significant advances with particular efficiency (forty years after that agreement, we are witnessing the access to public power of a great percentage of the people who were educated in private religious schools).

After the ascent to power of John Paul II and his visit to Mexico in 1978, a new activist church has begun to emerge in the country, a church that, in the words of Bishop of Hermosillo Carlos Quintero Arce, should attempt "the Polish way" in Mexico. That is, the Mexican church, as the Polish one before, should become a center of organization for civil society. It should do so in order to confront a very diversified and broad state, which, like the Polish state, seems to have wide areas of illegitimacy and a lack of credibility, penetration, and support in society.

After four decades of silent consolidation, the Mexican church seems predisposed to support the political decision, sent from Rome, of trying to win over and recover its independence as a center of power and organization of society. It won't be easy, because, like the country itself, the church has its own limits. The situation of the seminaries, the formation of priests, the quality of their cadres in general leave much to be desired, so it seems difficult for a long-term dominant class to emerge from those schools. In contrast with the state bureaucracy, in which there is a growing technological development and refining, in the church the level of the elites and the means to form them are in decline.

The Army

The Mexican Army has been transformed in the last forty years from a civilian institution into the awakening of a geopolitical challenge on the southern border. Like the bureaucracy in general, it has undergone a modernization. The "revolutionary generation" has disappeared, that of the military that participated in the Revolution or in some of the armed sequels of the 1920s or 1930s (from the De la Huerta rebellion in 1923 to the Cristiada). The last secretary of defense with those characteristics was Marcelino García Barragán (1964–1970).

Now, the key positions in the armed services are occupied by more recent generations, more technical cadres, graduated from the Military Academy or some of the numerous educational institutions that make up the University of the Armed Forces, and later on graduated in high command from the War School.

At the same time, the army has experienced a technical and budgetary stimulus, although it still remains relatively small. In the 1970s, the guerrillas and the drug trafficking revealed an army that was prehistoric, with armament, for example, very inferior to that used in drug-trafficking circles, a weakness that cost the lives of a good number of soldiers and officers. The recognition of that lag led to a new era in budget and attention to the military aspect of the army. The central feature of that resurgence, which would dominate in the following years, was the emergence, with the Nicaraguan Revolution and the Central American War, of a new geopolitical reality on the southern border of Mexico that was both unexpected and conflictive. There were refugees, the war, and the very real possibility, barely avoided several times, of a U.S. invasion of El Salvador and Nicaragua. It seemed impossible to draft serious policies given this scenario without a minimal capacity for a military response.

The U.S. Influence

The other actor usually missing in political analysis, despite the historical evidence of its active and frequently interventionist participation in the internal affairs of Mexico, is U.S. influence. Between 1940 and 1984, the relationship between Mexico and the United States went through several phases, whose extremes were the agreement on war in the 1940s and 1950s (the Second World War and the cold war), the impact of the Cuban Revolution in the 1960s, the Echeverría Third Worldism in the 1970s, and the active foreign policy initiated by José López Portillo, with respect to the Central American conflict, and the possibilities of international influence due to the Mexican oil boom in the second half of the 1970s. With greater moderation, the actions of the Contadora Group at the beginning of the 1980s attempted to steer the possibility of a Central American war toward political negotiation.

The relationship with the United States is also related to a central matter, which should be revised substantially: the issue of Mexican nationalism, which means, fundamentally, the struggle to conserve its identity and autonomy with respect to the United States. The analysis of the relationship with the U.S. government should also broadly describe the long line of problems that have defined in these past forty years the growing conflictive relationship with the United States: the downfall of Allende, the Echeverría Third Worldism, and, finally, the policy of oil power, or middle power, developed by López Portillo to confront the challenges of the Nicaraguan Revolution and the expansion of the Central American conflict. This sequence also constitutes an important change in the defensive policy, which has forced the development of an active Mexican foreign policy due to the military events in its immediate proximity.

The 1980s, under a U.S. government dominated by the conservative wing of the Republican party, also witnessed a transformation in the U.S. policy toward Mexico. The effects on Mexico of this new general orientation of the foreign policy of the United States have been summed up as follows by Wayne Cornelius:

The local problems and the political attitudes of both nations have become the main influence on their mutual relationships. The policies—some voluntary, others dictated by the economic reality of the times—have been, in many senses, contrary, and have placed both countries en route to a confrontation that already produced a bothersome change in the public attitudes and the official responses to what happens in Mexico; there has been a change from a "benign indifference" to a "unilateral protectionism," together with a renewed interventionist impulse. The U.S. desire to adjust and manipulate the Mexican foreign and internal policies in a more active fashion, will become a very important source of tension between Mexico and the United States. The Mexican economic crisis of 1975–76 and 1982–84, coupled with the drawbacks suffered by the United States both internally and abroad, have increased in a significant way the tension and distrust in the relationship. In particular, the economic crisis of the 1980s revealed the manner in which the United States can be affected in a negative fashion by events in Mexico. As the main creditors of Mexico are U.S. commercial banks, the health of the entire U.S. financial system seemed to be threatened by Mexico's insolvency, as well as by its inability to repay its external debt of 82 billion dollars (now 105 billion dollars).

The illegal entry of Mexicans in search of jobs to the United States increased by more than 40 percent, and the majority of U.S. citizens seemed to be convinced that this was the beginning of a new wave of permanent Mexican immigration. The end of the extended Mexican "economic miracle" (sustained growth with low inflation) created great skepticism in the United States with regard to the capacity of the Mexican economy to absorb the current and future generations of Mexican workers, and to offer them productive employment that would represent a viable alternative to the search for jobs in the United States, despite the discovery of huge oil reserves in Mexico. Finally, the obvious errors of the Mexican government, together with its defense of the revolutionary regimes and movements in Central America, generated doubts among U.S. officials on the political stability of Mexico and the ability of Mexican leaders to conduct themselves in such a way as to not threaten the vital economic and security interests of the United States.

The Mechanics of Consensus

No analysis of the general historical conditions of the second half of the twentieth century in Mexico would be complete without including at least a few words regarding two issues that seem to be enigmatic. First are what we could call the mechanics of consensus: What are the elements that have allowed a society as unjust as the Mexican one to live in peace, a society whose notorious economic development has not been able to improve, and in certain cases has worsened, these inequalities? How has this consensus been sustained at the core of society within a system that does not seem capable of responding to the elementary needs of the majority of society?

There are historical reasons and institutional reasons. At the heart of this enigma of Mexican peace we could perhaps find the persistence of a colonial political culture, in which the privileges and the inequalities are seen, both at the top and the bottom of the pyramid, as something "natural." There are some elements of that same culture repeated in the Mexican twentieth century, and that could perhaps help to explain some of the mechanics of consensus. First, there is the tradition of an authoritarian tutelage, in which power is portrayed as a venerable, unchallengeable, and superior institution, destined to protect the people, and the people are portrayed as an inert mass always in the position of needing redemption. Second, there is a corporative tradition according to which any measure, right, and/or demand has to be incorporated in some corporative fashion: the individual citizen does not count for anything, but rather his insertion into some of the levels of representation or privilege is what matters.

Together with this colonial heritage, or along with it, there is a notable bureaucratic establishment of modern appearance that, in effect, resolves concrete issues or satisfies basic needs day to day. The past and the present interweave in a mixture of traditions, laws, and customs, in whose interior, archaic and modern at the same time, agreements are adopted and the consensus is imposed.

The other enigma has to do more directly with the temporal time frame, and we could call it the mechanics of inertia. The postrevolutionary establishment has slowly declined, and it is undergoing, as we have repeatedly asserted, a great transition. Even one of its main features, the institution of the presidency—centerpiece of the system that is now suffering from a loss of prestige and growing citizen distrust—is now presenting proposals apart from the traditions and customs that we now regard as characteristic of the Mexican political system. Predisposed to effect the transition, the current government says that it seeks to put an end to the political and administrative centralization that has been the axis of stability and development in postrevolutionary Mexico; it wants to put an end to corruption and bureaucratic patrimonialism, which is the tradition of the corporative and authoritarian state in Mexico; it wants to do away with the political intermediaries and the subsidies, which have been the cornerstone of the lazy, lax, pluri-class, and subsidizing state that managed the historical pact of the 1910–1917 Revolution; and, finally, it wants to put an end to populism, which has been the main ideological instrument of the postrevolutionary "inter-classism."

At the same time, the country is changing its territorial appearance. A new Northern Mexico is appearing at an astonishing rate, subject increasingly to a process of reindustrialization and integration with the U.S. economy. This process does not have a lot in common with the old industrial North that was the pride and vanguard of the Mexican miracle in the 1950s and 1960s; it is an entirely different process. While the productive boom progresses along the border and plants are installed that work directly for the U.S. market, the Alfa Group, vanguard of the old northern industrializing bourgeoisie, not only is incapable of leading anyone, but is barely capable of surviving. The country is in crisis, but in this new North there is a production and employment boom—except in Monterrey, its former economic center—while the nonoil South is drowning in the reaffirmation of its marginality and is growing at a different rhythm.

In the context of these novelties, the central issue of the mechanics of inertia is that, to a large extent, the old formulas that have been tried before do not seem to be capable of confronting the new situations, but they are the only formulas that the society has to negotiate with the state and with itself. The conflict within the Mexican Union of Electricians (SME) that we mentioned before seems to be typical of this clash: in 1984, the SME defended its collective contract of 1936—the most advanced at the time—to confront an initiative of productive rationalization that today finds precisely in those old formulas the obstacle to the modernization that is now required.

This all results in a profound historical paradox: the fact that the objective requirements of production, economic development, and social pluralism are now in conflict with the only formulas that the society and the state have to manage and organize themselves. This is the deep conflict that characterizes our transition, a transition that, notwithstanding, is falling increasingly on the far side of what is coming, and less on this side of what has already been. It is certainly not a process that will take place in days or weeks, but rather in years and perhaps decades. Mexican society is witnessing the end of a fundamental agreement within itself, a true change of era, that makes us feel both disconcerted and desirous of change, the inert weight of the past and the magnetic and undefined clamor of the future.

)

Bibliography

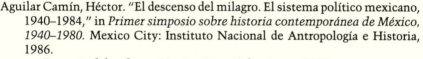

Aguilar Camín, Héctor. "El descenso del milagro. El sistema político mexicano, 1940–1984," in *Primer simposio sobre historia contemporánea de México, 1940–1980.* Mexico City: Instituto Nacional de Antropología e Historia, 1986.

———. *Después del milagro.* Mexico City: Cal y Arena, 1989.

———. *La frontera nómada: Sonora y la Revolución Mexicana.* Mexico City: Siglo XXI, 1977.

Aguilar Camín, Héctor, and Lorenzo Meyer. *A la sombra de la Revolución Mexicana.* Mexico City: Cal y Arena, 1989.

Ashby, Joe C. *Organized Labor and the Mexican Revolution under Lázaro Cárdenas.* Chapel Hill: University of North Carolina Press, 1967.

Bailey, John J. *Governing Mexico: The Statecraft of Crisis Management.* New York: St. Martin's Press, 1988.

Basáñez, Miguel. *La lucha por la hegemonía en México, 1968–1980.* Mexico City: Siglo XXI, 1981.

Bazant, Jan. *Breve historia de México de Hidalgo a Cárdenas 1805–1940.* Mexico City: Premia, 1980.

Benjamin, Thomas, and Mark Wasserman (eds.). *Provinces of the Revolution. Essays on Regional Mexican History.* Albuquerque: University of New Mexico Press, 1990.

Brailowsky, Vladimiro, and Terry Barker. "Recuento de la quiebra. La política económica en México, 1976–1982," in *Nexos,* no. 71 (November 1983), pp. 13–24.

Brandenburg, Frank R. *The Making of Modern Mexico.* Englewood Cliffs, N.J.: Prentice-Hall, 1964.

Calvert, Peter. *Mexico.* New York: Praeger, 1989.

Cardoso, Ciro (coord.). *México en el siglo XIX (1821–1910): historia económica y de la estructura social.* Mexico City: Nueva Imagen, 1980.

Carr, Barry. *El movimiento obrero y la política en México, 1910–1929* (2 vols.). Mexico City: Col. SepSetentas, 1976.

Castañeda, Jorge. *México: el futuro en juego.* Mexico City: Joaquín Mortiz, 1987.

Castañeda, Jorge G., and Robert Pastor. *Limits to Friendship: The United States and Mexico.* New York: Knopf, 1988.

Clark, Marjorie Ruth. *La organización obrera en México.* Mexico City: Era, 1979.

Clemente Orozco, José. *Autobiografía.* Mexico City: Ediciones Era, 1970.

Cockcroft, James D. *Precursores intelectuales de la Revolución Mexicana.* Mexico City: Secretaría de Educación Pública, Siglo XXI, 1985.

Comisión sobre el Futuro de las Relaciones México–Estados Unidos. *El desafío de la interdependencia.* Mexico City: Fondo de Cultura Económica, 1988.

Cordera, Rolando, et al. *México: el reclamo democrático.* Mexico City: Siglo XXI, 1988.

Córdova, Arnaldo. *La ideología de la Revolución Mexicana. La formación del nuevo régimen.* Mexico City: Era, 1973.

———. *La política de masas del cardenismo.* Mexico City: Era, 1974.

Cornelius, Wayne. "El mexicano feo. México y Estados Unidos en las décadas de los ochenta," *Nexos,* no. 84 (May 1985), pp. 15–27.

Cornelius, Wayne A., and Ann L. Craig. *Politics in Mexico: An Introduction and Overview.* San Diego: Center for U.S.-Mexican Studies, University of California, 1988.

Cornelius, Wayne A., Judith Gentleman, and Peter H. Smith (eds.). *Mexico's Alternative Political Futures.* San Diego: University of California, 1989.

Cosío Villegas, Daniel. *La constitución de 1917 y sus críticos.* Mexico City: Hermes, 1957.

———. *Historia moderna de México. El Porfiriato* (7 vols.). Mexico City: Hermes, 1955–1963.

———. *Historia moderna de México. La república restaurada* (various vols.).

———. (coord.). *Historia general de México.* Mexico City: El Colegio de México, 1976.

Costeloe, Michael P. *La primera república federal de México (1824–1835). Un estudio de los partidos políticos en el México independiente.* Mexico City: Fondo de Cultura Económica, 1975.

Cumberland, Charles C. *Mexico: The Struggle for Modernity.* New York: Oxford University Press, 1968.

———. *La Revolución Mexicana. Los años constitucionalistas.* Mexico City: Fondo de Cultura Económica, 1975.

Dulles, John W. *Ayer en México.* Mexico City: Fondo de Cultura Económica, 1977.

Eckstein, Susan. *The Poverty of Revolution. The State and the Urban Poor in Mexico.* Princeton, N.J.: Princeton University Press, 1977.

Falcón, Romana. *Revolución y caciquismo. San Luis Potosí, 1910–1938.* Mexico City: El Colegio de México, 1984.

———. *La semilla en el surco. Adalberto Tejeda y el radicalismo en Veracruz.* Mexico City: El Colegio de México, 1986.

García Díaz, Bernardo. *Historia de México.* Mexico City: Everest, 1985.

Gilly, Adolfo. *La revolución interrumpida. México, 1910–1920: una guerra campesina por la tierra y el poder.* Mexico City: Ediciones Caballito, 1971.

González, Luis. "El liberalismo triunfante," in *Historia general de México,* vol. 2. Mexico City: El Colegio de México, 1981, pp. 899–1015.

González Casanova, Pablo. *La democracia en México.* Mexico City: Era, 1965.

Green, Stanley. *The Mexican Republic. The First Decade 1823–1832.* Pittsburgh: University of Pittsburgh Press, 1987.

Guerra, François-Xavier. *Le Méxique. De l'ancien régime à la révolution* (2 vols.). Paris: Harmattan, 1985.

Hamilton, Nora. *The Limits of State Autonomy. Post-Revolutionary Mexico.* Princeton, N.J.: Princeton University Press, 1982.

Hansen, Roger D. *La política del desarrollo mexicano.* Mexico City: Siglo XXI, 1970.

Hellman, Judith A. *Mexico in Crisis.* New York: Holmes & Meier, 1978.

Hewitt de Alcántara, Cynthia. *La modernización de la agricultura mexicana, 1940–1970.* Mexico City: Siglo XXI, 1978.

Iturriaga, José. *La estructura social y cultural de México.* Mexico City: Fondo de Cultura Económica, 1951.

Johnson, Kenneth. *Mexican Democracy: A Critical View.* Boston: Allyn & Bacon, 1972.

Katz, Friedrich. *La guerra secreta en México, vol. 1.* Mexico City: Era, 1982.

———. (ed.). *Riot, Rebellion and Revolution. Rural Social Conflict in Mexico.* Princeton, N.J.: Princeton University Press, 1988.

Knight, Alan. *The Mexican Revolution* (2 vols.). Cambridge: Cambridge University Press, 1986.

Krauze, Enrique. *Por una democracia sin adjetivos.* Mexico City: Joaquín Mortiz/Planeta, 1986.

Levy, Daniel, and Gabriel Székely. *Mexico. Paradoxes of Stability and Change.* Boulder, Colo.: Westview Press, 1983.

Loaeza, Soledad (ed.). *México 1982–1988: los tiempos del cambio.* Mexico City: Fondo de Cultura Económica, 1992.

Loaeza, Soledad, and Rafael Segovia (comps.). *La vida política mexicana en la crisis.* Mexico City: El Colegio de México, 1987.

López Cámara, Francisco. *La estructura económica y social de México en la época de la reforma.* Mexico City: Siglo XXI, 1967.

Medin, Tzvi. *Ideología y praxis política de Lázaro Cárdenas.* Mexico City: Siglo XXI, 1972.

Medina, Luis. *Historia de la Revolución Mexicana, período 1940–1952. Del cardenismo al avilacamachismo.* Mexico City: El Colegio de México, 1978.

———. *Historia de la Revolución Mexicana, período 1940–1952. Civilismo y modernización del autoritarismo.* Mexico City: El Colegio de México, 1979.

Meyer, Jean, and Enrique Krauze. *La cristiada. La guerra de los cristeros* (3 vols.). Mexico City: El Colegio de México, 1973–1974.

———. *Historia de la Revolución Mexicana, período 1924–1928. Estado y sociedad con Calles.* Mexico City: El Colegio de México, 1977.

Meyer, Lorenzo, Rafael Segovia, and Alejandra Lajous. *Historia de la Revolución Mexicana, período 1928–1934. El conflicto social y los gobiernos del maximato.* Mexico City: El Colegio de México, 1978.

———. *Historia de la Revolución Mexicana, período 1928–1934. Los inicios de la institucionalización. La política del maximato.* Mexico City: El Colegio de México, 1978.

———. *México y los Estados Unidos en el conflicto petrolero, 1917–1942.* 2d ed. Mexico City: El Colegio de México, 1972.

———. *Su Majestad Británica contra la Revolución Mexicana, 1900–1950. El fin de un imperio informal.* Mexico City: El Colegio de México, 1991.

Meyer, Michael, and William Sherman. *The Course of Mexican History.* New

York: Oxford University Press, 1979.

Monsiváis, Carlos. Quoted in Héctor Aguilar Camín, "El descenso del milagro. El sistema político mexicano, 1940–1984," in *Primer simposio sobre historia contemporánea de México, 1940–1980*. Mexico City: Instituto Nacional de Antropología e Historia, 1986.

Moreno Toscano, Alejandra. "La semilla federal," *Nexos*, no. 99 (March 1986), pp. 24–26.

Mosk, Sanford A. *Industrial Revolution in Mexico*. Los Angeles: University of California Press, 1950.

Ojeda Gómez, Mario. *Alcances y límites de la política exterior de México*. Mexico City: El Colegio de México, 1976.

Padgett, Vincent. *The Mexican Political System*. Boston: Houghton Mifflin, 1966.

Palacios, Guillermo. "La idea oficial de la Revolución Mexicana." Master's thesis, Center of Historical Studies, El Colegio de México, 1969.

Paz, Octavio. *El ogro filantrópico. Historia y política 1971–1978*. Mexico City: Joaquín Mortiz, 1979.

Pellicer, Olga, and Esteban L. Mancilla. *Historia de la Revolución Mexicana, período 1952–1960. El entendimiento con los Estados Unidos y la gestación del desarrollo estabilizador*. Mexico City: El Colegio de México, 1978.

Pellicer, Olga, and José Luis Reyna. *Historia de la Revolución Mexicana, período 1952-1960. El afianzamiento de la estabilidad política*. Mexico City: El Colegio de México, 1978.

Purcell, Susan Kaufman. *The Mexican Profit-Sharing Decision. Politics in an Authoritarian Regime*. Berkeley: University of California Press, 1975.

——— (ed.). *Mexico–United States Relations*. New York: Academy of Political Science, 1981.

Revueltas, José. *México, una democracia bárbara: posibilidades y limitaciones del mexicano*. Mexico City: Editorial Posada, 1958 (2d ed., 1975).

Reyes Heroles, Jesús. *El liberalismo mexicano* (3 vols.). Mexico City: Fondo de Cultura Económica, 1950.

Reynolds, Clark. *La economía mexicana. Su estructura y crecimiento en el siglo XX*. Mexico City: Fondo de Cultura Económica, 1973.

Rodríguez, Jaime F. *The Revolutionary Process in Mexico. Essays on Political and Social Change*. Los Angeles: University of California Latin American Center, 1990.

Ross, Stanley. *Francisco I. Madero, Apostle of Mexican Democracy*. New York: Columbia University Press, 1955.

Ruiz, Ramón Eduardo. *La Revolución Mexicana y el movimiento obrero, 1911–1923*. Mexico City: Era, 1978.

Scott, Robert E. *Mexican Government in Transition*. Urbana: University of Illinois Press, 1959.

Shulgovski, Anatoli. *México en la encrucijada de su historia*. Mexico City: Fondo de Cultura Económica, 1968.

Sierra, Justo. *Evolución política del pueblo mexicano*. Mexico City: Fondo de Cultura Económica, 1950.

Skirius, John. *José Vasconcelos y la cruzada de 1929*. Mexico City: Siglo XXI, 1978.

Smith, Peter. *Labyrinths of Power: Political Recruitment in Twentieth-Century Mexico.* Princeton, N.J.: Princeton University Press, 1979.

Stevens, Evelyn. *Protest and Response in Mexico.* Cambridge: Massachusetts Institute of Technology, 1974.

Tannenbaum, Frank. *Peace by Revolution.* New York: Columbia University Press, 1933.

Tello, Carlos. *La nacionalización de la banca.* Mexico City: Siglo XXI Editores, 1983.

————. *La política económica en México, 1970–1976.* Mexico City: Siglo XXI, 1979.

Tello, Carlos, and Rolando Cordera. *La disputa por la nación.* Mexico City: Siglo XXI, 1981.

Tenembaum, Barbara. *The Politics of Penury. Debt and Taxes in Mexico 1821–1956.* Albuquerque: University of New Mexico Press, 1986.

Torres, Blanca. *Historia de la Revolución Mexicana, período 1940–1952. México en la Segunda Guerra Mundial.* Mexico City: El Colegio de México, 1979.

Townsend, William C. *Lázaro Cárdenas: Mexican Democrat.* Ann Arbor, Mich.: G. Wahr, 1952.

Trejo, Saúl. *El futuro de la política industrial en México.* Mexico City: El Colegio de México, 1987.

Tutino, John. *From Insurrection to Revolution in Mexico, 1750–1940.* Princeton, N.J.: Princeton University Press, 1986.

Ulloa, Berta. *Historia de la Revolución Mexicana, período 1914–1917. La encrucijada de 1915.* Mexico City: El Colegio de México, 1979.

————. *Historia de la Revolución Mexicana, período 1914–1917. La revolución escindida.* Mexico City: El Colegio de México, 1979.

————. *La revolución intervenida. Relaciones diplomáticas entre México y Estados Unidos, 1910–1914.* Mexico City: El Colegio de México, 1971.

Valadés, José C. *El porfiriato, historia de un régimen* (2 vols.). Mexico City: UNAM, 1977.

————. *Orígenes de la República Mexicana. La aurora constitucional.* Mexico City: Editores Mexicanos Unidos, 1972.

Vernon, Raymond. *El dilema del desarrollo económico de México.* Mexico City: Diana, 1967.

Villarreal, René. *El desequilibrio externo en la industrialización de México, 1929–1975. Un enfoque estructural.* Mexico City: Fondo de Cultura Económica, 1976.

Walker, David W. *Kinship, Business and Politics: The Martínez del Río Family in Mexico, 1823–1867.* Austin: University of Texas Press, 1986.

Warman, Arturo. *Los campesinos, hijos predilectos del régimen.* Mexico City: Nuestro Tiempo, 1972.

Weintraub, Sidney. *A Marriage of Convenience. Relations between Mexico and the United States.* New York: Oxford University Press, 1990.

Weyl, Nathaniel, and Sylvia Weyl. *The Reconquest of Mexico: The Years of Lázaro Cárdenas.* New York: Oxford University Press, 1939.

Womack, John. *Zapata and the Mexican Revolution.* New York: Vintage Books, 1976.

Index